The Unknown Life of Jesus

CORRECTING THE CHURCH MYTH

ROBERT SIBLERUD

New Science Publications
9435 Olsen Court
Wellington, CO 80549
(970) 568-7323

Other Sacred Science Chronicles

In the Beginning: Mysteries of Ancient Civilizations - Volume I

Keepers of the Secrets: Unveiling the Mystical Societies - Volume II

The Science of the Soul: Explaining the Spiritual Universe - Volume III

The Unknown Life of Jesus: Correcting the Church Myth

Printed and bound in the United States of America

Published by:
New Science Publications
9435 Olsen Court
Wellington, Colorado 80549

ISBN: 0-9666856-4-4

Library of Congress Catalog Card Number: 2003093344

Acknowledgements:

Cover Art: **Ron Russell** (Copyright ©1998, Ron Russell)
Editing: **Margaret Shaw**
Proof Editing: **Shirley Parrish**
Critique: **James Deardorff, Ph.D.**
Foreword: **Maury Albertson, Ph.D.**

TABLE OF CONTENTS

FOREWORD

Maury Albertson, Ph.D.*

Truth. One of Jesus' well-known statements is found in John 8:32, "And ye shall know the truth, and the truth shall make you free." So what is truth that can set one free? Truth is the quality of being true in accordance with fact or reality. It is considered genuine and authentic. A recent survey in the United States found more than 2,500 religions being followed, each professing the truth. If Jesus told us to know the truth, how can we discern which of these religions is really true?

A religion can be defined as a belief in a personal God or gods who are entitled to obedience and worship. Religion does not necessarily mean truth, but only a belief and worship of a god. It appears that to find the truth, one needs to step outside religion to find it. But where? It is my opinion that this answer lies within science, and only through science can we discern truth. Science can be defined as a branch of knowledge involving systemized observations and experimentation. Can we apply science to Jesus and spirituality? The answer is yes, and this book, *The Unknown Life of Jesus,* helps us do that.

As an engineering professor who has been involved in research most of my life, I always want to see the data before believing in a new idea or hypothesis. During the 1980s, Professor Ken Freeman, in the Department of Philosophy at Colorado State University, and I undertook a scientific study on reincarnation. We studied all of the major religions and spiritual teachings of many great masters. By assigning numerical values to certain teachings of death and rebirth, including those found in Christianity, the study concluded that in all probability, major religions should consider reincarnation a truth.

Adding support to this hypothesis was the research performed by Ian Stephenson, M.D., former head of the Psychiatry Department at the University of Virginia Medical School. He studied thousands of children who could remember their immediate past life. To document these memories, his research took him to locales where each child remembered living. In almost all instances, Stephenson verified a past life of the child by interviewing family members and friends that knew the child as an adult in the past life. This is yet more scientific confirmation that suggests that we have had past lives.

So why did Jesus not teach about past lives? In fact He did! As you will see in *The Unknown Life of Jesus,* ancient manuscripts written in Aramaic (the language of Jesus) were discovered in the past two centuries. In these manuscripts, Jesus teaches about the principles of reincarnation. The early Church edited out much of this information from the New Testament. However, you will also see that the New Testament has subtle references to reincarnation. Again, science confirms the probability of reincarnation. This is but one of many examples where the science of Jesus contradicts the Church.

If scientific evidence does not confirm Church teachings, why does the Church not change their teachings to conform to science? Good question. Religion is not based on truth, but belief. Church leaders ignore the science, believing their teachings are divinely inspired and therefore must be true. As a result, the science is ignored. One of the main purposes of religion is to teach people how to live morally, and the science underlying their teachings remains irrelevant. Why complicate things by changing dogma?

If science contradicts orthodoxy, our scientific community tends to avoid it. Scientific journals will not publish it, news media will not report it, proper research funding is difficult to attain, and often researchers are discredited by the establishment who question them. As in academia and medicine, preserving status quo in religion is of highest priority.

However, it is vitally important that scientists and lay people begin to think outside the "box," as this is where new discoveries are made and where "truth" is often found. Instead of condemning those who step beyond the orthodox boundary, they should be embraced and encouraged. This is the realm of "new science."

The Unknown Life of Jesus summarizes the findings of those new scientists who have looked beyond the "box" of orthodox religion and discovered an entirely different Jesus than that espoused by the Church.

* Dr. Albertson is the former Director of Research at Colorado State University and the co-founder of the Peace Corps.

PREFACE

The *Unknown Life of Jesus* is the fourth book of the Sacred Science Chronicles. The theme in all the chronicles has been there should be no separation between spirit and science. The spiritual world operates under laws of the universe, as does the physical world, and we are now just beginning to understand these spiritual laws that are supported by quantum physics. Can we apply some of this science to the life of Jesus? The answer is yes.

Probably the most influential person in the history of mankind has been Jesus the Christ. Great religions have been founded around Him and His teachings, and many wars and human atrocities have also occurred in the name of Jesus, the "Prince of Peace." One has to wonder if the dogma espoused by the Christian churches really is the teaching of Jesus, or is it a brilliant means to control parishioners? Few Christians have questioned the Church and its teachings, but during the time of the Inquisition, those who did were burned at the stake.

The laws of science should also apply to religion. It is not my intent to influence your Christian faith, and for those who have a strong fundamentalist faith, I urge you not to read the book. You are fortunate in a sense, because a strong faith can give you peace. For those of you who have questioned the history behind Church dogma, reading this book might give you a stronger faith in Jesus the man, who showed humanity how to live in this material world.

The sad thing about dogma is its reluctance to change despite evidence to the contrary. *Webster* defines dogma as, "a point of view or tenet put forth as authoritatively without adequate grounds." As you will see in the book, scientific evidence that is contrary to Church dogma is often destroyed, discredited, or ignored. Some people were even tortured and killed.

The purpose of this book is to allow the reader to think about alternatives to Church dogma regarding Jesus. I believe we are each responsible for our own spiritual health and should not be dependent upon organized religion. Organized religion can fill the needs of many who are on the spiritual path, a spiritual path that can also be followed outside religion.

Being raised in a Christian environment, attending Sunday school, two years of Lutheran confirmation, and church, I still had many questions about Christianity. How could religious leaders be so confident in the accuracy of the Bible? Why were there so many Bible interpretations? Why don't people have the same chance in life — some are born into poverty, some are unhealthy, and some are of different race? Why couldn't good people go to Heaven if they had not been exposed to Christianity? If one had to be a Christian to go to Heaven, how did people get to Heaven before the time of Jesus? Why is so little known about Jesus? And the questions went on. I wondered how many other people were thinking like me? For nearly three decades, I found my spiritual answers outside Christianity, and all were answered satisfactorily. During my spiritual journey, I came across well-researched books that explained the life of Jesus. Finally, the life of Jesus began to make sense.

I don't pretend to have all the answers. The Sacred Science Chronicles have been a synthesis of the research of many new paradigm scientists whose ideas have not been accepted within traditional society. After sorting out research about Jesus, I have tried to tie it together in a way that made sense to me. So was born this book, *The Unknown Life of Jesus* — a synthesis of the new science that helps explain who Jesus was. There is some research in this book that is contradictory, and I have included both sides. You, the reader, will need to decide if it resonates with your truth. I believe there are many paths to God, and hopefully this book will facilitate the journey along your path.

Robert Siblerud

Chapter One

THE EARLY CHURCH

Establishing The Myth

Is it possible the Christian Church has based its spiritual doctrine on erroneous facts, including the physical resurrection of Jesus Christ? The Apostle Paul admitted that the cornerstone of Christianity is the resurrection of Jesus. "And if Christ had not risen, then is our preaching vain, and your faith is also vain?" (1 Cor. 15:14). Can science, history, and legend substantiate the resurrection claims made by the Church . . . or should one accept the teachings solely on faith? At the time of Jesus, many pagan mystery schools incorporated the concept of resurrection into their initiation rites. Resurrection was symbolic as the rebirth of spirit, that is, enlightenment of a person's soul. As we will see, early Christians incorporated many pagan beliefs to entice those of pagan faith to join their ranks.

Gnostics, many of whom lived at the time of Jesus, were composites of freethinking, Christian sects competing with the Proto-orthodox Church (which was to become the Roman Catholic Church) to establish its spiritual doctrine. In the two centuries following Jesus' life, orthodoxy had not yet been fully established, so Gnosticism had a chance to become the orthodox Christian belief system. Gnosticism claimed the path to salvation was knowledge (gnosis), and knowledge of self was knowledge of God. Gnostics believed each individual was responsible for finding the spiritual truth, and that it was the Proto-orthodox Church who taught false dogma. Many Gnostics believed the God of the Old Testament was evil, unlike the God of Jesus. They did not believe in the virgin birth of Jesus nor in His death at the crucifixion.

A contentious rivalry developed between the Proto-orthodox Church and Gnosticism for several centuries, each trying to establish itself as the true Christian philosophy. The early Church Fathers began a slanderous campaign against the

Gnostics, as recorded in the anti-heretical literature. It was this campaign that made the Church victorious and allowed the victors to write history and establish doctrine.

The New Testament holds the history of the victors and is the document that established orthodoxy. Written history, however, can be biased in favor of the winners to enhance their belief system and support their position on controversial issues. Only texts supporting the position of the victorious Church were canonized in the New Testament, eliminating many manuscripts that shed light on Jesus. Because the printing press had not yet been invented, copies of the canons that eventually comprised the New Testament were transcribed by scribes. As we will see, the scribes had their own biases and agendas, and their corrections in the transcriptions enhanced the orthodox position. Scholars have studied more than 5,000 transcribed copies of Greek written scripture and found numerous errors in each, most accidental but many deliberate, to enhance the orthodox position. Most scholars thus reject the notion that the Bible was an act of inspiration. It appears that even in yesteryear, religious politics and corruption were alive and well.

Evidence will be given throughout this book that Jesus survived the crucifixion, attained His knowledge from the East, and then brought back His teachings to the East. Christian fear of the consequences of Christ not dying on the cross should be unfounded. In fact, rational minds would more readily accept the concept of resurrection if it was symbolic of spiritual resurrection rather than physical resurrection. Before we explore the unknown life of Jesus, it is important that we understand how orthodox Christianity became established.

ROMAN AND PAGAN INFLUENCE

Despite the negative image portrayed by the Roman Empire, it was this Empire that was largely responsible for the success of the Christian Church. Founded in 753 B.C., Rome was ruled by kings for 250 years. For nearly 500 years thereafter, Rome was governed by an aristocratic oligarchy called the Senate. The Empire arose in the Hellenistic (Greek) world ruled by Alexander the Great, who died in 323 B.C. Rome took advantage of the unity created by the Greeks and continued to promote the Greek language and Greek culture. Beginning in 264 B.C. and culminating in 146 B.C., Rome fought three major wars (the Punic Wars) with Carthage for control of the entire Mediterranean region. Victory ensured control of this vast Greco-Roman region surrounding the Mediterranean for four centuries.

Later, Julias Caesar tried to become a dictator of the Empire but was assassinated. His great-nephew and adopted son, Octavian, did what Julius Caesar could not. Octavian transformed the republic into an empire in 27 B.C., ruling under the assumed name of Caesar Augustus. He died in 14 A.D., leaving a legacy of peace for two centuries.

Under Caesar Augustus, the Empire was essentially an organization of city-states or provinces rather than a body politic, allowing rural inhabitants the same footing as urban dwellers. The Roman provinces were ruled by governors, appointed by the Senate or emperor, normally chosen from the elite sector of the population. A governor was responsible for keeping peace and collecting taxes and was given freedom to deal with local problems, including matters of life and death. Pontius Pilate held this office at the time of Jesus, and the Roman public-nuisance law authorized Pilate to condemn Jesus to death. It was this Roman government matrix that allowed the seeds of Christianity to germinate.

Christianity benefitted greatly from Rome's stability and unity as its doctrine was being established during the first two centuries. Many Christians enjoyed protection under Roman law. Greek was the common language throughout the Empire. Christian leaders used the road network to great advantage and frequently sailed to foreign countries from ports of the Empire, whose common language was Greek. The Apostle Paul said, "I am a Roman citizen," and moved freely around the Mediterranean in safety. As with Christianity, pagan religions were allowed to flourish within the Empire.

During the beginning era of Christianity, pagan religions were predominate throughout the Empire. The term *pagan* at that time referred to the wide range of polytheistic religions outside Judaism and Christianity. Pagans believed divine beings or gods of health, wealth, rain, etc. or their opposites were constantly involved with their everyday lives. Pagan religion had no overriding organization, no creed, and no ethical role in their religious practices. Many pagans did not believe in an afterlife. Educated thinkers of pagan religion believed in one almighty god such as Zeus or Jupiter, and below this god was a hierarchy of gods or spiritual beings. At one level were the great gods, below them the local gods, then the divine beings, demigods, immortals, and heros like Pythagoras. All these gods were hierarchically above humans. Everyone in the ancient world accepted as fact that there were many gods.

Doctrine played no role in the pagan religion. What mattered was showing devotion to the gods. Pagans worshiped the gods to gain favor and patronage, and in return, the gods often spoke to humans through divinations, such as dreams and oracles.

The pagan religion and the Roman government functioned to secure the same goal of a prosperous, meaningful, and happy life. The Roman emperor encouraged the cult of gods, and the Roman emperor himself was thought to be divine. Outside Rome, the living emperor was worshiped as the divine savior of the Empire. Local cults devoted to the emperors were found throughout much of Asia Minor. From Caesar Augustus forward, most Roman emperors were deified, and the entire population was required to show the emperor an outward sign of worship. Only the Jews were exempt from the requirement. Originally, the first Christians were also exempt, until they were not recognized as ordinary Jews. Basic tolerance became a central philosophy of ancient Greco-Roman pagan religions. All gods deserved to be worshiped in ways appropriate to them, and local practices were honored. Depending on the pagan religion, rituals and fixed prayers had to be performed in certain ways to secure the favor of the gods. Fortunately, no conflicts arose with the argument "your gods are false and mine are real" because during this era, most religions were respected.

During this time, mystery cults had developed in the Greco-Roman world; the cults, whose hallmark distinction focused chiefly on the well-being of the individual, were in contrast to most religions that centered on life in the here and now. Each mystery cult was unique and all emphasized rites of initiation for membership. Many centered around the mythology of death and resurrection of a god or goddess, a mythology that was rooted in ancient fertility religion, with the death of winter and the rebirth of spring. Those who worshiped a god or goddess were promised a more satisfactory existence now along with a more blissful afterlife.

Philosophy in the Greco-Roman world was not concerned with placating the gods to obtain community and family favors. Instead, the focus was on attaining well-being in this world. Philosophers of all types could be found on street corners proclaiming their views. In the first century after Christ, the three most prominent schools of thought were Stoics, Platonists, and Epicureans. These schools had several similarities: all tried to show how an individual could achieve well-being and inner peace in the midst of a difficult world, and all believed that only an exercise of the mind could provide a person with the tools necessary to live a fulfilled life. Thus, education and discipline were premiums in achieving this desired inner peace. In addition, philosophies were primarily concerned with doctrines defining what to think and ethics guiding one on how to live. Pagan cults in the Empire were largely tolerant of each other, but this was not true with different schools of philosophy. Proponents of various schools insisted on the validity of their own views and were intolerant of other views. They worked to convert people to their point of view, initiating missionary movements.

Interestingly, strong similarities existed between ancient mystery schools and Christianity. A secret society member of a mystery school worshiped a divine being, often of a virgin birth, who had died and was risen from the dead. This being would bring peace on earth and eternal life after death. Mystery school initiates went through a period of ritual purification (baptism) and instruction, just as Christians do today. Members periodically celebrated the myth of the cult's origin, such as Christians celebrate the Last Supper. Ritual similarity was found between the Mithraic religion that was popular in the Roman Empire and Christianity, which led the Church Fathers to attack the Persian Mithraic cult. During the time after Alexander the Great (died 323 B.C.), various religions were put into a common melting pot in the Greek-speaking world and Persian Empire. They borrowed from each other, and their various conceptions of divinity were modified by the identification of other people's gods. In other words, these religions were becoming similar.

Virtually all religions in the Empire were polytheistic except Christianity and Judaism, which were committed to the notion of one true God. (Although some pagans believed in Zeus or Jupiter as the supreme deity). Approximately seven percent of the 60 million people in the Roman Empire were Jewish. Jews believed in a powerful deity, God the Creator, who could benefit humanity and who showed special favor to His worshipers. Cultic acts of Judaism included animal sacrifices and prayer performed in a sacred temple led by a priest.

Most Jews lived outside Palestine because in 550 B.C. a large number of Jews were forced to leave their homeland due to the military invasion by Babylonia. During the time of Jesus, however, twice as many Jews lived in Egypt as in all Palestine. Most Jews had stopped speaking Hebrew, and by the second century B.C., many Jews read their scripture only in Greek. Jews believed they were the chosen people of Israel. In exchange for a covenant of obeying God's law, God would protect and defend them against all adversaries. The laws were found in the Torah, the first five books of the Old Testament given to Moses, consisting of Genesis, Exodus, Leviticus, Numbers, and Deuteronomy. The Jewish Temple was sacred to them, as they believed their deity dwelled there, in the Holy of Holies, the temple's most sacred spot that contained the Ark of the Covenant. During Jesus' time, the temple measured 1,500 feet by 975 feet with the mortarless walls of stone rising 100 feet from the street. In 63 A.D., the temple was completed, leaving 18,000 workers unemployed. Seven years later Rome destroyed it.

Jews believed, as did worshipers of other religions, in divine beings of lesser majesty and power than the creator God. These divine beings appeared in human form, sometimes as angels imparting divine revelation or perhaps performing a spectacular miracle. Jews believed that a Messiah would come to lead them to salvation. The Jewish Essene community, a Jewish sect, believed the coming of two Messiahs was imminent: one from Aaron lineage, who was to be the priestly Messiah, the other from Davidic lineage, to be a kingly Messiah. Coincidently, John the Baptist was from the Aaron lineage and Jesus from the Davidic.

Such is the background leading up to the establishment of the Christian Church. There were many pagan religions, whose members were potential recruits for the new Church. The teachings could not be too different if the Christians were to convert these pagans to Christianity. This explains why Christianity adopted some of the pagan doctrines in their religion. The Jews, however, who were scattered around the Roman Empire, were more resistant to accept the doctrine of the developing Church.

ORIGIN OF THE CHURCH

Initially, Christianity sprang from small, eccentric circles, a religion of humble people. As Christianity grew, it developed its own doctrine, and the books were distinctly its own. Interestingly, Jesus, who presented himself as an envoy of God, had no intention of founding a religion. Little information about His life and deeds was written during His lifetime, and oral communication kept the teachings alive before they were committed to print many years after the crucifixion. Following the apparent resurrection of Jesus and His appearance to the disciples three days later, the apostles dispersed, and we have little knowledge of what happened to them. Therefore, the history of primitive Christianity was much like a prehistory reconstructed from documents reflecting it, but not written for the purpose of recording it. We do know that a strong resentment by some conservative Jews did occur toward the Christian community. Stephan was the first Christian martyr stoned to death by an unruly mob, which included Saul, the future apostle Paul.

Christianity can credit most of its success as a religion to Saul, whose conversion took place on the road to Damascus, and thus became Paul. Considered a zealot, Paul was a highly controversial figure during his lifetime, having many enemies and many friends. Paul was a Jew raised by parents who strictly adhered to doctrines endorsed by the Pharisees. He was from the Greek city Tarsus in southeast Asia Minor, but educated in Jerusalem by a revered rabbi who taught him to read and write in his native Greek tongue. The Pharisee religion of Saul, centering around the Law of Israel's God, fervently focused on the belief in the physical resurrection of the dead. Unlike another

Jewish sect, the Sadducees, the Pharisees anticipated the intervention of God in the upcoming apocalypse. During these end times, they believed God would send a savior who would establish God's kingdom. Saul (Paul) was intent on persecuting the followers of Jesus and destroying the early Church, most probably because Christians proclaimed Jesus as the Messiah. According to the Book of Acts, Saul had received authorization from the high priest in Jerusalem to capture and imprison Christians.

The fate of Christianity changed, however, on Saul's journey to Damascus to persecute Christians when the resurrected Jesus appeared to him. In 1 Cor.15:8-11, he names himself as the last person to have seen the resurrected Jesus. This marked his change from the persecuter Saul to the Apostle Paul, as he was convinced that it was his duty to preach the good news of Christ to the gentiles. Scholars do not know how long after Jesus' death that Paul encountered Jesus, nor how Paul knew it was Jesus.

Paul believed he was living in the end times, and that he would be alive when Jesus returned from heaven. He spoke of Jesus as the "first fruit of the resurrection." For Paul, Jesus had already returned to life.

Following his conversion, Paul spent several years in Arabia and Damascus before he went directly into other regions of Syria and Cilicia, eventually becoming involved with the church of Antioch. His missionary work then advanced further west into Asia Minor, Macedonia, and Achaia. Paul saw himself as the apostle to the gentiles. Paul's plan was to establish a Christian community in cities that had previously been untouched by a Christian presence. After spending time creating a new church, he would move to another city and begin another church.

In his travels, Paul contacted local synagogues where he would be welcome as a traveling Jew and a businessman in leather goods. On occasion at the worship service, he would speak about Jesus as the Messiah who fulfilled Jewish scripture. His goal was to convert Jews and devout gentiles outside the synagogues. Paul's other targets were pagans, many of whom he brought to Christian faith and "converted from worshiping dead idols to serve the living and true God." He argued against the reality of deities worshiped in local cults. Paul emphasized that Jesus was going to come for His followers to save them from

God's wrath, emphasizing a strong, apocalyptic message. He appeared to be using fear to gain converts.

Those who accepted Paul's message formed a social group, called a church, mostly of lower-class converts. He spent one year and a half in Corinth, where he converted many pagans and then apostolised three weeks later in Thessalonica. Paul's message always emphasized death and resurrection, and upon Jesus' return, His followers would experience a glorious salvation. Teaching that Christ was the fulfillment of the law, Paul said believers did not have to perform the works of the law. In other words, faith supplanted deeds.

Paul sent letters, which eventually comprised 13 of the 27 books found in the New Testament, to congregations of churches. Seven of the Pauline Epistles are considered authentic by scholars, including Romans, 1 Corinthians, 2 Corinthians, Galatians, Philippians, 1 Thessalonians, and Philemon. Three epistles are possibly not from Paul's pen, including Ephesians, Colossians, and 2 Thessalonians. Scholars categorized three others as not likely genuine, those being 1 and 2 Timothy, and Titus.

In these letters, Paul showed a remarkable lack of concern for social inequities of his world. Although he claimed all people were equal in Christ, Jews and gentile, slaves and free, men and women, Paul maintained that slaves should stay enslaved, and that men should continue to dominate women. Christians, he said, should stay in whatever social role they found themselves. He was convinced that the history of the world they knew would come to a halt with the apocalypse. Equality would be manifested by God Himself when He destroyed the evil age.

In Romans, Paul said that everyone had sinned, and the wages of sin was death. The only way to be restored to right standing before God was to participate in Jesus' victory over death by being baptized, and, thus, becoming unified in His death and resurrection. Christ's death had conquered the power of sin. Jesus' resurrection showed He was not subject to the power of death. Paul emphasized that Christians died with Christ but were not resurrected as Jesus was. They would be resurrected when Christ returned at the end of time.

Scholars have commented on the different emphasis given to Jesus in the gospels compared with the emphasis Paul gives

Him in the Epistles. The gospel states that salvation to the world is found through the words and deeds of Jesus. In contrast, Paul says nothing about salvation through Jesus' words and deeds, but only through His death and resurrection. Some scholars question if Paul ever knew the stories about the earthly Jesus. He rarely mentioned anything about the historical Jesus nor about the teachings and experiences of Jesus. The life of Jesus seemed unimportant to Paul when he established the churches. Paul did know some of Jesus' apostles and Jesus' brother James, but spent very little time with them. When they did meet, they discussed the future of the gentile mission rather than the words and deeds of Jesus (Galations 1-2).

Scholars conjecture that the reason Paul did not discuss beliefs with the original disciples was that they differed on some issues. (1) Both expected a cosmic judge from heaven in the immediate future. According to the gospels, Jesus said this divine figure was to be the son of man, as predicted by the prophet Daniel. For Paul, there was no doubt it was to be Jesus Himself. (2) The gospels' Jesus believed that to escape judgement, a person must keep the central teachings of the law as Jesus interpreted it. For Paul, to escape judgement, a person must believe in the death and resurrection of Jesus and not rely on observance of the law. (3) According to the gospels, Jesus' faith involves trusting God to bring His future kingdom to His people. Paul preached that faith involved the past death and resurrection of Jesus. (4) For Jesus, His importance was determined by His proclamation of the coming of the end and correct interpretation of the Law. Paul taught that Jesus' importance lay in His death and resurrection for sins. (5) Jesus said the end of the age began for His followers who accepted His teachings and began to implement them into their lives. For Paul, the end of the age began with the defeat of sin at the cross of Jesus. The difference between the emphasis of the teachings given by Jesus and Paul is remarkable.

In the New Testament Epistles by Paul, the only historical information given about Jesus was that He was born of a woman, was a Jew, was from the lineage of David, had a brother James, had twelve disciples, conducted His ministry among Jews, had a last meal with the disciples, and was crucified and resurrected. The mystery is why Paul did not remind his congregation of

Jesus' teachings. Paul was developing his own form of Christianity, some call it Pauline Christianity, that states no amount of obedience to the law would help with God's judgment. It could only come to those who trusted in Christ's death and resurrection. Some people found Paul's Christianity inspiring, and others found it repugnant. In fact, the New Testament of James appears to attack Pauline Christianity. James writes, "A person is justified by works, not by faith alone." James insists that those who have true faith will do works that appear to be good deeds (2:14-16).

Another difference in Paul's teaching is that he urged celibacy for the sake of the gospels. If possible, Christians were to refrain from marriage and the fleeting pleasures of conjugal bliss because it was better to devote themselves completely to the Lord. Paul also urged silence from women. In 1 Cor. 14:34-35, Paul writes, "Women should be silent in the churches . . . For they are not permitted to speak." In 1 Timothy 2:11-15, "Let a woman learn in silence in full submission . . . I permit no woman to teach or have authority over a man. She is to keep silent." Paul's teachings were not always accepted by the authorities and did get him into trouble.

According to Book of Acts, Paul was arrested in Jerusalem and was sent to Rome to stand trial before the Roman Empire for alleged crimes. Later, historical tradition indicates that Paul became a martyr in Rome during the tyrannical persecutions of Christians by Nero (c. 64 A.D.). Nero had accused the Christians of starting the great fire of Rome.

The early Christian Church, mainly comprised of gentiles, was already established in Rome by 57 or 58 A.D., the probable date of Paul's letter to the Church in Rome. One tradition states that the Apostle Peter established the Church in Rome 15 years earlier and became the first bishop (Pope). The earliest books known to be written by members of the Roman Church were 1 Clement and the Shepherd of Hermas that have no indication about Peter starting the Church or being the first bishop. Paul's letter to the Romans, which is the earliest record of a Christian presence, greets 28 people in the community but mentions nothing about Peter's presence. All these instances make scholars a little suspect about Peter being the first bishop.

The efforts of Paul provided the foundation for the early Christian church. It probably took a strong personality and passion that few people had that enabled Paul to create the substructure of Christianity. Sometimes a strong personality can create a dogma, even if the facts are wrong. As we will see, there was strong competition with Pauline Christianity.

THE STRUGGLE FOR ORTHODOXY

During the second and third centuries A.D., intense rivalries and theological debates occurred among various Christian groups who advocated various understandings of Christianity. By the fourth century, one of the Christian groups (Proto-orthodox Church) had prevailed by overwhelming the opposition and designating itself as orthodox, thereby declaring the rival sects as heretics.

Christianity in the second and third centuries was in a great state of turmoil. Many belief systems were expounded: some believed in one God, others claimed two gods, while a few sects ascribed to multiple gods. Some sects believed Christ was both man and God; others said He was man inhabited by God; still others claimed Christ was God, but not man. During that time of transition the majority of church leaders and laity acknowledged no established orthodoxy nor theological system. Different local churches supported various understandings of the religion.

The term "orthodoxy" literally means "right opinion." Heresy is always second to the truth and is considered a corruption of orthodoxy. Early orthodoxy meant the teachings advocated by Jesus and His apostles, with heresy representing a contamination of the original teachings. Scholars, such as Walter Bauer, provided evidence that the early Christian Church did not comprise a single orthodoxy but instead emerged a variety of competing heretical minorities. Early Christianity embodied a number of divergent sects, with none representing a clear and powerful majority. Orthodoxy did not exist in the second and third centuries, nor was heresy derived from original teachings through an infusion of Jewish ideas and pagan philosophies. Beliefs that were during later times embraced as orthodoxy and condemned as heresy were in fact competing interpretations of Christianity. Thus, a battle for orthodoxy transpired during the early centuries.

One belief finally acquired dominance because of social and historical circumstances. This social Christian group exerted itself sufficiently over the rest of Christendom and resulted in the emergence of a majority opinion. It was only then that the "right" belief system represented the view of the Christian Church. It is this winner that writes history. The winner (the Proto-orthodox Church) preserves the writings of their theological forbearers and insists these represent the majority of Christians from apostolic times. It was the victor who destroyed the written manuscripts of competing viewpoints. The victors became the Church of Rome, which used its superior administrative prowess and vast material resources to influence other Christian sects. Through the use of hierarchial structure on other churches, the Church of Rome allowed various bishops to persuade the majority of church members to adopt certain doctrine. The Gnostics were considered the first heretics by the emerging Proto-orthodox Church. It was only after the discovery of the Gnostic writings at Nag Hammadi in 1945 that scholars realized that the Gnostics thought of themselves as orthodox. In fact, Gnostics appeared in many ways quite different from how they were depicted by their "orthodox" opponents.

All of the nontolerated sects were certain of their own interpretation of Christianity, meaning that every group considered itself orthodox and other groups heretical. However, writings of Ignatius of Antioch, Polycarp, Justin, Tertullian, Hippolytus, and Clement of Alexandria were all preserved by the victorious Prototype-Christian sect and established the foundation for orthodoxy.

Heretics were usually accused by the Proto-orthodox Church of being self-contradictory, absurd, and divergent. Proto-orthodox Christians, however, described themselves as consistent, sensible, and unified. Orthodoxy faithfully transmitted what they considered to be the true teachings of Jesus and His apostles, while heretics had no clear connection to apostolic tradition, and according to the Proto-orthodox Church, heretics perverted scriptural doctrine from Judaism and pagan philosophy. The orthodox Church often used tactics to portray their enemies (Gnostics) as promiscuous and in pursuit of evil ways. Although, the Gnostics were considered the first heretics, other heretics evolved during the debate of Jesus' divinity.

One Proto-orthodox view of Christ was that Jesus was both human and divine. He had preexisted, was virginally conceived, and was God on Earth. Three other viewpoints also competed for the description of Jesus' divinity. Adoptionists believed that Jesus was a human who was neither preexistent nor born of a virgin. At some point, probably during His baptism, Jesus was adopted by God to mediate His will on earth. In other words, they believed Christ was a man but not God. Separationists had another view and believed that at the baptism, Jesus became indwelt by God and was an emissary from the divine realm. Prior to the crucifixion, the divine Christ departed Jesus to return to the Pleorma. Lastly, the Docetists believed Jesus Christ was one unified, completely divine being. Christ was God Himself who had come to earth for redemption of humanity, only appearing human. With three competing views of Jesus' divinity, it is easy to understand the difficulty in establishing orthodoxy. The most organized group would probably win the battle of orthodoxy.

Signs of an organizational hierarchy developed early in the Proto-orthodox Church. In the Book of Acts, the elders, or presbyters, were distinguished from their superiors, or bishops. By the second century, a system of bishops developed based upon the imperial system of cities. As the Church grew, questions of proper behavior also arose. Scripture and tradition provided a basis of solving the Christian's life by giving guidelines, but who would interpret them? The Proto-orthodox Church decided it was to be the successor of the apostles. Special authority came to be recognized in the bishops of the capital cities, largely based upon writings of the "Apostolic Fathers."

During the first generation that followed the apostles, there were three "Apostolic Fathers" whose writings consisted largely of letters, including those by Clement of Rome, Ignatius of Antioch, and Polycarp of Smyrna. Other men were recognized as making a contribution to defining the Christian message, but not all of them were bishops. These individuals came to be known as the "Fathers of the Church."

In 178 A.D., the first important treatise against Christianity was written by Celsus, who claimed the Christian faith was one among many other faiths. Christianity needed to respond to this criticism on an equal, intellectual plane. Those who responded to this challenge were called the Apologists. Christian Apologists took on the task of showing that the pagan view of worshiping more than one god was wrong. Justin Martyr, the most famous Apologist and a Platonist before his conversion about 130 A.D., was considered the first to formulate Christian philosophy. He declared Christianity to be the perfect philosophy, but that all previous philosophy contained certain truths. According to Martyr, the God of Plato was the God of the Bible. During the Church's early development, new Church Fathers emerged to help establish Church orthodoxy.

The third generation of Church Fathers introduced something new, an attack on heretics. Following the appearance of Christian heresy, defined as doctrines different from the Proto-orthodox Church belief, anti-heretical writings became plentiful from this generation of Church Fathers. During the second century, there were three main heresies: (1) Montanism, (2) Gnosticism, and (3) Marcionism (an outgrowth of Gnosticism).

Montanism developed around 170 A.D. by a group of enthusiasts who followed the teachings of Montanus, a Phyrgian visionary. He believed the end of the world was at hand. His task was to lead a spiritual elite guided by the Holy Spirit, which was called upon to restore the Proto-orthodox Church to primitive purity. The Montanic sect was puritanical in principles and imposed rigorous discipline on its followers.

Gnosticism, a loose term applied to a variety of groups, some of which predated Christianity, was more difficult to generalize. "Gnosis" meant "knowledge," often restricted to a select few who believed knowledge of self was the path to salvation. Gnostics believed that all matter was evil, and they provided knowledge of how to overcome the entrapment of the material world. They believed the Universal God, the one above the God of Israel, sent a savior Jesus Christ, who taught us how to escape the rebirth cycle and overcome a destiny dictated by astrology. Most Gnostics did not believe in the virgin birth nor the physical resurrection, but thought they were only symbolic. Gnostics provided guidance on the soul's return to the Universal God after death, providing details of navigating through the spiritual world of the seven planetary spheres, whose rulers tried to prevent the soul's ascent to God.

Marcion, a partial Gnostic, taught that the Creator God (the demiurge, the god of Israel) was an evil god. This god of the material world was much different from the Jesus God of love. In other words, the God Jesus talked about was different from the Old Testament god. Marcion was the first to suggest a New Testament, believing the Old Testament should be rejected in favor of a New Testament, and that much of the Old Testament should be corrected. He believed the New Testament should include only the Gospel of Luke and ten Epistles of Paul. Although each of the three heresies had a substantial following, they lacked the power base of the Proto-orthodox Church.

Several writers challenged the teachings of Montanism, Gnosticism, and Marcionism. Father Irenaeus of Lyon (located in Gaul) was perhaps the most outspoken. Born in 135, he wrote five volumes against heresies. Much of the knowledge about Gnostics before the Nag Hammadi (Gnostic writings discovered in the desert of Egypt) discovery came from the biased writings of Irenaeus. Although Irenaeus believed the Gnostics were correct in declaring God unknowable through reason alone, he believed one needed the incarnation of Jesus for God to reveal Himself to man. Spirit and matter were different, but in man they were bound together. Irenaeus recommended 27 specific books to be included in the New Testament, a recommendation that was followed over a century later.

Another writer who challenged these heresies was Hippolytus, a theologian and Church Father, wrote ten volumes describing 32 different heresies. He was the last Western theologian to write in Greek. Around 220, he criticized Pope Callistus (an ex-slave) for laxity in dealing with Sabellianism (a heretical view of the Trinity) and claimed to be the Pope himself. Hippolytus was the first anti-Pope writer who was martyred in 235 along with the Pope he opposed.

Two important events arose from the response of the anti-heretical writers speaking for orthodoxy: the decision to form a New Testament canon, which would determine the books the Bible would include, and the formation of a "Rule of Faith" or creed within which the essential points of Christian belief would be woven into a consecutive narrative. The Muratorian Canon of 200 resulted, which consisted of a table of contents of the New Testament, which is essentially the same as the current New Testament except for the addition of Epistles of James and Peter. It wasn't until 382, however, that the Council of Rome recognized the canons of both the Old Testament and New Testament. World events also played a role in the development of the New Testament and the Proto-orthodox Church.

During the second century, at the end of Antonine's Rule, the Roman Empire, which included Gaul and Britain, plunged into a prolonged crisis from which it never reemerged in the West. In the Eastern part of the Empire, the crisis was surmounted by its conversion to Christianity of what is today called the Byzantine Empire, although it maintained formal continuity with the successors of Augustus. The Severan Dynasty of the Roman Empire ruled from 193 to 235, but four of its emperors were assassinated by soldiers within the regime. From 235 to 268, there was a period of military anarchy as both Gaul and Palmyra broke away from Rome. During the third century, astrology from Mesopotamia replaced Roman divination. Mithraism became a popular religion among Roman soldiers, expressing a lofty morality and declaring the need for salvation. Neo-Platonism became popular and provided Greek teachings that were comparable to Christianity. However, none of the philosophies enjoyed long time popularity, and none could compete with the growth of the Church. From 190 to 251, the Proto-orthodox Church in Italy grew from three bishops to 60.

Several important third century achievements occurred in the North African cities of Alexandria and Carthage. Clement of Alexandria converted from Greek paganism to Christianity, thereby establishing the intellectual dignity of Christianity. His pupil, Origen (184 - 254), wrote *On First Principle,* a systemic account of Christian doctrine. A fundamental biblical scholar, preferring symbolic interpretation of scripture, Origen worked to legitimize Gnostic concerns and reconcile them with Christian beliefs, but their efforts failed.

In Carthage, a biased progressive thinker named Tertullian, the son of a pagan centurion, was a fierce antagonist of Jews, pagans, and heretics. He was the first theologian to write in Latin, and the first to use the term "Trinity" to refer to the Christian God.

Unlike the second century heretics, the third century heretics insisted they were orthodox and entitled to stay in the Proto-orthodox Church, while heretics in the second century left the Church. The question of heresies in the third century, however, involved the Trinity. Modalists believed that God was one being, Father, Son, and Holy Spirit. Sabellians were the chief advocates of this belief. Adoptionists held that Jesus was a man adopted by God, and Subordinationism claimed that either the Son was subordinate to the Father or the Holy Spirit was subordinate to both. The Proto-orthodox view, however, saw the Father, Son, and Holy Spirit as separate entities. Because of this divergent thinking, Christianity was to fall upon difficult times in the third century.

During the third century, the imperial Empire of Rome began outright persecution. In 202, Seotimus Severus forbade the conversion of his subjects to Judaism or Christianity, but enforced conversion only against the Christians. Nearly a century later, Emperor Diocletian ordered all Christian churches demolished, prohibited Christians from meeting, and ordered them to renounce their faith. However, in the early fourth century, the outlook for Christianity improved. In 311, Emperor Galerius surprised the Empire by issuing an edict of toleration of Christianity, but he died shortly afterward. Following Galerius' death and benefitting Christianity, Constantine defeated his chief rival for rulership at the Battle of the Milvian Bridge. Prior to the battle, Constantine dreamed that by using a Christian symbol on his standard, he would win the battle and become the emperor. Following his victory, he proclaimed the toleration of all religions, including Christianity. Constantine paved the way for Christianity by becoming a Christian himself, but was not baptized until just before his death. He incorporated Christian attitudes into law by mitigating the severities of criminal law, improving slave conditions, and conciliating with the pagans. Constantinople became the new capital of the Empire in 330. For the next millennium, Christianity took advantage of its association with the imperial authority. Constantine had engendered the Middle Ages, and Christian orthodoxy was in place.

New members inundated the Church with minimal understanding of the faith. They often came with non-Christian beliefs and practices. With the newly protected position in the Roman

Empire, the orthodox Church was able to deal more effectively with heresy. The Church found the safest method by which to define and maintain orthodoxy was through the Ecumenical Council, the origin of representative assemblies in human history that transcended the limits of one people. The Church believed the voice of one people was actually the voice of God, and with this belief the Ecumenical Council could not err. Bishops from the whole Church were gathered at the Council, often elected by the Christians of their diocese with senior bishops named by secular authorities. When disputes of doctrine arose, they were settled based on historical claims that sided with the teachings of the original apostles. The Council defined once and for all the Christian teachings and fundamental doctrines of faith, especially concerning the nature of the Church, the Trinity, and Jesus' incarnation. Their objective was to end persistent "false" statements about these issues.

Constantine summoned the first Council, Nicea I in 325, to deal with the threat of a new heresy, Arianism, named after Arius, who later died in 336. Arius taught that the Father created Christ out of nothing, though Arius was later awarded the title "Son of God" by the same Father. Arianism appealed to converts who maintained the pagan ideas of a divine hero, half god and half man. By a vote of 300 to 2, the Council rejected Arius' claim and adopted the doctrine that Christ was of one substance with the Father. Historians write that not only was this argument heard at the Council, but bribery, abusive language, and even violence, were manifested during this conclave.

The second Ecumenical Council confirmed the decision of Nicea regarding Arianism, but also condemned Apollinarians, who denied the doctrine of Christ's full humanity. Apollonarius (died 390), bishop of Laodicea, believed that Christ, like all other men, possessed a body and soul, but lacked a human spirit, which was replaced by the Divine Logos or Word of God. Hence, Apollinarius believed Christ was fully God but not fully man.

The third Ecumenical Council at Ephesus met in 431 as the result of teachings by Nestorius, a Syrian who had become a patriarch of Constantinople. He objected to the term "God bearer" in reference to the Virgin Mary. Nestorius contended that Mary was the mother to the part of Christ that was man. In addition, Nestorius made a sharp distinction between man and the Godhood of Christ. The council condemned Nestorius and exiled him. And while Nestorianism did not become an important belief in the Empire, it was significant in the East, becoming a strong sect in Persia, Arabia, India, and Turkesta. A remnant of the Nestorian sect exists today, called Assyrian Christians.

The last era of Christian heresy was that of Monophysitism. Eutyches, the abbot of the Constantinople monastery and a zealous opponent of Nestorianism, was accused of going to the opposite extreme and confusing the two natures of Christ that Nestorius had insisted on separating too rigidly. At the fourth Ecumenical Council, which met in 451 at Ephesus, the Pope sent a statement entitled the "Tome" to the Council. Approved by the Council, the Tome set forth the classic orthodox statement that "Christ was God: He was also man, but a man without original sin. Christ is like us in all things but sin." Christ did not succumb to temptation, but was said to be one person with two natures.

A fifth council met in 553 that condemned the writings of three men who were sympathetic to Nestorius. At this Council, belief in the preexistence of the soul and reincarnation was decided to be heresy. A sixth Ecumenical Council (Constantinople III) met in 680 condemning Monotheletism as heresy and asserted that Christ had two wills, divine and human. Monophysites, a sect that exists today among the Coptics of Egypt and Ethiopia believe Christ had two natures, but only one mode of activity or will.

Later, the final seventh Council developed the process of theological definition within the Eastern Orthodox Churches. Christ was the bridge between God and man because He was both. Dogma had now been completed within Christianity, and formed a basis by which to instruct about one-third of the Roman Empire population who had become Christian.

Chapter Two

THE NEW TESTAMENT

Preserving The Myth

As the Proto-orthodox Church was developing orthodoxy, the Church Fathers thought it wise to have a document that substantiated the dogma they were professing. The Torah and Old Testament were a "Rock of Gibralter" for the Jewish faith, and perhaps a New Testament could provide the same anchor for the newly developed Church. The debate concerned which writings to include in the New Testament, which finally decided upon the letters of Paul and writings by the apostles or disciples of the apostles. However, all these writings did not quite substantiate the dogma being taught by the Church. As we will see, the scribes and Church Fathers took liberties to change these writings to correspond to Church doctrine.

ESTABLISHING THE NEW TESTAMENT

The New Testament emerged from the conflict among various Christian groups. Dominance by the Proto-orthodox position (Roman Church) led to the development of the Christian canon as we have it today. Originally written in Greek except for Matthew, according to Papias and the early Church Fathers, the New Testament contains 27 books written by 15 or 16 authors addressing Christian individuals or communities between the years 50 and 120 A.D.

The first four New Testament books are known as the gospels, a term that means "good news." They tell stories about the life and death of Jesus, including His birth, ministry, miracles, teachings, last days, crucifixion, and resurrection. Matthew, Mark, Luke, and John comprise the gospels. Proto-orthodox Christians of the second century claimed that two of the four authors were disciples of Jesus: Matthew, the tax collector, and

John, the beloved apostle. The other two gospels were assumed to have been written by Mark, the secretary of Luke, and by Luke, a physician and traveling companion of Paul. Many modern day scholars, however, doubt the accuracy of these authorships.

The book Acts of the Apostles was written by the same author as the third Gospel of Luke. Acts describes the history of early Christianity, beginning with the events following Jesus' death. It portrays the spread of Christianity throughout parts of the Roman Empire, principally through the missionary work of the Apostle Paul.

Following Acts is a section that comprises 21 epistles, letters written by Christian leaders to various communities and individuals. Thirteen epistles focusing on Christian beliefs, practices, and ethics are attributed to Paul, a claim that many scholars question.

The Book of Revelations concludes the New Testament and describes a future apocalypse. Written by a prophet named John, it describes the course of future events leading up to the coming destruction of the world. Principally, Revelations is concerned with the end of Christianity.

Interestingly, more than 60 other books written in the first 150 years of Christian history were excluded from the New Testament, but they still provide insight and history of the times. A body of writings called the "Apostolic Writings" by Christians living in the second century were considered by Proto-orthodox circles to be on a level with the gospels and Paul's writings. These writings include the Epistle of Barnabas, Shepherd of Hermas, 1 and 2 Clement, and the Epistle of Polycarp.

A most important discovery in 1945 at Nag Hammadi, Egypt unearthed 52 manuscripts written in the ancient Egyptian dialect of Coptic. Transcribed in the mid-fourth century from Greek, the manuscripts were based on writings of Gnostic origin from the second century and were thought to have been buried in a jar by monks of a nearby monastery. Most of the texts, which included epistles, apocalypses, and secret teachings, were not included in the New Testament. Several Gnostic gospels were allegedly written by the Apostle Philip and Didymus Juda Thomas, who some early Christians thought was Jesus' twin brother. These books rejected Proto-orthodox Christian beliefs and were used by the Gnostics during the orthodoxy struggle of the second, third, and fourth centuries.

During the past 100 years, the discovery of manuscripts resulted in the origination of the *Apocrypha,* a modern collection of early Christian writings that were often preserved in fragments. Often, the Greek original was not preserved, and all that is available are translations in Latin, Coptic, Syriac, Armenian, and Arabic, having been composed at the end of the first century. The Apocrypha has become a good source for history regarding early Christianity, a source some scholars believe to be as important as the New Testament.

Scholars have concluded that the authors of all New Testament Gospels are anonymous, with not one autograph on any New Testament book. One might ask how the authors acquired their stories about Jesus. Luke sheds some light at the beginning of the gospel that he acquired information from earlier written accounts of Jesus' life, and that he and his predecessors acquired information from Christians who had told stories about Jesus (Luke 1:1-4).

An interval of time occurred between the death of Jesus around 30 A.D. and the first writings. Scholars believe Mark was the first gospel, written between the mid 60s and 70s, over 30 years following the crucifixion. Matthew and Luke were written around 80 or 85, and John was written in 90 or 95.

Opportunities to tell stories about Jesus presented themselves for decades prior to the writing of the gospels, for Christianity spread throughout the Mediterranean, mainly in private settings. Stories were generally not told by eyewitnesses, but were passed by word of mouth from convert to convert. They were told in different countries, different languages, different contexts, and for different reasons. The religion grew as the Christian converts spread the stories of Jesus. However, storytellers had no independent knowledge of what really happened, perhaps helping to explain the many contradictory stories. Many scholars believe it is possible that stories may have been fabricated if a story would prove useful in a certain situation. Hard evidence even suggests some stories in the gospels have been changed. However, most believers were not interested in the historical facts, but in the moral truth of the story. Studies have found that people in oral cultures typically do not share the modern concern for preserving tradition intact, nor did they repeat the exact story every time.

Sometimes the gospel represents irreconcilable conflicts. Christians retold stories about Jesus to convince people that Jesus was a miracle worker who was the Son of God. Many early Christians appear to have willingly changed an historical fact to make a theological point. For example, both Mark and John indicate the day and hour of Jesus' death. In John's account, Jesus was executed on the day that preparations were being made to eat the Passover meal, sometime after noon. Mark describes Jesus being killed the following day, the morning after the Passover meal had been eaten, sometime around 9:00 A.M. Scholars believe that John's account is more accurately historical because it coincides with Jewish sources that describe how criminal trials were to be conducted by the Sanhedrin, the ruling body in Jerusalem.

Authors of the gospels, according to the Proto-orthodox Church, claimed two of the gospels were written by the disciples Matthew and John. The Bible infers that the disciples were uneducated peasants from Galilee who apparently spoke Aramaic, the language of Jesus. The Book of Acts infers that John, the son of Zebedee, was uneducated and unable to read and write. Authors of these gospels were absolutely fluent in Greek, and most scholars believe the Apostles did not go back to school to learn to read and write. They ask, why would Matthew, who accompanied Jesus and witnessed the things Jesus said and did, take most of his stories, sometimes word for word from someone else? Of course, he may have told the story to someone else who wrote it down.

In summary, scholars believe the gospel authors inherited a number of stories from earlier written sources, most often circulating by word of mouth. As stories circulated, they were changed and often modified when they were written down. Those who passed along the traditions were interested in proclaiming their faith in Jesus, not historical accuracy.

Biblical researchers believe that Matthew and Luke used the Gospel Mark as a source for many of their stories about Jesus. By observing the editing, one can determine their distinctive emphasis. Matthew, Mark, and Luke are called the Synoptic Gospels because they have so many stories in common, often using the same words. They agree extensively with one another, but also disagree. But why?

Besides using Mark as a source, authors of Matthew and Luke had access to another source, what biblical scholars call Q, which provided common stories for Matthew and Luke, not found in Mark. Matthew had another source called M, and Luke used another source called L. Many scholars believe the author of John did not use the Synoptic Gospels as a reference. Many stories found in John, other than the Passion story (the suffering and death of Jesus), are found only in John. Scholars believe the Gospel John was probably not the literary work of a single author, but a compilation of works by one person who was responsible for the completed product. The author was believed to be a native speaker of Greek living outside Palestine.

The original idea of a Holy Scripture or New Testament canon came from Marcion (early second century), who many consider to have been a Gnostic. Marcion, a radical theologian from the Pauline church tradition, believed that Christ did not really live in the flesh, but was a spiritual manifestation of the Father. Marcion created a Holy Scripture consisting of the Gospel of Luke and ten letters attributed to Paul, believing that other Pauline letters (now included in the New Testament) were forgeries. Marcion believed that salvation through Jesus came from a different God than that of the Old Testament, causing him to reject the Old Testament. As history shows, other Christians wanted a larger canon.

The New Testament canon as we know it today was essentially created by Bishop Irenaeus (130 - 202), an anti-heretical writer from Lyon. He wanted to place the New Testament side by side with the Old Testament and wanted it to include all the Pauline letters and some Catholic epistles directed to all the churches. Iranaeus also wanted to include the Johannine writings, which included the Book of Revelations. Most writings that had been in the Christian communities from the beginning were included, if the tradition of the churches had conformed to its use. Writings from the early period of Christianity were also included, even if they had not been written by an apostle. Authors of the New Testament were to be either apostles or disciples of apostles, with Paul categorized as a disciple. Originally the term "apostle" was identified with Paul, but Irenaeus broadened it to include the 12 disciples. Later writings were excluded.

The question of inspiration played no role for the process of canonization. Eusebius, the great early Christian historian, raised doubts whether the Revelations of John should be included. Finally a consensus about the 27 writings eventually emerged in 367, over two centuries following the first writings concerning Jesus. Compiling the New Testament had not been an easy ordeal, and some of the important writings that shed light on the life of Jesus were quickly forgotten and ignored. As we will see, the New Testament canon was transcribed from its original form many times, becoming corrupted by scribes to reinforce the orthodox view that helped to create the myth of Jesus.

THE CORRUPTION OF SCRIPTURE

Most Christians believe the Bible to have been divinely inspired and a true representative of spiritual truth. However, when one applies the rigors of science to the New Testament, the conclusion is that this cornerstone of Christian faith is seriously corrupted. The research and scholarship of Professor Bart Ehrman from the University of North Carolina, a New Testament scholar, have provided biblical students great insight into scripture corruption. His two books, *The Orthodox Corruption of Scripture* and *The New Testament, A Historical Introduction to the Early Christian Writings,* describe his research and explains how and why the New Testament was edited to support the theosophical position of the victors, the Roman Catholic Church.

Proto-orthodox Christians used literature in the early struggle for dominance over competing Christian sects. They produced controversial treatises, forged supporting documents under the names of earlier authorities, collected apostolic works into an authoritative canon, and insisted on their "correct" interpretation of these works. Documents of this new canon could be circulated only to the extent that they were copied by scribes familiar with the debates over Christian doctrine. Some felt at liberty to make changes or insert anything they felt was missing or needed to be added or to make the documents say what the scribes believed them to mean. In other words, scribes corrupted the texts that were eventually included in the New Testament. As mentioned earlier, during the first two and one-half centuries fol-

lowing the crucifixion, there were a number of competing Christian groups that advocated a variety of theologies. The winner was the group with the documentation supporting their belief, no matter how the documentation was acquired.

The New Testament canon that survives today consists of copies made over the course of centuries. No two of these copies are exactly the same in all their particulars, excepting a few fragments. No one knows how many differences or variant readings occur among the surviving copies, but Professor Ehrman believes they number in the hundreds of thousands. The vast majority of differences are purely accidental and can be explained by scribal ineptitude and carelessness, such as misspelled words or omissions of a word or line. Other mistakes found were inversions of letters, omissions of whole groups of words, corrections based on other manuscripts, biblical quotations changed to match Old Testament quotations, and additions to the text, including dogma additions. As can be seen, many of these changes were deliberately made by the scribe. Ehrman's research has proven that orthodox Christians produced copies of scripture that supported their own biases. An uncounted number of quotations by Church Fathers of the second century were also found in the writings. In some cases, the text of a passage had become so corrupt that the scribe had no choice but to hypothetically reconstruct whatever he thought might have been the original meaning.

Scribes became quite innovative in their editing of the New Testament. When a scribe provided an additional 12 verses to the end of the Gospel of Mark, it was not an accident. Some changes in text were made to harmonize with parallel passages. Others were made to eliminate grammatical embarrassments, and some to heighten clarity. The most disturbing editions were those deliberately made to establish character that conformed to Proto-orthodox Christianity. The majority of textual variants are preserved in surviving documents that originated during the first three Christian centuries as well as later ones. The oldest documents display a remarkable degree of variation. A number of variant readings reflect the conflict between competing Christian groups, and the scribes rendered them more orthodox. The scribes literally rewrote the texts, claims Professor Ehrman, making the manuscript a completely different text. Only a small portion of the New Testament writings and other early Christian literature can be viewed as the single work of an individual.

Ehrman, having access to ancient copies, researched a hypothesis that scribes had altered texts to further a particular Proto-orthodox view. As mentioned previously, there were three competing views of Proto-orthodoxy describing the divinity of Jesus: the Adoptionist view, the Separationist view, and the Docetic view. Ehrman found that scribes altered the New Testament to counteract these differing viewpoints.

Christians of the first three centuries agreed that Christ was the Son of God, but they could not agree what the Sonship entailed. Some believed that Jesus was a man adopted by God to be His son. By the second century, most believed the adoption occurred at Jesus' baptism when a voice called from heaven, "You are my son, today I have begotten you." (Luke 3:22).

The Proto-orthodox view that finally prevailed insisted Christ was divine, He had preexisted, had been virginally conceived, and that He was God on earth. A variety of passages from the merging New Testament can be used by both sides of this debate. Ehrman claims the victor's manuscripts survived antiquity, and opposition to Adoptionism made a significant impact on the textual meaning. In several passages (Mark 1:1, Luke 3:22), the corruption virtually displaced the original text. Some scribal changes emphasized that Jesus was born of a virgin. Targets for changes were passages that originally spoke of Joseph as Jesus' father or parent (Luke 2:33, 43, 48). Others were changed to emphasize Mary's virginity (Matt 1:16). In several instances, the concept of Jesus' miraculous birth was imported into passages that originally had not mentioned it (John 1:13, John 5:16). These scribal changes were important in establishing orthodoxy and creating the myth surrounding Jesus.

Dr. Ehrman's research shows that orthodox scribes frequently altered texts that might be interpreted to mean that Jesus became the Son of God only at the baptism (Luke 3:22, 10:37, John 1:34), or at His resurrection (Rom. 1:4), or at some unspecified moment (Luke 9:35, 1 John 5:18). Many highlighted their view that Jesus was already the Son of God before His baptism (Mark 1:1), or even before coming into the world (Matt 1:18).

Most commonly, the Adoptionist scribes simply designated Christ as God, providing more evidence to illustrate the corruption to establish orthodoxy. Occasionally, the changes could be dated to the period of concern (2 Pet 1:2, Jude 5).

Despite the many changes made by the scribes, scribes never eliminated the notion that Jesus was fully human. However, they did eliminate texts that could implicate Christ in human weaknesses, not appropriate to one who was understood to be divine (Matt 24:36) or spiritually perfect (Luke 2:40). One passage even suggests He was purely mortal (John 19:5). One can begin to understand why there are so many contradictions in the Bible.

Both the Gnostics and Separationists had strong opinions about the divinity of Jesus. Intrinsic to the Gnostic sects was the belief that a redeemer figure, a savior, descended from heaven to bring divine knowledge. This knowledge was required for salvation of the soul, which was imprisoned in the realm of matter. According to the Gnostics' belief, this figure could not belong to the earthly world because this Savior would have become entrapped in matter and enslaved to the demiurge, whom they considered the devil. The Separationist view believed the Savior made a temporary residence entering into the man Jesus at His baptism, empowering Him for a ministry of teaching and healing, but departing prior to the crucifixion. Early church leaders had to resolve these conflicting beliefs. Several corruptions challenged the Gnostic claim that Jesus and the Christ were distinct beings, by pronouncing an apostolic anathema (expulsion to Satan) on anyone who was foolhardy enough to advance such a view (1 John 4:2, Matt 12:30, Luke 11:23, 2 Cor 11:4).

In the altered form, these New Testament texts as we know them emphasize that Jesus was the Christ from birth and not from baptism (Matt 1:16, 18, Luke 1:35). The texts were altered by claiming that Christ did not enter Jesus when the spirit descended upon Him as a dove (Mark 1:11, Matt 3:16, Luke 3:22), nor leave before His Passion (Mark 15:34, Heb 1:3, 2:9, Rom. 8:34). Again, editing was necessary to be done to emphasize the orthodox view. Orthodox scribes affirmed their belief in Christ's death and resurrection by inserting the title "Christ" into relevant passages that otherwise lacked it (1 John 1:17, Matt

16:21, 2 Cor 4:10, Acts 3:13, 4:33, 13:37). Additionally, the scribes altered His name as it occurred in the biblical text, revealing their preference for the phrase "our Lord Jesus Christ." The Gnostics disdained the title "Lord" and denied the unity of Jesus and the Christ. So who do you believe on such an important issue?

The Docetists also had their opinion. Second and third century Proto-orthodox Christians opposed those who espoused Docetic views of Christ. Docetists claimed Christ was not human and therefore did not experience pain and suffering. They claim He was not raised bodily nor exalted into the heavens, and they deny His birth from a human mother. Most even denied a connection between God of the Old Testament and Jesus.

Orthodox opposition influenced scribes to edit Docetist views out of scripture, but some were edited into them. A few of the most interesting alterations speak of the physical reality of Christ's Passion (Luke 22:43-44, John 19:28, Matt 20:22-23, Mark 9:12). Orthodox beliefs in the bodily ascension of Jesus into heaven were incorporated into Luke 24:51-52 and Mark 16:4, 19. Also incorporated was the statement that He would return during judgment, found in 1 John 2:28, Acts 20:31, and Luke 23:42. In contrast, Proto-orthodox modifications speak directly to the physical dimension of Christ's existence (John 5:9, 7:46, Matt 8:27) and emphasize His physical birth (Gal. 4:4, Rom. 1:3). Because the early Christians believed in the Old Testament, scribes sometimes modified texts to link Christ more closely with the Old Testament and the God of Israel (John 10:8, Rom. 9:5, Gal. 5:16, 17).

Generally, alterations by scribes were very significant, showing how orthodox Christian views became cemented in the evolving Christian tradition, endowed with canon authority through corrupt editing of texts. Scribes usually modified texts that would have served as proof for the opposition. Proto-orthodox Christians had to defend Christ's deity against Adoptionists, His humanity against Docetists, and his unity against Separationists. These are the reasons why scribes modified the New Testament, often in contrary directions: some heightened His divinity, while others diminished it.

Adding to the mystique of the New Testament is the question about the original authors whose writings were corrupted.

The early Church Fathers believed the author of the Gospel of Luke and Acts of the Apostles was a travel companion of Paul. Scholars now believe this not to be true, as the book contains many invented speeches, and the author more than once confuses literary conjecture with reliable information. The source of information from Acts seems to have been derived from legendary materials, perhaps from an itinerary of a travel report written by a travel companion of Paul. Some biblical analysts believe the literary genre of the Acts of the Apostles, supposedly written by the author of Luke, indicate it was written long after Luke's original gospel writings and should, therefore, have been included in the Apocryphal Acts.

Other contradictions are found in the Bible that are difficult to explain. Two genealogies of Jesus were produced by authors of Matthew and Luke that contradict each other. Both agree in naming Joseph as father of Jesus, but they assign different fathers to Joseph and both take him back on a different lineage to David. Old Testament prophecy claimed the Messiah was to be of Davidic lineage. By listing the genealogy lines of Jesus, they confirm the original belief that Jesus was not of a virgin mother. If a virgin birth occurred, what was the point of explaining the lineage of Joseph? Professor Alfred Loisy, a French biblical scholar, believed the genealogies were invented in circles that had no idea of the miraculous conception. He argues that gospel stories used Old Testament texts and current myths, adapting them to the New Testament texts.

Loisy argues that early in the studies of Jesus, no one knew the day or hour of the resurrection. Quite early, a particular day was chosen to consecrate Jesus. This was the first day of the week, the day of the sun, a pagan day. Loisy states that the day of the sun was not consecrated to Jesus because the Christ had risen on that day, but because it was a fitting day for the resurrection.

Loisy believed the assignment of Nazareth as the family home of Jesus was an attempt to explain Nazorean, which had been added to the name of Jesus. Nazorean was the name of a sect having no connection with the town of Nazareth, thought to have been the name of an Essene sect that believed in baptism.

Bethlehem, the birthplace of Jesus, claims Loisy, was a myth, as were the star and magi. The author of Luke contradicted himself by dating the birth of Jesus under the reign of Herod, whose reign ended in 4 B.C. Most scholars now believe that Jesus was born earlier than commonly thought. Some believe that Jesus was born in the sun sign Virgo, meaning virgin. Loisy also believes the baptism of Jesus was a myth as was the temptation in the desert. He writes that the gospels are not historical records of the death of Jesus. The chronology of the Passion was edited in a way that separated the Christian Passover from the Jewish Passover. Other incidents, according to Loisy, were also introduced for the fulfillment of prophecy. So who do you believe?

Scientific research has shown that the Christian religion has been largely based on corrupted scripture. For nearly two millennia, parishioners have accepted falsehoods based on biased Church Fathers who allowed scribes to alter scripture, in the belief they were correcting faulty accounts. The teachings of Jesus seem to have been ignored by Church leaders whose primary purpose was to achieve orthodoxy. As we will see, the story of Jesus is much different from that which we have been told by Church authorities. Scholars have been able to analyze scripture to determine which verses have not been corrupted and have determined that one of the earliest writings that the Gospels were based upon was a source called the Quelle.

THE QUELLE

Researchers today are capable of dissecting texts in a variety of ways. One of the dissection techniques used in analyzing the New Testament results in the revelation of concealed subtexts, thus providing a foundation for the completed work. However, because of the multiple editorial changes made by scribes, an untrained observer would have difficulty recognizing these subtexts.

One of the earliest sources for the gospels was the Quelle. Scholars who believe the Gospel of Mark was written at the end of the 60's are incorrect because it refers to events during the Jewish War (66 - 73 A.D.). The gospels of Matthew and Luke, according to current thought, were written after Mark. Most scholars assume that authors of these two gospels used Mark as a source along with a second source called "Q," an abbreviation for "quelle," which means "source" in German. Existing texts and oral traditions were employed by the authors of Matthew and Luke as references, but the authors had no way of verifying what was true and what was invented. Gospel writers for Luke and Matthew are thought to have relied on different versions of both Mark and Q. In summary, Q is scripture found in Matthew and Luke, but not in Mark.

The source Q remains a promising, yet controversial source of Jesus' life. Historians and theologians believe that Q is the oldest written source that circulated among Jesus' followers, much older than Mark. Some believe that the teachings were most likely written down immediately after His crucifixion. (Evidence will be presented in another chapter that they may have been written down during the life of Jesus). Scholars claim that Q is the lost original gospel that preserved the sayings of Jesus.

Scholars were hopeful the discovery of ancient Gnostic texts could shed light on the Q source. In 1945, a discovery of great importance occurred in the desert cliff region near Nag Hammadi on the Nile River. A jar containing 52 manuscripts of Gnostic writings was found. Most texts were dated between 350 - 400 A.D. and were Coptic translations made from an original Greek version. Some were dated no later than 120 - 150 A.D. Sometime during the fourth century, an edict came from the Pope to destroy all Gnostic writings. Located in Nag Hammadi during that time was a Christian monastery, and historians hypothesize that the monks decided to bury the manuscripts instead of burning them. Scholars were hopeful this discovery would answer many unanswered questions about the Gnostics. Before the Nag Hammadi discovery, about the only source of the Gnostic belief system came from the anti-heretical writings of the early Church Fathers. The Nag Hammadi discovery, however, contradicted many of these biased writings.

Also included in the Nag Hammadi discovery was the Gospel of Thomas manuscript, a loosely structured collection of 114 sayings of Jesus. Scholars found the Q material was to be somewhat similar in structure, and many sayings found in Q paralleled the Gospel of Thomas. Many scholars believe that Thomas makes use of material in Matthew, Luke, and John, plus the Gnostic material. So much so that Thomas is considered a continuation of Q without fundamental changes in the form. Many aphorisms found in Thomas are less developed than parallel versions found in the gospels, suggesting that the content of Thomas is from an earlier stage in the process of oral tradition. Thomas preserved sayings not appearing in any of the canonical gospels, which seems authentic in view of their structure and contents. The Gospel of Thomas is also saturated with Buddhist ideas.

Analysis of Q provides insight into both the personality of Jesus and the makeup of His group of followers. Three elements characterize Q's contents: (1) wisdom discourses, (2) prophetic and apocalyptic declarations, and (3) biographical materials. Some scholars determined that Q was revised, reordered, and enriched at three different periods. Q-1 is the oldest material, comprising the wisdom and sayings of Jesus, characterized by radical ethics that break with social conventions. Q-2 consists of prophetic and apocalyptic texts added afterwards and portrays a symptomatic confrontation of followers directed against the Jews for their response to the teachings of Jesus. Belonging to a later date is Q-3, the story of the temptation and additional biographical information of Jesus.

Q was unified through the three editorial revisions, which laid a systematic, theological foundation. Scholars believe the final edition was circulated among the followers of Jesus after the Jewish War. In addition, the authors of Matthew and Luke used information from Q in their writings because it was a coherent, written structure of discourses and anecdotes. Linguistic analysis suggests that Q must have been written in Greek. However, it has often been mentioned how incoherent Q is, with no evidence that there has ever been a Q document as defined.

By comparing the writings of Q with the gospels, scholars determined the amount of embellishment in the gospels that the Proto-orthodox Church intentionally added to enhance their viewpoint. An examination of Q allows one to assess the values and traditions established by the Proto-orthodox Church, which differed greatly from the writings of Q.

The followers of Jesus who circulated the Q-1 sayings were not Christians, as they viewed Jesus as neither the Messiah nor Christ. They did not comprehend His teachings as an attack on Judaism, nor did they believe His death was a divine event or a means of redemption. None of the followers believed that Jesus rose from the dead to rule over a new world. Instead, they viewed Jesus as an exceptional, spiritual teacher whose wisdom would assist them during difficult times.

In contrast, the New Testament gospels suggest that Jesus made His appearance to reform Judaism. This is not reflected in the Gospel Q, however, which has no mention of the disciples nor an agenda to reform the politics and religion of Judaism. Gospel Q tells of no encounter with authorities in Jerusalem, no martyrdom for a cause, nor any mention of a first church in Jerusalem. Jesus' followers were not aware of the cause they were to uphold to change the world and prepare the way for a new religion based on His teachings. Q does not proclaim the view that Jesus was the Son of God. These ideas developed much later, having nothing to do with the original followers of Jesus. Individuals who espoused these later views had no first-hand contact with Jesus' teachings and intentions. Some scholars suggest that neither Jesus nor the Q followers were Christians.

In summary, Q is the compilation of New Testament verses that scholars believe were untainted by the scribes. Q was deduced by linguistic and editorial analysis of biblical scholars. The complete book of Q contains 62 short phrases. Twenty-one of them, Q-1, form the oldest teachings of Jesus. The following are words from the original teachings of Jesus:

1. "How fortunate are the poor; they have God's kingdom
   How fortunate the hungry; they will be fed
   How fortunate are those who are crying; they will laugh."
2. "I am telling you, love your enemies, bless those who curse you, pray for those who mistreat you.
   If someone slaps you on the cheek, offer your other cheek as well.
   If anyone grabs your coat, let him have your shirt as well.
   Give to anyone who asks, and if someone takes away your belongings, do not ask to have them back.
   As you want people to treat you, do the same to them.

If you love those who love you, what credit is that to you? Even tax collectors love those who love them, do they not? And if you embrace only your brothers, what more are you doing than others? Doesn't everybody do that? If you lend to those from whom you expect repayment, what credit is that to you? Even wrongdoers lend to their kind because they expect to be repaid.
Instead, love your enemies, do good, and lend without expecting anything in return. Your reward will be great, and you will be children of God.
For he makes his sun rise on the evil and on the good; he sends rain on the just and the unjust."

3. "Be merciful even as your Father is merciful.
Don't judge and you won't be judged.
For the standard you use (for judging) will be the standard used against you."
4. "Can the blind lead the blind? Won't they both fall into a pit? A student is not better than his teacher. It is enough for a student to be like his teacher."
5. "How can you look for the splinter in your brother's eye and not notice the stick in your own eye? How can you say to your brother, 'Let me remove the splinter in your eye,' when you do not see the stick in your own eye? You hypocrite, first take the stick from your own eye, and then you can see to remove the splinter that is your brother's eye."
6. "A good tree does not bear rotten fruit; a rotten tree does not bear good fruit. Are figs gathered from thorns, or grapes from thistles? Every tree is known by its fruit.
The good man produces good things from his store of goods, and treasures; and the evil man evil things. Or the mouth speaks from a full heart."
7. "Why do you call me, 'Master, master,' and not do what I say?
Everyone who hears my words and does them is like a man who built a house on a rock. The rain fell, a torrent broke against the house, and it did not fall, for it had a rock foundation.

But everyone who hears my words and does not do them is like a man who built a house on sand. The rain came, the torrent broke against it, and it collapsed. The ruin of that house was great."

8. "When someone said to him, 'I will follow you wherever you go,' Jesus answered, 'Foxes have dens, and birds of the sky have nests, but the son of man has nowhere to lay his head.'
   When another said, 'I will follow you, sir, but first let me say goodbye to my family,' Jesus said to him, 'No one who puts his hand to the plow and then looks back is fit for the kingdom of God.' "
9. He said, "The harvest is abundant, but the workers are few; beg therefore the master of the harvest to send out workers into his harvest.
   Go. Look, I send you out as lambs among wolves.
   Do not carry money, or bag, or sandals, or staff; and do not greet anyone on the road.
   Whatever house you enter, say, 'Peace be to this house!' And if a child of peace is there, your greeting will be received (literally, 'your peace will rest upon him'). But if not, let your peace return to you.
   And stay in the same house, eating and drinking whatever they provide, for the worker deserves his wages. Do not go from house to house.
   And if you enter a town and they receive you, eat what is set before you. Pay attention to the sick and say to them, 'God's kingdom has come to you.'
   But if you enter a town and they do not receive you, as you leave, shake the dust from your feet and say, 'Nevertheless, be sure of this, the realm of God has come to you.' "
10. "When you pray, say
   'Father, may your name be holy.
   May your rule take place.
   Give us each day our daily bread.
   Pardon our debts, for we ourselves pardon everyone indebted to us. And do not bring us to trial (into a trying situation).' "
11. "Ask and it will given to you; seek and you will find;

knock and the door will be opened for you.
For everyone who asks receives, and the one who seeks finds, and to the one who knocks, the door will be opened.
What father of yours, if his son asks for a loaf of bread, will give him a stone, or if he asks for a fish, will give him a snake?
Therefore if you, although you are not good, know how to give good gifts to your children, how much more will the Father above give good things to those who ask him!"

12. "Nothing is hidden that will not be made known, or secret that will not come to light.
What I tell you in the dark, speak in the light. And what you hear as a whisper, proclaim on the housetops."
13. "Don't be afraid of those who can kill the body, but can't kill the soul.
Can't you buy sparrows for two cents? Not one of them will fall to the ground without God knowing about it. Even the hairs of your head are all numbered. So don't be afraid. You are worth more than many sparrows."
14. "Someone from the crowd said to him, 'Teacher, tell my brother to divide the inheritance with me.' But he said to him, 'Sir, who made me your judge or lawyer?' "
15. "He told them a parable saying, 'The land of a rich man produced in abundance, and he thought to himself, What should I do, for I have nowhere to store my crops?' Then he said, 'I will do this. I will pull down my barns and build larger ones, and there I will store all my grain and goods. And I will say to my soul, soul, you have ample goods stored up for many years. Take it easy. Eat, drink, and be merry.' But God said to him, 'Foolish man! This very night you will have to give back your soul, and the things you produced, whose will they be?' That is what happens to the one who stores up treasure for himself and is not rich in the sight of God.'"

16. "I am telling you, do not worry about your life, what you will eat, or about your body, what you will wear. Isn't life more than food, and the body more than clothing?
Think of the ravens. They do not plant, harvest, or store grain in barns, and God feeds them. Which one of you can add a single day to your life by worrying?
Aren't you worth more than the birds? And why do you worry about clothing? Think of the way lilies grow. They do not work or spin. But even Solomon in all his splendor was not as magnificent. If God puts beautiful clothes on the grass that is in the field today and tomorrow is thrown into a furnace, won't he put clothes on you, faint hearts?
So don't worry, thinking, 'What will we eat?' or 'What will we drink?' or 'What will we wear?' For everybody in the whole world does that, and your Father knows that you need these things. Instead, make sure of His rule over you, and all these things will be yours as well."
17. "Sell your possessions and give to charity (alms). Store up treasure for yourselves in a heavenly account, where moths and rust do not consume, and where thieves cannot break in and steal.
For where your treasure is, there your heart will also be."
18. "He said, 'What is the kingdom of God like? To what should I compare it? It is like a grain of mustard which a man took and sowed in his garden. It grew and became a tree, and the birds of the air made nests in its branches."
He also said, 'The kingdom of God is like yeast which a woman took and hid in three measures of flour until it leavened the whole mass.'"
19. "Everyone who glorifies himself will be humiliated, and the one who humbles himself will be praised."
20. "A man once gave a great banquet and invited many. At the time for the banquet he sent his servant to say to those who had been invited, 'Please

come, for everything is now ready.' But they all began to make excuses. The first said to him, 'I've bought a farm, and I must go and see it. Please excuse me.' And another said, 'I've just bought five pair of oxen and I need to check them out. Please excuse me.' And another said, 'I've just married a woman so I can't come.' The servant came and reported this to his master. Then the owner in anger said to his servant, 'Go out quickly to the streets of town and bring in as many people as you find.' And the servant went out into the streets and brought together everybody he could find. That way the house was filled with guests."

21. "Whoever does not hate his father and mother will not be able to learn from me. Whoever does not hate his son and daughter cannot belong to my school.
Whoever does not accept his cross and so become my follower, cannot be one of my students.
Whoever tries to protect his life will lose it; but whoever loses his life on account of me will preserve it."

22. "Salt is good; but if salt loses its taste, how can it be restored? It is not good for either the land or manure pile. People just throw it out."

(Text from Mack, Burton L., *The Lost Gospel: The Book of Q and Christian Origins*, Element Books, 1993)

So concludes the story of Q that included some of the unedited versions of Jesus' teachings according to biblical scholars. Many of these scholars have marveled that Q-1 is so uniformly Buddhistic, and some have concluded that Jesus may have derived his ideas and teachings from the wisdom of Buddha.

Chapter Three

THE EASTERN INFLUENCE

Similarities Between Jesus And Buddha

During the past two centuries, scholars began to realize that Christianity may have been influenced by Buddhism. Some even went so far as to claim that Jesus was not a Christian. He was a Buddha. How could this be? Later chapters will explore evidence that Jesus spent His lost years in India, studying the teachings of Buddha. But first, we will examine some of the historical sources used in researching Jesus' life. Then we will look at the similarities between the teachings and stories of Jesus and Buddha.

Historians remain frustrated with the lack of historical evidence regarding Jesus, making it difficult to determine who Jesus, the person, was. Books written during the first two centuries seldom mention Jesus as a real person. Later theological writings assume a belief in Jesus Christ as the Son of God and as the Messiah, most which have been edited for orthodoxy purposes.

One of the first sources that mentions Jesus is a non-Christian text written in the first century. The Roman historian, Tactius, wrote of a superstitious sect of Christians deriving their name from an individual they called Christ, who was executed under the direction of Pontius Pilate, governor during the time of Emperor Tiberius. Other writings do not refer to Jesus directly. For example, Philo Judaeus (20 B.C. - 50 A.D.) wrote extensively about Pontius Pilate, but does not mention Jesus. Pliny the Younger (62 - 113 A.D.) wrote about Christians living in Bithynia, but does not mention anything about their founder. Flavious Josephus (37 - 100 A.D.), the great Jewish historian, published his *Jewish Antiquities* around 92 A.D. In it, he described the history of the world beginning with the creation and ending with the reign of Nero. Josephus provided a detailed account of politics and society at the time of Jesus, referring to John the Baptist, Herod, and Pilate. He described the stoning of a man called James and mentioned his brother Jesus, "whom people call Christ." Even the gospels provide little information on Jesus' childhood and youth. Even the year of Jesus birth remains in question. We do know for certain, Jesus was born while Herod was in power between 37 - 4 B.C.

The only source for historical research of Jesus is found in the collection of writings in the New Testament. As mentioned earlier, writers for the early Christian Church modified and distorted early manuscripts. These copies were used and modified by scholarly theologians to promote their particular views of orthodoxy. Copies were eagerly reproduced by scribes, who often made changes both intentionally and unintentionally, and then disseminated them throughout the world. Many of these early manuscripts were contradictory to one another, and the young Proto-orthodox Church believed the only way to prevent the faith from fragmenting further was to assemble a canon of writings, the New Testament. Once the canon was decided upon, apocryphal texts were rejected and destroyed. Adulterated texts became the only source of knowledge about Jesus. Early Christianity succeeded in pushing the historical Jesus into the background. However, as previously mentioned in the first chapter, the unedited version of Jesus's teachings as found in the Quelle are very similar to the teachings of Buddha, and some have concluded that Jesus may have derived His ideas and teachings from the wisdom of Buddha.

SIMILARITIES BETWEEN THE NEW TESTAMENT AND BUDDHISM

For 1,500 years, Jesus has been depicted in accordance with official theology, with all writings strengthening Church doctrine. During the last two centuries, however, German Protestant theologians began scholarly investigation of the New Testament, leading the way in biblical research. Their findings armed the Protestant Church in Germany with evidence to accuse the Roman Catholic Church of falsifying Christianity. In 1835, David Friedrich published *The Life of Jesus,* in which he rejected the historical authenticity of Jesus. In the mid-1800's,

Bruno Bauer declared that the life of Jesus was a myth. Albert Schweitzer, M.D., the well-known physician and theologian, viewed research into the life of Jesus as a test of Church truthfulness. Additionally, Gruber and Kersten, historical researchers of Jesus, wrote that the Jesus portrayed to us by the Church is not the true Jesus. All of this research concluded that the Jesus of Christianity is merely a literary creation. Throughout history his image has been artificially constructed from false fragments of his biography, from invalid statements, and with a great deal of inventiveness by Christian writers.

Other scholars became outspoken as well. Wilhelm Nestle, a religious historian, wrote, "Christianity is the religion founded by Paul, which replaces Jesus' gospel with a gospel about Jesus—a religion that should be called 'Paulism.' This Paulism is a misinterpretation and falsification of Jesus' real teaching—a fact that has also been recognized by modern theological research. All the beautiful aspects of Christianity are linked with Jesus, all the unbeautiful with Paul." Additionally, Ernst Kaiserman, a New Testament scholar, concluded from his research about Jesus that "Only a few words from the Sermon on the Mount, the dispute with Pharisaism, a number of parables, a scattering of other things date back in all probability to the historical Jesus." In addition, he claims those who read the authentic words of Jesus find nothing about original sin of death and resurrection. Instead, they learn about love.

Scholars in the early 19th century began to see parallels between Buddhist teachings and New Testament stories. They found in the Gospel of John that Buddhist ideas occur verse after verse. J. Edgar Brum wrote about this similarity in *The Christian Buddhism of St. John.* In one example, the Buddha said, "Whosoever sees the Dharma (the great cosmic law) sees me." Jesus says in the Gospel John, "He that seeth me, seeth him that sent me" (John 12:45). Based on this and many more similarities, the author concluded from his research that Jesus was a Buddhist.

This research continued in the 20th century with similar findings. In the 1930's, Burnett Hillman Streeter, an Oxford New Testament scholar, established that the moral teaching of Buddha resembled that of the Sermon on the Mount. Also, Elaine Pagels, a Gnostic Christian scholar, wrote that Jesus' teachings sounded more Eastern than Western. Other scholars have suggested that if the names were changed, the "living Buddha" could have said what the Gospel of Thomas attributed to the "living Jesus."

Historical events led to the connection of East with West. Centuries before the birth of Jesus, India was with the West. Since King Solomon's time, Jews had contact with India. Following the captivity of Israel by Babylonia in the sixth century B.C., the Jewish dispersement resulted in Persian and southern India communities maintaining direct intellectual and spiritual links between East and West. During the third century B.C., King Asoka brought most of India under his rule and devoted his life to spreading the teachings of Buddha. Missionaries were sent to Syria, Egypt, Macedonia, and Cyrene, and the West became familiar with Buddhism. This Buddhist influence also played an integral role in literature of the Hellenistic world.

Gruber and Kersten suggest the authors of the New Testament believed the teachings of Jesus had much in common with Buddha. This close relationship of the two masters attracted the attention of scholars who wondered how these similarities came about. Recent research strongly suggests the beginnings of Christianity were dependent on Buddhism but has not answered the question of how Buddhism became so influential that it was adopted by Christianity.

Childhood stories of the young Jesus were similar to those of Buddha. Scholars discovered that the older Buddhist texts were borrowed by the West, concluding that the stories of Jesus may have originated from Buddhism outside of Judaism. Their research showed that some stories were imported from India and incorporated into the gospels. Because Jesus' biographers knew little about Jesus' childhood, they had to improvise, according to these biblical researchers. They used mythical narratives appropriate for the early years of a divine child, based on the early years of Buddha. Texts of the Mahayana schools in India made the human being Siddharta Gautama (Buddha) into a god. These scholars conjecture this was the model that the gospels followed when describing Jesus' early years.

The similarities between Jesus and Buddha are many. In fact, it is believed that both masters preexisted before their incarnations. The ancient Indian view was that gods occasionally came to earth in human form, today called an "avatar." The Gospel of John speaks of Jesus being an incarnation of the word, synonymous with God. Similarly, Buddha is said to have spent time in Tushita heaven before descending to earth. Another similarity is that the genealogical trees of both Gautama (Buddha) and Jesus show them to be of royal lineage.

The stories of the immaculate conception and virgin birth are found in Buddhism as well as in Christianity. On a full-moon night, King Shuddhodana's wife, Maya, had a strange dream that a white elephant with six tusks and a lotus blossom entered her womb. At this time, Buddha consciously and willingly entered Maya's body. In the "Story of Hannah," Mary's conception is described in a similar manner. Mary, in a dream-like vision, sees a white dove descending from heaven and entering her body. Writers of the gospels interpreted the white dove as symbolic of the Holy Spirit.

Even the resulting explanations to the women's husbands share a similar theme. Joseph understandably became upset about Mary's pregnancy, knowing he was not the father, until an angel explained the background of the pregnancy. King Shuddhodana was also informed by angels (devas) about his wife's miraculous conception. During Guatama's conception and birth, a great light shone over the world. Similarly, a great light is said to have shone at the time of Jesus' birth.

Krishna, another Indian avatar, shared similarities with Jesus. Mary gave birth on a trip to another town to pay taxes. A similar story exists regarding Krishna, the eighth avatar of Vishnu, as his mother also delivered on a journey similar to Mary's, and Krishna was also born in a manger among shepherds. Both Krishna and Jesus escaped infanticide ordered by an unscrupulous ruler and were both taken into exile.

According to the Gospel of Luke, 40 days after His birth, Jesus was brought to Jerusalem for presentation in the temple. A pious man named Simeon learned from an angel that he would not die before he had seen the Lord anointed. While in the temple, Simeon took the infant in his arms; he then knew he would die in peace. A similar story occurred with Buddha, involving an old man named Asita, who saw Buddha in the temple as a newborn son. In India, the custom was common for a newly born infant to be brought to a temple as a show of respect for the gods. This was not a Jewish custom.

In Luke 2:41-52, the twelve-year-old Jesus vanished while in Jerusalem for Passover. His parents found Him in the temple teaching His views. A Buddhist parallel exists with the young Prince Siddartha (future Buddha) who became lost. His father found him beneath a tree, contemplating religion. It could well be that the author of Luke was aware of these Buddhist traditions and so invented these stories for that reason.

Two of Jesus' most famous miracles were the multiplying of loaves and walking on water. A similar miracle occurred with Buddha, who multiplied bread for his disciples and monastery inhabitants, a total of 500. Jesus satisfied 5,000 people with five loaves. Additionally, in several of the oldest Buddhist texts, Buddha walks on water as one of his many magical abilities. Some scholars believe the correspondence between the two miracle stories are too numerous to be independent, and therefore, must be viewed as more than a coincidence.

In yet another similarity, in Matthew 14:28-33, the disciple Peter attempts to walk on water, but begins to sink. A similar Buddhist story occurs with Sariputta, a disciple of Guatama, who also tries to walk on water but sinks.

Both Jesus and Buddha treated people equally, no matter their status or caste. They both stressed equality of all people. A New Testament story tells of a poor widow who tithed two lepta, a lot of money considering her financial situation. In the story, Jesus taught His disciples that a poor person's modest offering is worth more than a rich person's larger gift. A similar story occurs with Buddha. Some scholars conjecture that the story of Buddha was handed down by the Christian community and recorded by Luke as being part of Jesus' life.

A biblical scholar, Rudolf Seydal discovered 51 similarities between New Testament scripture and Buddhism, analyzing each in depth. Seydal believes the evangelists did not make use of the legends about Buddha, but used a Christianized, poetic gospel, which employed the Buddhist structure and many Buddhist themes. This was believed done in order to be a Christian work of art similar to the Buddhist writings that stimulated a thinker to imitate Buddha. Another theologian, Van din Bergh van Eysinga, concluded there were 11 strong correspondences between Christ and Buddha, with six being worthy of consideration.

Some researchers assert the Gospel of Mark was the result of desk work. They believe the author had in front of him stories of miracles, collections of prophecies, an incomplete collection of Jesus' sayings, the parables, and books of the Old Testament. Also available were Jewish, Hellenistic, and Buddhist material. To portray Jesus as the Messiah, the writers of Mark borrowed from the Jewish holy books. Some scholars even conclude that those responsible for writing the gospels were more interested in reforming Judaism than establishing a new religion, especially in the Gospel of Matthew.

SIMILARITIES BETWEEN THE TEACHINGS OF JESUS AND BUDDHA

Roy C. Amore, a religious historian, was the first to realize the astonishing correspondences between Buddhist texts and Q. He could not explain why the Jesus' teachings in Q sounded Buddhistic, and he made the assumption that both Jesus and later evangelists had access to Buddhist sources. The later insertions into scripture were in no way linked with Buddhist ideas. Almost without exception, the Buddhist sayings are concentrated in Q, in the original words of Jesus.

Some Buddhist works were written in verse, a form that Jesus often followed. Researchers have found precise Buddhist precedents for the Beatitudes (passages from the Sermon on the Mount declaring what makes a man blessed) and other major declarations made in that sermon, which many believe to be the heart of Jesus' teachings. The sayings of Jesus are not only reminders to act rightly, but are deeply rooted principles of karma, which is the intention behind one's words and deeds.

One of the most difficult tasks for both Jesus and Buddha was to convince their serious followers that they had to leave their families behind. A path out of entanglement in the outer world could be achieved only by making a radical break with all ties, whether they were emotional, intellectual or familial. In the

Gospel of Thomas (42), Jesus instructs His disciples to disseminate His teachings by abandoning family ties and domesticity, that is, to become transient. Similarily, Buddha left his family on his path toward enlightenment.

Reincarnation is a cornerstone in the Buddhist teachings. Buddha spoke of the eight spokes of the wheel symbolizing the noble Eight Fold Path. Those who want to be released from the cycle of rebirths must adhere to the eight demands. For example, there cannot be right thinking and right action without right speech. If the path is not followed, a person will once again fan the flames of the wheel of rebirths. A similar teaching is found in the Epistle of James (3:6), which states the speaker of the tongue inflames the "cycle of life." The correct translation was circle of births.

A precondition for breaking through the rebirth cycle is the realization of the second stage of the Eight Fold Path—a complete renunciation of material things. Buddha taught that material possessions do not endure. Buddhist monks practice this principle by remaining without possessions and calling themselves homeless. Buddha said, "In this world, the wise man holds onto faith and wisdom. Those are his greatest treasures: all other riches he pushes aside." Jesus also taught a similar message in Matthew 9:21, which states that only someone who sold all his or her possessions and followed Jesus could be perfect. Jesus said one should sell possessions and give them to charity. A detachment from material possessions was important for spiritual evolvement in both Jesus' and Buddha's teachings.

Jesus did not seek out the company of stubborn people, and He taught the disciples that they should not stay with, or strive to convince people by whom they were rejected. Buddha had a similar philosophy, "If a Buddhist disciple does not find a companion, either better or his equal, he should pursue a lonely way. There can be no association with fools" (Dh 5:3).

Both Jesus and Buddha told their followers not to worry. Jesus said, "I am telling you, do not worry about your life, what you will eat, or about your body, what you will wear . . . ."(QS-34). Similarly, Buddha often told his disciples how useless worrying about anything was. Buddhist teachings advise that we should be composed, tranquil, satisfied, and free of fear.

Buddha and Jesus both taught about humility. Buddha taught that his disciples should always be humble. Similarly, Jesus said, "Everyone who glorifies himself will be humiliated, and one who humbles himself will be praised."

Buddha emphasized self-knowledge, a hallmark Buddhist characteristic. Buddhists proclaim that by studying Buddhism, we study ourselves. Jesus also placed a high value on self- knowledge. He said, "He who knows everything, but fails to know himself misses the knowledge of everything" (Thomas 67). Self-knowledge was the basic philosophy of the Christian Gnostics, as gnosis means "knowledge."

Buddha was against the caste system of the Brahmins, who kept spiritual knowledge among themselves. Jesus opposed the scribes who did not allow everyone access to true knowledge in order to maintain their influence. "The Pharisees and scribes took the keys of knowledge, and they hid them. Neither did they enter, nor did they allow those who wished to enter . . ." (Thomas 39). Jesus also said, "Nothing is hidden that will not be made known, or secrets that will not come to light" (Q-35).

Common sense would dictate that the two greatest spiritual beings that inhabited this world would have a similar message. The unadulterated teachings found in Q-1 substantiate the similar teachings of Jesus and Buddha. Evidence will be presented in the following chapters that Jesus did in fact travel to the East and was taught about Eastern spirituality.

THE APOCALYPTIC JESUS

The first layer of Q writings, Q-1, is considered by Q scholars to include the original teachings of Jesus, closely related to the teachings of Buddha. In Q-1, Jesus is remembered as an independent, wise teacher, with a strong compassion for suffering humans in search of redemption. The portrayal of Jesus in Q-1 showed a Jesus full of compassion and love. His followers, until the Jewish War (66 - 73 A.D.), were a small, insignificant group spread throughout Judea and Galilee.

Some scholars doubt if Jesus was His real name, but perhaps given to Him by His followers around the time of the Jewish War. At that time great personalities were viewed as different embodiments of the spirits of the Chosen People. These personalities, usually leaders, were seen as reincarnations of Joshua. In the Jewish tradition, Joshua is the prototype of the liberation from foreign rule. The land was full of Joshuas. The name Jesus is the Greek translation of Joshua, with "Jah" meaning "redemption." Biblical scholar James Deardorff claims "Jah" comes from "Jahweh" (JHWH = God) and "shua" gives the "save" meaning. Scholars have suggested that the followers called their leader Jesus (Joshua) to identify Him with other religious prophets. False prophets acted similarly to the Jesus portrayed in the Gospels, such as leading people into the wilderness and giving them a divine sign, the miraculous increase in loaves. Similar to the other prophets, Jesus of the New Testament went to the Mount of Olives telling His disciples His last days were ahead.

The second layer of teachings, Q-2 and Q-3, was gathered long after Jesus left His followers. They are from the time of the Jewish War, and, unlike Q1, introduce a tone of anger and condemnation into the writings. The Q-2 and Q-3 people transformed Jesus into the eschatological Jesus, that is, the Jesus who taught about the end of man and the world. This Jesus uttered threats and denunciations of entire cities and classes, aligning with expectations of that time. The transition from Q-1 to Q-3 occurred during threatening times, around the Jewish War. Also, the original Jesus movement of wandering monks became an apocalyptic sect in Q-2 and Q-3 times. The original Jesus in Q-1 spoke about loving one's enemies and not getting angry, while the new Jesus displayed anger toward cities that resisted His teachings, one of the many contradictions introduced by the author of Matthew. While the Q-1 Jesus persuaded His followers to be merciful and non-judgmental, the new Jesus did not, as the Q-2 and Q-3 writings viewed anger about not being received. Q scholars conjecture that Jesus propagandists took the old Gospel of sayings out of hiding (Q-1) and edited denunciations into it.

Because the original Q-1 followers had little success in developing the early Church, their successors, the Q-2 and Q-3 people, inserted apocalyptic prophecies to gain converts. In the Gospel of Thomas, which includes Q-1, Jesus teaches that true knowledge entails self-knowledge, which allows one to break away from the world. This group revered Jesus as a great esoteric teacher, not an apocalyptic prophet. The Q-2 and Q-3 people knew little about Jesus' life, however, losing this information before the war. They added to the Q-1 material based on their group's sociological situation.

Gruber and Kersten believe that someone in the Q-2 and Q-3 group had knowledge about the connection between Jesus and Buddha. The Q-2 and Q-3 people made use of Buddhist's legend to depict Jesus. The story of Jesus' temptation closely models Buddha's temptation. As mentioned earlier, some scholars believe the stories of Jesus' childhood found in the gospels and *Apocrypha* were borrowed from India. Both Jesus and Buddha emancipated themselves from their respective mentors (Jesus from John the Baptist), and both retreated to the wilderness and fasted.

REBIRTH

The first question that may come to mind when comparing Jesus with Buddha is the concept of rebirth. Christianity teaches that the soul does not reincarnate but goes through a process of bodily resurrection on Judgment Day, when the decision is made whether one spends eternity in heaven or hell. In contrast, Buddhism is based on the principle of reincarnation, where the soul comes back to the physical plane for repeated lives. The soul's purpose is to perfect itself through rebirth, so it can eventually return to his or her divine home. To reach perfection, the soul must live many lives. In this life, one is held accountable for misdeeds, and one's karma is the result of misdeeds that often occurred in a past life. Until the lesson is learned, a soul will undergo multiple rebirths to overcome this ignorance. A soul is under the auspices of destiny to learn particular lessons, which in turn falls under influence of the heavenly bodies. According to Buddhism, astrology maps out the particular fate for an individual in the current life.

Evidence from Gnostic literature does suggest that the early Christians believed in reincarnation, but as orthodoxy grew, the church edited out this doctrine from scripture. Surprisingly, there are still references to rebirth in the New Testament.

However, it appears that in the traditional texts the concept of rebirth was actually taught by Jesus. In a later chapter about the *Gospel of the Nazirenes,* we find that Jesus spoke frequently about reincarnation.

In an earlier copy of a New Testament text before it was corrupted, Nicodemus asks Jesus, "What must I do to enter the kingdom of God?" Jesus answered, "Verily, verily, I say unto thee: except a man be born again and again, he cannot be readmitted into the kingdom of God." Nicodemus asks, "How can a man be born into his mother's womb and be born again?" Jesus replies, "Marvel not that I said unto thee, Ye must be born again and again" (Jesus Evangelism 5:12-16). The quotation was an original Aramaic text. The corrupted version is now found in John 3:1-4, 7:9-11.

The theme of the preexistence of the soul is found in the Gospel of Thomas of the *Apocrypha.* In Thomas 49, Jesus said, "Blest are the solitary and chosen—for you shall find the kingdom. You have come from it, and you shall return into it."

There are more discussions of rebirth in the Bible. For instance, the Hebrew prophet Elijah was to have lived in the 9th century B.C. Four centuries later, Malachi recorded a prophecy in the closing lines of the Old Testament: "Behold, I will send Elijah the prophet before the coming of the great and dreadful day of the Lord." The first Gospel of Matthew refers to the prophecy on three occasions, and the remaining gospels speak of it seven times. In Matthew 16:13-14, "When Jesus came into the coasts of Caesara Philippi, He asked His disciples, saying, 'Who do men say that I the son of man am?' And they said, 'Some say thou art John the Baptist; some Elias; and others, Jeremias, or one of the prophets.'" This statement from Matthew 16 is repeated almost verbatim in Mark 8:27- 28 and Luke 9: 18-19.

Additional instances of rebirth are found in Matthew. Matthew 17:9-13 states, "And as they came down from the mountain, Jesus charged them saying, 'Tell the vision to no man, until the son of man be risen again from the dead.' And his disciples asked him, saying, 'Why then say the scribes that Elias must first come?' And Jesus answered him, 'Elias truly shall first come and restore all things. But I say unto you, that Elias truly is come already, and they knew him not, but have done unto him whatsoever they listed. Likewise shall also the son of man suffer of them.' Then the disciples understood that he spake unto them of John the Baptist' [who already had been beheaded by Herod]."

In Matthew 11:7, 10-11, 14-15, Jesus said unto the multitudes concerning John, "This is he, of whom it is written, behold I send my messenger before thy face, which shall prepare the way before thee. Verily I say unto you, among them that are born of women there hath not risen a greater than John the Baptist . . . and if ye will receive it, this is Elias, which was for to come. He that hath ears to hear, let him hear."

Jesus, Himself, often spoke of His own previous, external existence. "Ye shall see the son of man ascend up where he was before" (John 6:62). "I am living bread which came down from heaven" (John 6:51). Did Jesus exist previously on earth, and not only in heaven? According to John 8:55-59, He did. Jesus is taunted by the Israelites for setting Himself up as greater than Abraham. Jesus replied, "Your father Abraham rejoiced to see my day: and he saw it, and was glad." Then said the Jews unto Him: "Thou are not yet fifty years old, and hast thou seen Abraham?" Jesus said unto them, "Verily, verily, I say unto you, before Abraham was, I am." In another verse, John the Baptist said of Jesus, "This was he of whom I spake, He that cometh after me is preferred for me: for he was before me" (John 1:14-15).

Jesus also spoke about the pre-existence of the soul, "Glorify thou me with thine own self with the glory which I had with thee before the world was" (John 17:5). This suggests other souls incarnated during Jesus' time that had preexisted with Jesus.

Jesus also discussed His future life. In John 14:3 He told of His coming reappearance on Earth, "I will come again, and receive you unto myself: that where I am, there ye may be also." Christians interpret this second coming as Jesus returning to Earth in an adult form. In Revelation 22:12, Jesus predicts, "Very soon now, I shall be with you again, bringing the reward to be given to every man according to what he deserves." Even Saint Paul suggested that He may return to earth life again until mankind is redeemed, "My little children, of whom I travail in birth again until Christ be formed in you, I desire to be present with you now, and to change my voice; for I stand in doubt of you" (Galatians 4:19). All of these subtle rebirth references made it into the New Testament.

The rebirths of the savior and prophets are clearly stated in the Bible, but does rebirth occur in ordinary humanity? The disciples questioned this truth about the man being blind, "Who did sin, the man, or his parents?" They must have had the idea of reincarnation in mind. Jesus had the opportunity to clarify the statement if the disciples were in error, but He did not. Jesus replied that the blindman's sight would be restored so that "the works of God should be manifest in him." Perhaps Christ's words should be taken literally when He said, "Except a man be born again, he cannot see the kingdom of God." Scripture does suggest the rebirth of the common man.

Many early Church Fathers believed in the pre-existence of the soul. For example, Justin Martyr (died 65A.D.) spoke of the soul inhabiting a human body more than once, but that it cannot remember previous experiences. Souls who have become unworthy to see God, he said, are joined to the bodies of wild beasts. He defended the concept of transmigration, where human souls enter the body of an animal.

Another Church Father, Clement of Alexandria (died 220 A.D.), also believed in the preexistence of the soul when he wrote, "Before the foundation of the world were we, who became destined to be in Him, preexisted in the eye of God before—we the rational creatures of the Word of God, on whose account we date from the beginning: for in the beginning was the Word . . . The Savior, who existed before, has in recent days appeared . . ." Clement,a Platonist and Church Father, headed the famous catechetical school in Alexandria from 190 to 203 A.D.

Origen, considered the most distinguished and influential of all the theologians of the early Church, was believed by historians to be the father of Church science and founder of Christian theology. At one time, Saint Jerome considered Origen "the greatest teacher of the church after the apostles." As a pupil of Clement of Alexandria, Origen replaced him as head of the Alexandria Catechetical School. Origen taught about the pre-existence of the soul and said, "The soul is immortal and therefore has neither beginning of days nor end of life." He could not restrain his impatience at the crude beliefs of traditionalists about the last days and resurrection of the dead. Origen said the resurrection in the gospels could not have been intended literally. He asked, "How can material bodies be recompounded, every particle of which has passed into many other bodies? To which body do the molecules belong?" Origen claimed that men fall into the lowest depths of absurdity and take refuge in the pious assurance that "everything is possible with God." He said souls animate bodies successively, and their transmigrations are regulated according to the soul's merits and demerits. Obviously, Origen was a Platonist riddled with strong Gnostic tendencies. It was not until three centuries later that the Church condemned Origen's teachings at the Fifth Ecumenical Council.

Christian Gnostics also believed in reincarnation. Gnosticism, according to some scholars, was one of the most powerful currents of thoughts that influenced Christian doctrine and practice. In orthodox circles, Gnosticism was regarded as a psuedo-Christian religion whose religious philosophy paralleled Christianity. Carl Jung, the famous psychiatrist, was convinced that "the central ideas of Christianity are rooted in Gnostic philosophy." Some scholars believe the Gnostics were the descendants of the original Christians and inheritors of the esoteric teachings of Jesus. In Mark 4:11, Jesus told His disciples, "Unto you it is given to know the mystery of the kingdom of God; but unto them are without, all these things are done in parables." He continued, "And when they were alone, Jesus expounded all things to his disciples, but without a parable spoke he not to the others" (Mark 4:33-34).

In 1900, more evidence in the Gnostic belief of reincarnation was provided by G.R.S. Mead who wrote in *Fragments of a Faith Forgotten,* "The whole of (Gnosticism) revolved round the conception of cyclic law for both the universal and individual soul. Thus we find the Gnostics invariably teaching the doctrine not only of the pre-existence but also of the rebirth of human souls . . . They held rigidly to the infallible working out of the great law of cause and effect."

Some Gnostics boasted to be in possession of genuine traditions that derived their doctrines from Paul, Peter, Judas, Thomas, Philip, and Matthew. Other Gnostics were close to James, the brother of Jesus, and Mary Magdalene. They professed that they had received secret doctrines orally from the apostles. For example, Basilides taught in Alexandria in about 125 A.D. and founded a number of Gnostic schools; he maintained that he received all his doctrines from the disciples Matthew and Peter through his disciple Glaucus. The orthodox Christian historian Eusebius wrote that Basilides published 24 volumes of *Interpretation of the Gospels,* which were later burned by the Church, containing information he had received from the disciples such as the concept of rebirth.

Gnostics believed Jesus represented the personal name of their teacher, while Christ was the divine spirit in every being. In a divine incarnation like Jesus, the spirit was fully manifest. Therefore, it was proper to add to His personal name a title (Christ) to express this fact. An advanced Gnostic disciple was called a *Chrestos;* when fully illuminated, a *Christos.* To become perfect through the ages of compassionate striving (through past lives) was worthy of deep admiration and reverence by the Gnostics. In other words, the soul perfected itself through successive incarnations. The Gnostics emphasized that Jesus did not take the position of uniqueness. He continually referred to Himself as son of man, not son of God, according to the Gospels. When the Jews accused Him of setting himself up as God, He replied, "Is it not written in your law . . . Ye are gods?" (John 10:4). Jesus did not think of people as terrible sinners. When the disciples marveled at His miracles, Jesus said, "Even greater things than these can ye do also."

All outward manifestations of Christian Gnosticism were eventually suppressed by the Pope and emperor, the death penalty being the penalty for their expressed belief. It was in the 6th century A.D. when Emperor Justinian, the ruler of the Eastern Roman Empire, declared war against the followers of Origen. At Justinian's demand, a local synod convening in Constantinople condemned the teachings of Origen. Ten years later Justinian issued his anathemas (curses) against Origen and submitted them for final ratification at an extra conciliary (unofficial) session of the Fifth Ecumenical Council, called the Second Council of Constantinople. The anathemas cursed, among other teachings of Origen, the doctrine of the pre-existence of the soul.

The Catholic Encyclopedia now portrays some startling information concerning the Fifth Ecumenical Council, according to Elaine Pagels. This information was recently revealed by

Catholic scholars, who now have access to the original records. On technical grounds, one can conclude that the Catholics have no barrier to believe in reincarnation based on a technical error.

The Council was attended entirely by Eastern bishops with no representation from Rome. Pope Vigilius was in Constantinople at the time but refused to attend the Council. Presiding was Eutychius, patriarch of Constantinople and head of the Eastern Church. Apparently, there had been a conflict between Justinian and Pope Vigilius. For eight years the Pope had been Justinian's prisoner, having been kidnaped from Rome in November of 545. To bring peace between the Eastern and Western branches of the Church, the Fifth Ecumenical Council was formulated with the purpose of deciding the fate of three supposed heretics, none of whom were Origen's followers. However, when Justinian refused Pope Vigilius' request for equal representation of bishops from East and West, the Pope refused to attend. As a result, of the 165 bishops at the meeting, 159 were from the Eastern Church.

The bishops at the extra conciliary session subscribed to the 15 anathemas against Origen proposed by the emperor. However, there is no proof that the Pope approved the anathemas, because he protested the convocation of the council. This extra conciliary sentence was later mistaken for a decree at the actual Ecumenical Council.

The far-reaching effect of the Council's decision is that orthodox Christianity has condemned the belief of the pre-existence of the soul, and by implication, reincarnation. For centuries, the so-called anathemas against Origen have been part of the proceedings of the Fifth Ecumenical Council, which now appear to be a mistake because the Pope did not give his stamp of approval. Four of the 15 anathemas were aimed at the pre-existence of the soul. Anathema one reads, "If anyone asserts the fabulous pre-existence of souls and shall assert the monstrous restoration which follows from it: let him be anathema." To anathema is to be cursed and committed to eternal hell fire for disagreeing with a particular Church doctrine. Some New Age scholars believe the early Christian community, who remembered Jesus' teachings, took the belief of reincarnation for granted until that belief became a victim to that fateful error at the Fifth Ecumenical Council.

The concept of the rebirth doctrine in early Christianity is still debatable. Enough evidence exists in scripture that suggests that people did believe in it. An early manuscript, entitled *The Gospel of the Nazirenes* written in Aramaic that will be discussed in the following chapter, emphasizes the doctrine of reincarnation through the words of Jesus. Evidence has been presented in this chapter about the similarity between the teachings and life of Jesus and Buddha. The cornerstone of Buddhism is the belief in reincarnation, and as we will see, Jesus did study the teachings of Buddha.

Chapter Four

THE GOSPEL OF THE NAZIRENES

An Ancient Account of Jesus

Most biblical scholars believe the four Gospels were based upon an earlier source, probably written in Aramaic, that was lost centuries ago. The ancient Essenes had such a document that was preserved in one of the Tibetan Buddhist monasteries, hidden for safety reasons from corrupt hands. Named *The Gospel of the Nazirenes,* it has proven to be the oldest of all accounts of Jesus' life. It was published in London around 1870 as *The Gospel of the Holy Twelve.* This gospel is one of the most ancient and complete of the early Christian writings. It provides evidence that many of Jesus' teachings that contradicted the developing biased dogma were edited out of the Bible by the early Church Fathers. This gospel was referred to by a number of Church Father historians, including Clement, Iranaeas, Origin, Eusebius, and others. Its historical authenticity is validated with ancient teachings found in the Torah and Talmud. *The Gospel of the Nazirene* explains Jesus the Nazirene's ancient way of life, taught since the time of Enoch and Noah.

This Aramaic original is quoted by many Church historians as the most likely source from which the four gospels (Matthew, Mark, Luke, and John) emerged. The original text is called *Aramaic Matthew* and is also known as the *Gospel of Hebrews, Gospel of Nazirenes, Gospel of the Ebionites,* or *Gospel of the Holy Twelve.* A large portion of the text of the *Gospel of the Nazirene* is identical to another scroll, supposedly preserved and hidden in Tibet from corrupters by the Mount Caramel branch of the Essenes (Carmelites), sometime in the mid to late first century. This text is considerably older than the New Testament.

The Gospel of the Holy Twelve entered into the contemporary era untouched and almost forgotten, but with a syntax that was difficult to read or understand. Modern editing has made the text more understandable by rewording much of the archaic language. This chapter is based on the resultant edited version that led to the book entitled *The Gospel of the Nazirenes*. Although this book answers many questions, several questions remain for me: Where is the original text located today? Was the original text ever carbon-dated? And what do biblical historians have to say about the original text?

THE NAZIRENES

The Nazirenes were a mystical Essene subsect that Jesus, His brother James, and their cousin, John the Baptist belonged to. Another Essene subsect was the Ebionites. The specific spelling which differentiates these Nazirenes from the rest is derived from a blending of two words - "Nazirite" and "Essene" or in Hebrew, "Nazir - Yesseyen" (Nazir-yen/Nazirenes). "Nazirene" comes from the Hebrew word "Nazir," which means a guard, the guardian of the truth, "the way," or a "warner" against lies or heresies, according to Josepheus, a first century Jewish historian. Many historians spell "Nazirenes" with an "a," Nazarenes.

There is strong evidence that these Nazirene teachings are essentially the same as the Bet Hillel school of Pharisees and Essenes of that time. Some historical evidence suggests that Jesus studied with Hillel the Elder, who had founded the Bet Hillel branch of the Pharisees. Jesus was raised in the Nazirene sect of the Essene branch of Judaism. Many of the Essenes during that era were previously Hillel Pharisees, who were forced to leave the sect because of the spiteful attacks by the Shammai Pharisees, who also persecuted the Hillel Pharisees.

Following the Pompey invasion of Jerusalem in 63 B.C., the Essene community began to break up. Some of the Essenes split into subgroups, while others went underground, joining with others of like mind to gain strength in numbers.

Nazirites, similar to the Essenes, existed in four basic groups—neophytes, devotees, first-level initiates, and adepts/high priests. The Nazirite adepts and high priests differed from the Essenes only in varying degrees. They lived in small, family villages, unlike the Qumran Essenes who lived in an all-male, celibate community. Nazirenes, as compared to their Essene mentors, were called household devotees as compared to in-temple initiates or adepts. Barbara Theiring writes in *Jesus and the Riddle of the Dead Sea Scrolls:*

> "The Essene Nazirite (Nazirite Essene) order was under the authority of the David Crown prince, as it was of the lower status than the celibate order . . . Between village Essenes (Nazirenes) and high monastic Essenes stood the Therapeutae of Egypt and other Diaspra Essenes. They were called the 'Joseph' tribes of Ephrain and Manasseh. In many ways they were like monastics, having similar views on purity. They were not secluded, but very much involved in the world and politics."

The beliefs of Nazirenes differed markedly from the Proto-orthodoxy Church. According to the history of the two main Essene subsects (Nazirenes and Ebionites), they believed the Holy Spirit officially entered Jesus at His baptism by John the Baptist in the Jordan River and not at conception. They also believed, as did the Gnostics, the term "First Begotten" as opposed to "Only Begotten" that linked Jesus to the reincarnation of Adam as a mortal who strived to an achievable initiate perfection. The perfection was reached at Jesus' baptism by John. The "Only Begotten" view was that Jesus was an immortal made into flesh. Nazirites believed Jesus was augmented to fulfill the Divine potential of humanity, as he received the God consciousness when baptized.

The teachings of the Essenes included similarities to Christianity, such as immortality of the self, love thy neighbor as self, and the desire to share the One Lord Creator with the world. Unlike Christians, they believed in vegetarianism, karma, and reincarnation. The Essenes also repudiated sacrifice and animal cruelty.

The Nazirites, also called the Yessenes, strongly resembled the Therapeutae, Pythagoreans, and the Buddhists, who also practiced community of goods, daily ablutions, and daily worship. All these religions renounced consuming flesh, strong drink, animal sacrifice, and the doctrine of "atonement" for the sins by vicarious and involuntary sufferings of others, a belief that was held by the Pharisees and Sadducees. The Nazirenes strongly opposed any belief system that proposed blood sacrifice of the innocent, either human or animal. The traditional Christian teaching that God sent His only begotten son to die in a grotesque blood sacrifice as a ransom for the sins of the world and forgiveness unto salvation is literally opposite of what history tells us the Nazirenes believed.

HISTORICAL ACCOUNTS OF THE NAZIRENE WRITINGS

Over the years, biblical scholars have commented on *The Gospel of the Nazirenes* to try and bring clarity to its relationship with the New Testament gospels. Some of these observations are listed below.

Baigent, Lincoln, and Leigh write in *Messianic Legacy,* "In Constantine's time, Nazarene teaching was still thriving and being disseminated. The Bishop of Rome, in A.D. 318, is reported to have had a meeting with Nazarenes . . . leaders directly descended from Jesus' family." They then quote Eusebius: "They held that . . . the Epistle of the Apostle (Paul) ought to be rejected altogether, calling him a renegade from 'the Law' and only using the *Gospel of the Hebrews* they treated the rest with scant respect."

Also referring to the Apostle Paul, Ian Wilson writes in *Jesus, The Evidence:*

> "The canonical gospel writer mentions that in his time there were many other gospels in existence, most of which have been unfortunately lost to us . . . The writings of the early Church Fathers provide clues to the existence of a few of these: *A Gospel of the Hebrews* . . .a Gospel of the Ebionites, apparently strongly opposed to the writings of the Apostle Paul, mentioned in a condemnation of heresies by the fourth century writer Epiphanius. Clearly the manuscripts discovered so far are a drop in the ocean of early documentary material circulated about Jesus."

In addition, Dr. U. C. Ewing claims in *The Prophet of the Dead Sea Scroll,* "The first gospel was set down in Aramaic, not in Greek.

It featured the mother tongue of Jesus and the brethren of the scrolls . . .It was used by the Essian followers of Jesus who were known as Nazarenes, the Ebionites, i.e., the Palestinian or Hebrew Christians under the leadership of James (Jesus' brother) . . ." Ewing continues, "Thus it was referred to by Jerome, Epiphanius, and others as *The Gospel of the Holy Twelve, Gospel of the Ebionites,* and *Gospel of the Hebrews.* The last [latter] meaning the gospel used by the Hebrew Christians . . . connected with the word as it came sweet and clean from the mouth of Jesus himself."

Dr. Hugh Schonfoeld writes in *The Passover Plot,* "There are links with the *Nazorean Gospel of the Hebrews,* which came to be regarded as the Hebrew original of Matthew." He later writes in *The Jesus Party,*

> "The Nazoreans who were the Jewish adherents of Jesus were still very active and flourishing in the fourth century A.D., where Epiphanius and Jerome were acquainted with them. Their communities and synagogues were spread over an arc extending from the Syrian coast through northern Transjordan down into Peraea (sic). They were in possession of and used exclusively, a gospel in Aramaic known as the *Hebrew Matthew* or *The Gospel of the Hebrews* . . . Indeed, the Gospel of the Hebrew, according to Jerome, claimed that Jesus' brother Jacob (James) who became leader of the Nazoreans had taken part in The Last Supper."

Dr. Edgar Goodspeed states in *History of Early Christian Literature:*

> "Eusebius lists the gospel *(Gospel of Nazirene)* among the disputed - or non-conforming books. Jerome, toward the close of the century, could not find a Greek copy of it, but saw an Aramaic text of it in Palestine, which he says he translated into Greek and Latin, probably meaning for the parts he wished to copy or use in his works. This Aramaic version so often regarded as 'the original' was for the use of Jewish Christian sects–perhaps Ebionites but probably Nazarenes—who in the third century were using this book, and finally gave their name to it, so that it came to be known as the *Gospel of the Nazarene.* Epiphanius says that

> Nazarenes or Gnostic Jewish Christians used a gospel resembling Matthew . . .This gospel disappeared sometime during the latter part of the fourth century."

Rev. Adam Findlay, M.A., D.D., writes in *The History of Christianity–In the Light of Modern Knowledge,* "The most primitive of the non-canonical gospels, *The Gospel of the Nazarenes,* was used up to the end of the fourth century in a community which set special store by it. Another, a *Gospel of Peter* which was episcopally condemned at the close of the second century, was found in an Egyptian grave."

During the time of Jesus, anyone in or around Judea who referred to any man as God or His only Begotten Son committed a crime punishable by death. Therefore, many late versions of the gospel were either not authorized by Jewish scribes or those of Hebrew descent, or their work was edited.

During the Nicene era of 325 A.D., gatherings organized by the Roman Emperor Constantine met to unify and canonize the many diverse religious texts and the traditions that were in existence at that time. To gain favor with Constantine in order to attain a secure future for Christianity, the correctors of the gospels expanded the life and teachings of Jesus into a concept of external divinity, which could be more easily merged with Greek and Roman religions. Many of the obvious traditions mentioned in the first and third century writings about the life of Jesus were edited out in the ensuing emotional and intellectual debates.

In 527 A.D. Emperor Justanians' first official edict regarding the Church was to outlaw all teachings considered to differ from official Church canon. For example, anything considered to be of a heathen philosophy such as Buddhism, Hindu, or Eastern mysticism was forbidden. The result was that anyone caught teaching about karma, reincarnation, vegetarianism, or related forms of ascetism, such as compassionate treatment of animals or anti-slavery, could be arrested and executed.

Finnish historian, Dr. John Forsstrom, writes in *The King of Jews,* "Jesus belonged to a political party called the Nazireans or Nazirites, and according to another source had a line (part) in the middle of his head in the manner of the Nazireans (Nazirites)"

Dr. Hugh Schonfield writes in *The Passover Plot:*

> "The oldest root of the Christian movement in Galilee is to be sought in a group of dedicated sectarians who continued the ancient Israelite institution of the lifelong Nazirite . . . We have every reason to hold that the family to which Jesus belonged was nurtured in this tradition and much of his teachings confirm this. . . The followers of Jesus the 'Nazoreans of Galilee' simply established in Jerusalem a community of their 'Way' a kinship as can be seen from the Acts with the communal 'Way of the Wilderness' followed by the various Essene groups bearing different names and having distinctive characteristics, but also have a family resemblance to one another." Schonfield continues: "Jacob (James), as reported by Hegesippus, was a lifelong Nazirite like John the Baptist, who followed the ascetic Essene way of life and consequently he could be another link between the Galilean Apostles and the group of 'saints' at Jerusalem."

The earliest Christians called themselves Nazoreans and came from within the framework of the Essenes. What distinguished the Christian Nazoreans was the claim that Jesus, their Master, was the Davidic Messiah.

THE NAZIREAN GOSPEL

Much of the *Gospel of the Nazirenes* is similar to the four gospels, given credence to the hypothesis that the New Testament gospels may have been based on this ancient text. If, in fact, this is the case, it is interesting to note what has been edited out of the New Testament gospels. One of the predominant themes not found in the biblical Gospels is the emphasis on the proper treatment of animals. All through the Nazirene text, it is emphasized that one should not eat flesh nor be cruel to animals. Another theme missing in the four gospels is the concept of reincarnation that is found in the Nazirene Gospel. Another major departure is that the *Gospel of the Nazirenes* tells of Jesus' early life, confirming that He was married, to Miriam, but also leave the door open about a later marriage to Mary

Magdalene after Miriam died. It also confirms His travels to India and Tibet. The Nazirene Gospel also leaves open the question about whether Jesus survived the crucifixion suggesting He may have walked over the mountain rather than ascending into the clouds. However, much of the *Gospel of the Nazirenes* does confirm many of the passages in the four biblical gospels. The following verses listed in chronological order are some of the important ones that differ from the Bible.

Mary and the Angel

Chapter 2, Verse 6: "Then said Mary to the angel, 'How shall this be, seeing I know not a man?' And the angel answered and said to her, 'The Holy Spirit shall come upon Joseph thy spouse, and the power of the Most High shall overshadow you, O Mary, therefore also that Holy One, which shall be born of you shall be called the Messiah, and his name on Earth shall be called Jesus, for he shall save the people from their sins, whoever shall repent and follow in the Way of the Law.'"

2v7: "Therefore you shall keep your covenant to eat no flesh, nor drink strong drink, for this child shall be filled with the Holy Spirit, consecrated to the Lord a Nazarite from his Mother's womb, and neither flesh nor strong drink shall he take, nor shall razor touch his head."

Jesus' Youth and Travels

6v13: "Then in his thirteenth year, when an Israelite should take a wife, the house of his parents became a place for seekers who desired that they should gain him through marriage; Jesus being already known throughout the land for his clarity in the Word of the Lord. Jesus then also came to the Temple to fulfill his place among them and grow strong with the Law and those teaching in the Temple saw his grace and wisdom, and sought counsel with his parents that he should travel afar with a noble one, who, visiting the Temple had heard Jesus speak with the authority of one who knows."

6v14: "So it was that for several years he traveled in India and other holy places and they loved him as he taught the Holy Scriptures. And Jesus went into the desert, meditated, and fasted and prayed, and obtained the power of the Holy Name, by which he wrought many miraculous deeds."

Jesus' Marriage

6v15: "And in the eighteenth year of his age, Jesus returned to his homeland and was espoused to Miriam, a virgin of the tribe of Judah. And after several years, Jesus journeyed with his brother James down into Egypt that they might learn the wisdom of the Egyptians, even as Moses did."

Jesus' Education

6v16: "And they went into the holy lands and conversed with the Most High face to face, and traveled, learning the language of birds and beasts, the healing powers of trees, herbs, and flowers, and the hidden secrets of precious stones; and they learned the motions of the Sun, the Moon, and the stars, the powers of the letters, and mysteries of the square and circle, and the transmutation of things, of forms, and numbers and signs."

Miriam's Death

6v17: "Then being fulfilled, they returned to Nazireth to visit their parents. And for a time they taught in Jerusalem. Then one came to Jesus saying, 'Miriam, your wife is ill even unto death.' And as he approached, she departed from among the living. He was distraught, and grieved that he could not seek her further, for it was not yet his time to awaken the sleeping again unto the body. But this came to pass that he may go on to the higher things that he must do."

Jesus' Travels

6v18: "Jesus then departed at once and went again into India and Tibet: throughout Persia, Assyria, the land of the Chaldeans, Greece, and Egypt. He visited their temples and conversed with their priests and their wise men for many years, doing many wonderful works."

Jesus on War

6v21: "And none shall hurt or destroy in my holy mountain, for the Earth shall be full of the knowledge of the Most High even as the waters cover the bed of the sea. And in that day I will make again a covenant with the beasts of the Earth and the fowls of the air, and the fish of the sea and with all created things. And I will break the bow and sword and all instruments of warfare will I banish from the Earth, and will make them to lie down in safety, and to live without fear."

Jesus on Hunting

6v23: "And on a certain day as he was passing by a mountain side near the desert, there he met he a lion and many men were pursing him with stones and javelins to slay him."

6v24 "But Jesus rebuked them saying, 'Why do you hunt creatures which are more noble than you? By the cruelties of many generations they were made the enemies of man, who should have been his friends.'"

6v25: "If the power of the Almighty is shown in them, so also is shown his long suffering and compassion. Cease to persecute this creature who desires not to harm you. See how he flees from you, and is terrified by your violence?"

6v26: "And the lion came and laid at the feet of Jesus, and showed love to him; and the people were astonished, and said, 'This man loves all creatures, and has power to command even those beasts from the desert, and they obey him.'"

Mary Magdalene

10v2: "Now this Mary was of the city of Magdala in Galilee. And she was a great sinner, and she seduced many by her beauty and comeliness. And the same came to Jesus by night and confessed her sins, and he put forth his hands and healed her, and cast out of her seven demons, and he said to her, 'Go in peace, your sins are forgiven you.' And she arose and left all and followed him, and ministered to him of substance, during the days of his ministry in Israel."

Jesus and Animal Cruelty

14v8: "A grain of wheat will produce ten thousand heads, and every head will have ten thousand grains, and every grain will produce ten pounds of fine clean flour, and other seeds, fruits, and grass will produce in corresponding proportion, and all the animals will use those foods that are products of the soil and become in turn peaceable and in harmony with one another, and with man. Woe to the crafty who hurt or abuse the creatures of the Earth. Woe to the hunters for they shall be hunted."

14v9: "And the man marveled and stopped training the dogs to hunt, and taught them to save life rather than destroy it. And he learned of the doctrines of The Way and became his disciple."

Jesus on Truth

17v15: "He that finds his life on account of a lie, shall lose it; and he that loses his life for the sake of The Truth, shall find life eternal."

Jesus on Cause and Effect

18v12: "As you do to others, so shall it be done to you. As you give, so shall it be given to you. As you judge others, so shall you be judged. As you serve others, so shall you be served. For the Lord is just, and rewards everyone according to their works. That which they sow they shall also reap."

Jesus on Sacrifice

21v8: "He also said, ' I have come to do away with the sacrifice and feasts of blood, and if you cease not sacrificing and eating of flesh and blood, the wrath of the Lord shall not cease from you; even as it came to your father in the wilderness, who lusted for flesh, and they ate to their content and were filled with rottenness, and the plagues consumed them!'"

Jesus on Karma

24v4: "And he also said, 'As you do in this life to your fellow creatures, so shall it be done to you in the life to come.'"

Jesus on Loving Your Enemies

25v13: "You have heard that it has been said, 'Thou shall love thy neighbor and hate thine enemy. But I say to you which hear, love your enemies, do good to them which hate you.'"

Jesus on Killing Animals

28v1: "It came to pass one day as Jesus had finished his discourse, in a place near Tiberias where there are seven walls, a certain young man brought live rabbits and pigeons, that he might have them to eat with disciples."

28v2: "And Jesus looked on the young man with compassion and said to him, 'You have a good heart and the Lord shall give you Light; but do you not know that the Lord Creator in the beginning gave to man the fruits of the Earth for food, and did not make him lower than the ape, or the ox, or the horse, or the sheep, that he should kill and eat the flesh and blood of his fellow creatures.'"

Jesus on Blood Offering

33v2: "And Jesus answered, 'No blood offering of beast, or bird, or man, can take away sin, for how can the conscience be purged from sin by the shedding of innocent blood? No, it will increase the condemnation.'"

Jesus on Rebirth

37v2: "And he said to them, 'Blessed are they who endure many experiences, for they shall be made perfect through them; they shall be as the angels of the Most High and shall die not more, neither shall they be born any more, for death and birth have no dominion over them.'"

37v4: "And a certain Rabbi (Nicodemus) came to him by night for fear of the Sanhedrin, and said to him, 'How can a man be born again when he is old? Can he enter a second time into his mother's womb and be born again?'"

37v5: "Jesus answered, 'Verily I say to you except a man be born again of flesh and of spirit, he cannot enter into the kingdom . . . .'"

37v7: "When Life comes from beyond one sight, it is that we have lived before, and whence it returns from whence it came, it is that we may rest for a little, and thereafter be reborn unto flesh."

37v8: "So through many changes must we be made perfect, as it is written in the book of Job. 'I am a wanderer, changing place after place and house after house, until I come to the city and mansion which is eternal.'"

Jesus on Vegetarianism

17v7: "And eat that which is set before you, but of that which is gotten by taking of life, touch not, for it is not lawful to you."

38v2: "And Jesus said to them, 'They who partake of the benefits which are gotten by wrongdoing of the Creator's creatures cannot be righteous: nor can they touch or teach holy things, or speak the mysteries of the kingdom whose hands are stained with blood, or whose mouth are defiled with flesh.'"

38v3: "The Lord has given the grains and the fruits of the Earth for food; and for righteous man truly there is no other lawful substance for the body."

38v4: "Wherefore I say to all who desire to be disciples, keep your hands from bloodshed and let no flesh meat enter your mouths, for the Lord is just and bountiful; who ordains that man shall live by the fruits and seeds of the Earth alone."

38v5: "But if any animal suffer greatly, and if its life be a misery unto it, or if it be dangerous to you, release it from its life quickly, and with as little pain as you are able. Send it forth in love and mercy, but torment it not, and the Lord will show mercy unto you, as you have shown mercy to those given into your care."

38v6: "Wherefore I say unto you: Be kind one to another, and to all creatures of the Earth."

Jesus on the Mysteries

40v1: "And the disciples came and said to him, 'Why do you speak to the multitudes in parables?' He answered and said to them, 'Because it is given to you to know the mysteries of the Kingdom, but to them it is not given.'

40v3: "Therefore I speak to them in parables because seeing, they see not, and hearing, they hear not, neither do they understand."

Jesus on Divorce

42v7: "And I say to you, whoever shall put away a wife, except it be for a just cause, and shall marry another in her place, commits adultery. His disciples said to him, 'If the case of the man be so with his wife, it is not good to marry?'"

Jesus on Reincarnation

54v5: "But they, which being worthy, attain the resurrection from the cycles of rebirth, neither marry, nor are given in marriage, neither can they die anymore, for they are equal to the Angels and are Children of the Most High, being children of the resurrection."

Jesus and Mary Magdalene

66v10: "Again I say to you, I and my Bride are one, even as Mary Magdalene whom I have chosen and sanctified as a type, is one with me: I and my congregation are One. And the Congregation is the elect of humanity for the rebirth of all."

Jesus on Resurrection

69v1: "As Jesus sat by the west side of the temple with his disciples, behold there passed some carrying one that was dead to burial, and a certain one said to him, 'Jesus, if a man die shall he live again?'"

69v2: "And he answered and said, 'I am the resurrection and the life, if a man live in Truth he shall not die, but live eternally. As in Adam, all are bound to cycles of rebirth, so in the Lord shall all be made eternal. Blessed are those who are made perfect in image and likeness, for they do rest from their labors and their works do follow them. They have overcome evil, and are made Pillars in the Temple of the Lord, and they go out no more, for they rest in Eternal.'"

69v3: "For them that persist in evil there is not rest, but they go out and in, and suffer correction for ages, till they are made perfect. But for them that have done good and attained unto perfection, there is endless rest and they go into life everlasting. They rest in the Eternal."

69v4: "Over them the repeated birth and deaths have no power, for them the wheel revolves no more, for they have attained unto the Center, where is eternal rest."

A Purpose of Jesus

75v9: "Verily I say unto you, for this end have I come into the world: that I may put away all blood offerings and the eating of the flesh of the beasts and the birds that are slain by men."

Following the Resurrection

87v1: "Then the same day at evening, being the first day

of the week, when the doors were shut where the disciples were assembled for fear of the Pharisees, came Jesus and stood in their midst and said to them, 'Peace be unto you.' But they were afraid and supposed that they had seen a spirit."

87v2: "And he said to them, 'Behold it is I myself, as you have seen me aforetime. A spirit can indeed appear in bones and flesh as you see. Behold my hands and my feet, handle and see.'"

87v3: "And when he had so said he showed to them his hands and side. Then were the disciples glad, when they saw Jesus."

87v4: "For Thomas, called Didiymus, had said to them, 'Except I shall see in his hands the print of the nails, and thrust my hand into his side, I will not believe.' Then said to Thomas, 'Behold my hands, my side, and my feet; place here your hands, and be not faithless but believing.'"

87v5: "And Thomas answered and said, 'Messiah!' And Jesus said to him, 'Thomas, because you have seen me, you have believed; blessed are they that have not seen and yet have believed."

Involution of Spirit

88v12: "For by involution and evolution shall the salvation of all the world be accomplished: by the descent of spirit into matter, and the ascent of matter into spirit and the Highest Heavens, through the ages."

Jesus and the Truth

90v2: "And as they were speaking, Jesus appeared in the midst and said, 'Truth, One, and Absolute, is in the Most High alone, for no man, neither any body of man, knows that which the Most High alone knows, who is the unbegotten. To men is truth revealed, according to their capacity to understand and receive.'"

90v3: "The Truth has many sides and one sees one side only, another sees another, and some see more than others, according as it is given to them."

90v10: "The Lord gives you all Truth, as a ladder with many steps, for the salvation and perfection of the soul, and that which seems true today, you will abandon for the higher truth of morrow. Press unto Perfection."

90v14: "There abide Goodness, and Truth, and Beauty, but the greatest of them is Goodness. If any have hatred to their fellows, and harden their hearts to the creatures of the Earth, how can they see Truth unto salvation, seeing their eyes are blinded and their hearts are hardened to all creation!"

90v15: "As I have received the Truth, so have I given it to you. Let each receive it according to their light and ability to understand, and persecute not those who receive it after a different interpretation."

Jesus and the Body

94v4: "The body that you lay in the grave, or that is consumed by fire, is not the body that shall be, but they who come shall receive other bodies, yet their own, and as they have sown in one life, so shall they reap in another. Blessed are they who have worked righteousness in this life, for they shall receive the crown of life."

Jesus After the Resurrection

95v1: "And Jesus after he had shown himself alive to his disciples after his resurrection and sojourned with them for ninety days, teaching and speaking of the kingdom, and the things pertaining to it: and had finished all things that he had to do, led forth the Twelve with Mary Magdalene, and Joseph his father, and Mary his mother, and the other holy women as far as Bethany to a mountain called Olivet, where he had appointed them."

95vs2: "And as stood in the midst of them, they honored him, but some doubted. And Jesus spoke to them saying, 'Behold, I have chosen you from among men, and given you The Law and The Word of Truth.'"

Jesus and the Future

95v3: "I have set you as the Light of the world, and as a city that cannot be hid. But the time comes when a darkness shall cover the Earth, and gross darkness the people, and the enemies of truth and righteousness shall rule in my name, and set up a kingdom of this world, and oppress the peoples, and cause the enemy to blaspheme, putting for my doctrines the opinions of a man and of men, and teaching in my name that which I have not taught, and darkening much that I have taught by their tradition."

95v4: "But be of good cheers, for the time will also come when The Truth they have hidden shall be manifest, and the Light shall shine, and the darkness shall pass away, and the true kingdom shall be established which shall be in the world, but not of it, and the Word of Righteousness and Love shall go forth from the Center, even the Holy City of Mount Zion, and the mount which is in the land of Egypt shall be known as an alter of witness to the Lord."

The Ascension

95v6: "And having said these things, he lifted up his hands and blessed them. And it came to pass that while they were walking near the base of the Mount of Olives, a great cloud descended, and he was departed from them."

95v7: "Many among them, questioned whether he was taken up in the cloud by angels as was Enoch or Elijah, or simply disappearing up into the mountain and beyond as Moses did . . ."

95v8: "And while they gazed steadfastly into the heaven, behold two stood by them in white apparel and said, 'You men of Israel, why do you stand gazing into the heavens: this same Jesus whom you seek will one day come again.'"

The teachings by Jesus in *The Gospel of the Nazirenes* are definitely more similar to the teachings of the Buddha than they are to orthodox Christianity. The physical resurrection is not a part of Jesus' teachings, but the concept of rebirth is emphasized. Treating life with great respect for all animal species is another great emphasis. As Jesus had prophesied, His teachings would be falsified and misinterpreted, a prophecy manifested by the actions of the Church. As we will see in the following chapter, another Aramaic manuscript was discovered 40 years ago, again emphasizing the concept of reincarnation by Jesus.

Chapter Five

THE TALMUD OF JMMANUEL

The Gospel Prototype?

In 1963, a Greek Catholic ex-priest and his friend, Eduard Meier, made an intriguing discovery in a half-buried tomb just outside Jerusalem, following the discovery of the burial cave by the ex-priest. Encased in a preservative resin and lying underneath a flat rock were papyrus scrolls written in the literary language of old Aramaic, spoken at the time of Jesus. The Lebanon-born priest had coincidently studied the ancient language of Aramaic. The author of the papyrus scrolls was thought to be a disciple of Jmmanuel, known as Judas Iscariot. What the ex-priest discovered made him fearful for his life. The scrolls appeared to be the prototype of the Gospel of Matthew, containing information heretical to the Church and contradicting the New Testament.

Knowing the might of organized religion and what might happen to him for finding the scrolls, the ex-priest wanted to conceal his name and the original manuscript from those who had learned of its existence. His fear was not unfounded, as he was later assassinated. In years prior to the discovery, he had withdrawn from the Church and lived incognito with the family he had started in the interim, using a pseudonym, Isa Rashid. In August 1963, Rashid and Meier agreed that Rashid would translate the scrolls and mail the translations to Meier, but Rashid would maintain custody of Aramaic scrolls. His good friend, Eduard Meier, lived in German-speaking Switzerland. Under the oath of secrecy that his name never be mentioned, Rashid mailed the translations to Meier. On several occasions, Rashid took Meier to the burial cave that Meier initially described as filled with sand and dirt. According to the contents of the scrolls, the scrolls had been placed in the burial cave which belonged to Joseph of Ariamathea, years after the crucifixion. Meier wrote that during the excavation of the burial cave, he found various items confirming the authenticity of the manuscripts; however, he did not elaborate. Fearing pursuit and persecution, the excursions were made under the cover of night. Rashid began translating the Aramaic scrolls, titled *The Talmud of Jmmanuel,* into German with the later aid of Meier as editor. Several years passed before Meier again heard from Rashid; he received two packets containing the first 36 chapters of the *Talmud of Jmmanuel,* about one-fourth of what made up the original scrolls. Several years later, a letter arrived from Rashid dated September 14, 1974 in which Rashid related to Meier that he was barely able to escape from Jerusalem with his family. The original Aramaic manuscripts were lost or destroyed in a Lebanese refugee camp where Rashid and his family had fled suddenly from an Israeli raid in 1974. He believed the manuscripts were all burned when the Israelis destroyed the homes in the camp. Rashid told Meier that he was going to withdraw from the whole matter, not wanting to endanger his family further. In March of 1976, Meier learned Rashid was indeed killed in Baghdad.

After 1975, Meier worked on the text to prepare it for publication, and then in 1978 self-published it in German as *The Talmud of Jmmanuel,* referred to as the *TJ* in this book. Meier distributed the book at cost, but only to the few who were interested. Interestingly, once it became known that Meier had the material and was also a UFO contactee with many UFO photos, Meier reported he experienced numerous assassination attempts.

Meier, himself, became somewhat of a controversial figure a dozen years after the discovery of the scrolls, when his status as a UFO contactee became known. He had acquried some of the best photographs of spacecraft ever published. Meier claimed he was in communication with beings associated with the craft, who claimed they were from the Pleiades and who persuaded him to publish the *TJ* material because it was close to the truth. With Meier's involvement in a UFO controversy, it would be almost impossible for anyone to take these scrolls seriously. Few people today are even aware of the *TJ,* including biblical scholars and theologians.

Professor James Deardorff of Oregon State University, however, discovered the *TJ* in 1984 and felt it merited good research. Knowing that Oregon State University would not authorize such research, Deardorff took an early retirement to research the *TJ*. His findings were published in a book titled *Celestial Teachings: The Emergence of the True Testament of Jmmanuel (Jesus)*. He investigated the possibility that the translation of the scrolls could have been a hoax, but concluded it was not and is in all probability the prototype of the Gospel of Matthew. The following is a summary of Deardorff's research concerning the *TJ*.

THE DEARDORFF RESEARCH

Deardorff emphasized that a grand hoax must always be kept in mind regarding the *TJ*. However, one must be aware of the possibility that the scrolls were genuine, and if true, there is an entirely different perspective of Jesus and the events surrounding Him. The *TJ* portrays Jmmanuel as an even greater prophet than does the New Testament. Teachings found in the *TJ* are heretical and depict Jmmanuel surviving the crucifixion and teaching reincarnation, not resurrection. In fact, the Gnostic philosophy that flourished in the early 2nd century can easily be explained by the teachings found in the *TJ*. As we will see, it answers many mysteries concerning the New Testament, including the virgin birth, the Star of Bethlehem, the resurrection of Jesus, and Jesus' appearance to Saul. The *TJ* also helps explain why the custodians of Christian literature edited the writings to make it understandable and believable for the masses.

Deardorff believes the *TJ* supports the theory that Matthew greatly "Judaized" his source material in forming the gospel, and Mark "de-Judaized" it while incorporating portions of the Matthew Gospel into his short gospel. Deardorff's research compares the *TJ* with biblical scholar Francis Beare's critique, which analyzed the Gospel of Matthew. Beare wrote of 194 criticisms of Matthew that would not have applied to the *TJ*, suggesting to Deardorff that the *TJ* could have been the prototype of the synoptic gospels. In other words, the *TJ* answers the criticism that Beare levied against the Gospel of Matthew, which suggested that Matthew was highly edited or redacted in literary terms.

The *TJ* encompasses that which is in the Gospel of Matthew, including five additional chapters at the end. For example, the ordering of verses in Matthew closely parallels that of the *TJ*. Approximately 21 percent of the *TJ* verses, which were defined and numbered by Rashid, are very close in meaning to the Matthew verses. Another 23 percent were recognized as "distant cousins" according to Deardorff, yet were cognate to other Matthew verses, that is, related in origin, order, and word content. However, in these verses, the meaning was rather different, sometimes entirely different. Deardorff found one percent of the *TJ* verses cognate to verses in the Gospel of Luke; 0.4 percent cognate to verses in Acts 9; and 1.7 percent cognate to the Gospel of John.

Before commencing his research, Deardorff asked a number of questions. Does the *TJ* solve a sufficient number of outstanding New Testament problems in a creative manner? Does it resolve major uncertainties of scholars over the centuries of how the New Testament gospels originated and who wrote them? Does it overcome objections that scholars have made to a large number of gospel passages? In Deardorff's mind, the *TJ* satisfactorily addresses all these issues, convincing him that the *TJ* does meet the criteria for biblical scholars to provide serious study. However, his concern remains that the *TJ* contains verses too occult for both Christians and scientists, which discourage them from seriously studying it. Deardorff also believes the heretical nature of the manuscript, along with the Meier UFO connection, would hinder those who are interested from studying it. Reputations of scholars in responsible positions understandably need to be protected. These are the reasons, hypothesizes Deardorff, that the *TJ* has not come to the attention of scholars or laypeople. Throughout his scholarly research, Deardorff remained hopeful that biblical scholars would risk their academic careers to study this intriguing manuscript. He has attempted to interest scores of other scholars to research the *TJ* by sending pertinent material to them. In almost all instances, he has been ignored or refused. To assist scholarly research, reliable English versions of the *TJ* are now available following a first edition, which was full of errors, causing Meier to insist that the German version be published alongside any English or foreign version.

In summary, Deardorff was in possession of a document that could settle centuries of debate about the life of Jesus. First of all, he needed to find out if an Aramaic version of Matthew had ever existed.

WAS THERE AN ARAMAIC GOSPEL?

Several clues in early Church history suggest the existence of a gospel written in Aramaic. Papias, a 2nd century bishop, wrote, "Matthew compiled the logia in the Hebrew language and each interpreted them as best he could." This was according to the early Christian historian, Eusebius, a 4th century bishop from Caesarca. Modern day scholars do not know how to interpret this. They believe "Hebrew" can probably be taken to mean Aramaic, since the language incorporated Hebrew characters used by Jesus and the people of Palestine.

This statement by Papias suggests the existence of a prototype to the Gospel of Matthew written in Aramaic. According to Deardorff, the statement suggests the precursor to the Gospel of Matthew may have been heretical in nature and could not be authorized for use by the early Church. For this reason, one can infer that referring to an early prototype was even difficult for other writers. The Papias statement implies that the logia had been used primarily in forming the Gospel of Matthew. Deardorff hypothesizes that if this were the case, these logia may have constituted the proto-Matthew text, the original teachings of Jesus.

Early Church Fathers support the view of Papias. Origen, the 3rd century Christian theologian, believed that Matthew compiled his gospel in Hebrew or Aramaic. According to the early Christian historian Eusebius, Irenaeus said in 180 A.D. "Matthew brought out a written gospel among the Jews in their own dialect, while Peter and Paul were evangelizing in Rome and founding the church." Again, more evidence for an early prototype.

Biblical scholars question the existence of a proto-Matthew text, as the modern view, but believe that Matthew was copied from Mark. According to this view, the logia could be interpreted as various sayings of Jesus, probably in oral form, that were interwoven into the edited copy of Mark's gospel, forming the Gospel of Matthew.

Deardorff's research suggests the *TJ* is evidence for the proto-Matthew theory, supporting at face value the interpretation of Papais. He believes the *TJ* we have today represents the first portion of the original *TJ*, which was the only portion the compiler of Matthew could use because of the heretical nature of the *TJ*'s narrative following the crucifixion. No amount of editing could overcome that.

Other scholars suggest that Jesus' teachings may be contradictory to today's orthodoxy. Marcus Borg, a leading scholar of the historical Jesus, once claimed a new scholarly consensus is developing that Jesus was a teacher of subservient wisdom. If the *TJ* is authentic, it supports Borg's claim, but the teachings were even more heretical or subversive than modern scholars can at this time tolerate, perhaps explaining why the heretical Aramaic version was ignored.

Supporting the hypothesis of an early Aramaic Gospel of Matthew is information received by Eusebius. He received a report from an Alexandrian named Pantaenus, who had been to India. After returning from India, Pantaenus claimed that one of the 12 disciples had preached to the people from a writing in Hebrew (assumed to mean Aramaic), and the text was identified as the Gospel of Matthew. If this report was true, the writing in question would have been a proto-Matthew text resembling the later Gospel of Matthew. Scholars seem to forget this item of history, and Deardorff believes biblical scholars often ignore the historical items rather than trying to connect them to other hypotheses.

Before the 20th century, scholars believed that Matthew was the primary gospel, and the other three gospels came later. Much of the evidence came from Papias, who was supported by other Church Fathers. For that reason, Matthew was placed first in the New Testament. In the 20th century, however, scholars began to believe that the Gospel of Mark was the first gospel, copied by Matthew and Luke. If true, the Gospel of Matthew would not have been seeded from a proto-Matthean document. Because of this now orthodox opinion, scholars ignore the evidence that an Aramaic version of Matthew existed in India. With this mindset, rejecting the authenticity of *TJ* is easy for scholars. Deardorff rebuts this view, saying that dismissing the *TJ* as a hoax would be more difficult for scholars if it supports a proto-Matthew theory rather than the prevailing theory that a literary hoaxer would be well aware of.

Verse location in the gospels may shed light on their origin. Researchers of the New Testament found that when arranging the various grouping of verses, teachings, and stories in Mark alongside a complete listing of parallel teachings and stories in Matthew, the verse number of the transposed Mark Gospel jumped around until chapter 12 of Matthew. At that point, they corresponded with Matthew's verses with increasing order. Researchers then placed Matthew verses where they fit correspondingly alongside a complete listing of Mark verses. This resulted in the break point occurring later in Matthew, with the perfect correlation of their order of events beginning with chapter 14. Deardorff says this supports the hypothesis that Mark is based upon Matthew, as the first arrangement explains more orderliness.

Historical evidence confirms that early Christianity was being taught in India. However, scholars argue that it was impossible that Bartholomew was teaching in India; and therefore, one should discount the Aramaic-Matthew story from Pantaenus. If the *TJ* is authentic, it should explain this discrepancy, and it does. A Muslim sect called the Ahmadiyyas, claimed evidence that Thomas, a brother of Jesus, traveled to India and that Jesus survived the crucifixion and entombment. Thomas means "twin" in Aramaic, and the Ahmadiyyas regarded Thomas as both a twin of Jesus and one of the disciples. However, the *TJ* does not support this claim. It discloses that Thomas was one of Jesus' brothers, Judas Thomas, who played a crucial role in post-crucifixion events and traveled to India with Jesus after the crucifixion. In contrast, the Apostle Thomas traveled separately to India and never reconnected with Jesus..

Deardorff has provided enough evidence that strongly suggests the existence of an Aramaic prototype. He believes the *TJ* should seriously be studied, and this is what Deardorff did.

JESUS IN THE EAST

Evidence will be presented in future chapters that suggests Jesus spent His "lost years" in India, where He studied the teachings of Buddha and Eastern philosophy. This information is confirmed by the *TJ*. Legends from the Ahmadiyyas also state that Jesus spent years in India, but after the crucifixion. Confirming this legend also is the *TJ*, describing how Jesus survived the crucifixion and traveled to India with His mother and brother. These legends trace Jesus' journey, first to Syria, then Iraq and Iran, from there to Afghanistan and finally, India. The *TJ* states that Jmmanuel lived for two years without being recognized in Damascus, Syria, following the crucifixion. Near Damascus is a place today called Mayuam-isa, meaning "the place where Jesus lived." Following the crucifixion, Jesus became known as Yuz Asaf, or Yuz Asaph. Deardorff thinks the topic of Jesus surviving the crucifixion cannot be treated seriously within scholarly literature and Christian journals. This hypothesis remains unknown by many biblical scholars.

Both scholars and non-scholars have puzzled over the biblical silence concerning Mother Mary following the crucifixion. What happened to her? Verses in the *TJ* account for her as she accompanies Jmmanuel to India. According to the *TJ*, Jmmanuel's mother became very sick, possibly due to the effects of the long journey, and died when He was 38 years old. Substantiating this claim is evidence found in eastern Pakistan, in a tiny town called Murree. This is where Mary was buried; the tomb still exists today and is known as the Tomb of Mary.

Islamic records dating from the 10th century confirm the identification of Jesus as Yuz Asaf. An Islamic scholar, Al-sa'id-us-Sadig, wrote in *Ikmal-udDin* about a Hindu story that Yuz Asaf lived during the reign of the Raja Gopadatta (49 - 109 A.D.), placing Him at the right period following the crucifixion around 32 A.D. Verses translated from Sanskrit identify Yuz Asaf as Jesus quite easily, with one parable told by Yuz Asaf almost identical to the parable of the sower of the seeds told by Jesus.

A 5th century account of the appearance of Jesus in India is found in the ninth volume of the *Puranas*. The book contains ancient Hindu narratives whose earliest origins date from the 5th century B.C. and continues to the 17th century. The anecdote leaves little doubt that it was Jesus appearing on a Himalayan mountain to King Shalivahan sometime between 39 to 50 A.D.

Further evidence that Jesus was in India comes from the Ahmadiyyas, who tell of Jesus spending the last part of a long life in Kashmir, where He married a beautiful woman and fathered some sons. A burial tomb that venerates Him still exists in Srinagar. One resident, a newspaper editor in Srinagar, vouches that one branch of His family lineage traces back to Yuz Asaf.

Additionally,at least 21 historical documents exist that confirm Jesus lived in Kashmir, India.

There is much evidence that Jesus survived the crucifixion, including the belief system of Islam. This Middle Eastern religion teaches that Jesus did not die at the crucifixion, but attributed His survival to divine intervention. Again, confirming that Jesus survived the crucifixion. The Ahmadiyyas, who revere Jesus almost as much as the Christians, have their own scenario about Jesus surviving the crucifixion. They believe that Jesus fell into "a deep state of unconsciousness on the cross so that heart action, circulation, and respiration were greatly suppressed," and the spear thrust into Jesus missed His heart. Contrary to the usual crucifixion custom, Jesus' legs were not broken, and He was removed quickly from the cross, after only a few hours. Jesus' early death even surprised Pontius Pilate (Mark 15:44). If Jesus survived the crucifixion, He would have needed some help within the tomb. As we will see, the *TJ* provides the scenario on how it was done. One clue may be the medicinal ointment known as "Marham Isa" or "Ointment of Jesus" that still exists today in the Moslem world. The legend associated with it states that it was prepared to treat Jesus' injuries.

Supporting facts that Jesus survived the crucifixion are also found in the Bible. Jesus is reported to still have looked, talked, and felt like a mortal to His disciples, and He still required ordinary food to nourish His body. Rationalists argue against resurrection, saying that it is highly improbable that upon resurrection the body is reconstructed from the same atoms once possessed in the former life.

Other evidence follows. Jawahar Lal Nehru, a former prime minister of India, writes in his book *Glimpses of World History,* "All over Central Asia, in Kashmir and Ladakh, and Tibet and even farther North, there is still a strong belief that Jesus or Isa traveled about there. Some people believed he visited India also." This statement is confirmed in the *TJ*. Irenaeus, the most influential of the early Church Fathers, may have believed that Jesus had been seen in the East and survived the crucifixion. He wrote,

> "But from the fortieth to the fiftieth year a man begins to decline toward old age, which our Lord possessed while he still held the office of teacher, even as

> the Gospel and the elders testify; those who were conversant in Asia with John, the disciple of the Lord, (affirming) that John conveyed to them that information, and he John remained among them up to the times of Trajan (which commenced 98 A.D.)."

Deardorff interprets this quotation as Irenaeus having access to Asian reports that Jesus lived long after the crucifixion.

One scholarly criticism of the Bible is the witness problem, where witnesses are supplied to the text in events believed to be unwitnessed. They believe the witness was edited in after the fact. The *TJ* addresses this problem. If a disciple accompanied Jesus to India, the witness problem would be solved. Jesus would have been available to supply the missing information and recall the teachings. From the crucifixion to other events in Jesus' life, the *TJ* portrays Jesus much differently than the Bible.

A DIFFERENT PORTRAYAL OF JESUS

The *Talmud of Jmmanuel* provides a startling new perspective on the life of Jesus. "Talmud" means a collection of teachings by one or more disciples. In the *TJ,* "Jmmanuel" represents the name "Immanuel," with the letter J pronounced as the i, e, or y sound. The name Jesus does not appear anywhere in the *TJ*. The original name Immanuel was prophesied in Isaiah and is quoted in Matthew 1:23, its Aramaic meaning "God with us." Scholars should wonder why "Jesus" rather than "Immanuel" appears in Matthew 1:21, especially if He were prophesied to be called Immanuel. Jesus is an abbreviated form of the Hebrew name Y'hosua, (Joshua) meaning "Yahweh saves" (God saves). Since the Hebrew language was not in vernacular use at that time, why would the compiler of Matthew have said in Matthew 1:23 that Isaiah prophesied Immanuel and then refer to Him as Jesus? And why would the compiler of Matthew think the man was the fulfillment of the Isaiah prophecy if he didn't even have the name that Isaiah had prophesized?

Deardorff now believes that Paul was most likely to have given Jesus this name, because Paul had attained enough authority to make the name stick. The meaning of Jesus fits Paul's redemption theology emphasizing man's sinfulness, "God saves." "Immanuel"(God with us) did not fulfill that purpose, while "God saves" (Jesus) does, since it is an abbreviated form of "God saves us from our sins." However, Irenaeus twice referred to Jesus as "Him who was born Emmanuel of the Virgin."

The Virgin Birth

The *TJ* also explains the virgin birth. Mary became impregnated by the guardian angel Gabriel, a distant descendant of the celestial son, Rasiel. Joseph was filled with anger after hearing about Mary's conception and thought seriously about leaving her. While pondering his decision, the angel Gabriel convinced Joseph to marry her because Mary was chosen for a great purpose. He was instructed to name the child Immanuel to symbolize "God's knowledge with us." According to Matthew, Gabriel told Joseph that the Lord is generous in His love, but also terrible in His anger when laws are disobeyed. Mary's impregnation was God's law, according to the *TJ*.

The Gods

Who is the angel Gabriel? Six centuries after Jesus, Gabriel appeared to the prophet Muhammed on a regular basis, giving sacred knowledge that now comprises the Koran. Some equate the gods with angels.

The ancient Sumerians might provide light on the subject of the gods. In Genesis, when gods were inhabiting the earth, they came onto the daughters of men begetting children. Genesis 6:2 explains, "That the sons of God saw the daughters of men that they were fair: and they took them wives of all which they chose." Genesis 6:4 states, "There were giants in the earth in those days: and also after that when the sons of God came unto the daughters of men, and they bare children to them, the same became mighty which were of old, men of renown." Ancient cuneiform writings of Sumer, 5000 years ago in Mesopotamia, explain who the sons of God were. The writings tell of the gods coming from a celestial body named Nibiru, who created humans to be workers, according to Sumarian scholar Zecharia Sitchin. These Sumerian writings tell how the gods genetically combined the DNA of the *homo erectus* with their own to create humanity. This would explain why the sons of God (Nefilim in the

Hebrew texts and Anunnaki in the Sumerian texts) could produce children with humans as they were genetically compatible. (The original Hebrew word "Nefilim," from which "giant" was translated, means "those who were cast down, not giant.") In Egypt, the earliest rulers were gods, but the middle epoch of the pharaohs was semi-divine, meaning half-human and half-god. Christians believe that Jesus was the son of God, perhaps not too far off, if the gods from Nibiru were genetically compatible with the daughters of men. Evidence exists that the Nefilim, Anunnaki, and Pleiadians were one and the same. Deardorff raises the question that the angel Gabriel may have been a Pleiadian, as could be inferred from the *TJ*.

Many references in the Sumerian writings describe the Anunnaki as having flying machines, which would make sense if they were from Nibiru. These ancient writings tell of a space port being in Sumer (in southern Iraq) before the Great Flood, and afterward it was located in the Sinai. Throughout the Old Testament are referrals to strange things in the heavens, such as when Ezekiel was taken to heaven. A common generic term used to describe these heavenly vehicles is "chariots of the gods," suggesting a similarity to today's unidentified flying objects.

The Star of Bethlehem and Chariots of the Gods

Several times the *TJ* describes these unusual heavenly phenomena, the Star of Bethlehem being such a case, suggesting it may be what we today call an unidentified flying object. Wise men came from the Orient to Jerusalem, saying,

> "Where is the newborn king of wisdom of the Jews? We have seen a bright light in the sky and heard a voice saying, 'Follow the tail of the light, because the king of wisdom of the Jews is born, who will bring great knowledge.' Therefore, we have come to adore the newborn king of wisdom. He shall possess the knowledge of god and be a son of the celestial son Gabriel. His knowledge will be boundless, and his power will rule the spirit of human beings, so that they may learn and serve Creation. When Herod Antipus heard this, he was frightened, and with him all of Jerusalem, because they feared that

> the newborn child might exercise dreadful power" (*TJ* 2:2-8).

The wise men departed Jerusalem with Herod instructing them to keep him informed of the child's whereabouts.

> *TJ* 2:14, "When they heard Herod Antipas, they departed. And behold, the light with the long tail, which they had seen in the Orient, went ahead of them with a high-pitched singing sound until it came to Bethlehem and stood directly over the stable where the infant was born. When they saw this they rejoiced exceedingly. They went into the stable and found the young child with his Mother, Mary, and Joseph. They fell down and worshiped the infant and offered their treasures, which were gold, frankincense, and myrrh."

In *TJ* 30:30-34, another mystical light appears at the Baptism of Jmmanuel,

> "When Jmmanuel had been baptized, he soon came out of the water of the Jordan, and behold, a metallic light dropped from the sky and descended over the Jordan. A voice spoke, 'This is my beloved son with whom I am well pleased. He will be the king of truth who will lift this human race to knowledge.' Behold, after these words, Jmmanuel entered into the metallic light, which climbed into the sky. . .After that, Jmmanuel was no longer seen for forty days and nights,"
>
> *TJ* 4:1 continues, "From this day Jmmanuel no longer lived among the human races."
>
> *TJ* 4:4, "There he lived for forty days. The guardian angels taught him the wisdom of knowledge."
>
> *TJ* 4:8, "They also taught him the omnipotence of the creation of the universe."
>
> *TJ* 4:9-10, "They also taught him about the immortality of the spirit through rebirth. There he saw the forefathers, the saints of ancient times, who were the fathers of the human races, the celestial sons."

Jmmanuel was then taken to three celestial gates.

TJ 4: 20-23, "Not far from these celestial gates was the palace of god, the ruler of these human races and those who had traveled from afar, the celestial sons, or guardian angels. In his palace, god ruled over the three races created by him and over his following, the celestial sons. He was immortal, ancient and of giant size like the celestial sons. In the palace of gods there appeared to Jmmanel two very tall men, the likes of which he had never seen on Earth."

TJ 4: 26-28, "These two men from the constellation of the seven stars (Pleiades) were venerable teachers and were together with two smaller men who said thy were from Baawi. They said, 'People have come from the heavens to Earth, and other people have been lifted from earth into the heavens, and the people coming from the heavens remained on Earth a long time and have created the intelligent human races. Behold, humans begotten by the celestial sons were different from other people on Earth. They were not like Earth humans, but like the children of the celestial angels."

TJ 4: 31-35, The human races will now retain their inherited beauty and propagate it further. But in the course of centuries and millennia they will mix with other races of the Earth and the heavens, so as to generate new human races and special lineages, as celestial sons did with the earth people. Jmmanuel, you are an informed insider begotten from our ranks by a celestial son. With your knowledge you will make the impossible possible and accomplish things that the human races will attest to as miracles. You know the power of the spirit, but beware of abusing it."

TJ 4:36, "Your own wisdom and knowledge obtained through us will contribute to the well-being of the human races, though the road leading thereto will be very difficult for them and you."

TJ 4:37, "You will be misunderstood and renounced, because the human races are still ignorant and given to delusionary beliefs."

> *TJ* 4:38, "They believe that god is Creation itself and not the ruler of the celestial sons and these human races."
> *TJ* 4:39, "Earth people attribute to him the omnipotence of Creation and glorify him as Creation itself."
> *TJ* 4:40, "But god is a human being, like all the celestial sons and the human races, except that he is vastly greater in consciousness than they."
> *TJ* 4:41, "Creation, however, is of immeasurably higher standing than god, the lord over the celestial sons and human races, because Creation is the immeasurable secret."
> *TJ* 4:47, "Fulfill your mission unperturbed in the face of irrationality, disbelieving people and false teachings of the scribes and Pharisees."
> *TJ* 4:48, "Hence, following the fulfillment of your mission, centuries and two millennia will pass before the truth of your knowledge brought among the people will be disseminated by some humans."
> *TJ* 4:51, "Thus they spoke, the celestial sons between the north and the west, before they took Jmmanuel in the metallic light back to Israel, to the land of Galilee."

If one has studied the ancient Sumerian writings from five thousand years ago, it might be hypothesized Jmmanuel was brought to Nibiru, where our creator gods lived, such as Anu and Enki. The Egyptian writings confirm the gigantic size of some gods that Jmmanuel saw, with Osiris and Horus being 15 feet and 30 feet tall respectively.

Gabriel is said to be the biological father of Jesus, which is somewhat confirmed in a Gnostic text, the Letter of the Apostles, "Christ came down through the various heavenly spheres and entered Mary in the guise of the angel Gabriel."

Judas Iscariot

The Buddha realized the importance of his teachings and had an assistant record his wisdom. Likewise, Jesus knew the higher purpose of His life mission, and thought it logical that He had a man who could read and write to record His teachings as well. According to the *TJ*, this was the case, and, surprisingly, it was Judas Iscariot, who was portrayed in the New Testament as betraying Jesus and committing suicide following the betrayal. The author of the *TJ* was

Judas Iscariot, who did not hang himself nor betray Jmmanuel, but traveled to India with Jesus after the crucifixion.

Several Gnostic gospels support this scenario of the *TJ,* suggesting Judas Iscariot did not commit suicide and could have been the true scribe who recorded Jesus' life, from which the synoptic gospels originated. The Church Fathers, Irenaeus and Epiphanius, mentioned the Gnostic gospel, "The Gospel of Judas," that suggested Judas Iscariot knew how to read and write.

Other clues suggesting that Judas did not commit suicide are found in the Gnostic Gospel of Peter, which mentions that after the crucifixion, the 12 disciples of the Lord wept and were afflicted. This happened much before Matthais was elected to replace Judas, but after Judas supposedly committed suicide. Three other similar instances occur in the Gnostic writings, found in the Ascension of Isaiah 3:17 and 11:12, and in the Coptic manuscript.

Paul writes, in 1 Cor 1:5, that Jesus appeared to the twelve after the resurrection, conflicting with the gospel account that Judas had committed suicide. In John 20:24 and Revelations 21:14 are two more references to 12, where 11 would have been appropriate. How could such a monumental error have been made? The *TJ* explains:

> *TJ* 14:1, "It happened that Jmmanuel and his disciples went to Bethlehem where he taught and advised people."
>
> *TJ* 14:2, "However, Judas Iscariot has become disloyal to the teachings of Jmmanuel and lived only for his desires."
>
> *TJ* 14:3, "Secretly he was collecting from Jmmanuel's audience and accumulating gold, silver, and copper in his money bag so he could live vainly."
>
> *TJ* 14:4, "And it happened Juda Ihariot, the son of Simeon the Pharisee, informed Jmmanuel of the wrongdoing of Judas Iscariot, since he hoped to be paid off for this."
>
> *TJ* 14:5, "Jmmanuel thanked him and did not pay him with any gifts whatever, so Judas Ihariot thought of revenge, because he was greedy for gold, silver, and goods."
>
> *TJ* 14:6, "But Judas Iscariot was led into the desert by

> Jmmanuel where, for three days and three nights, he was taught by him the concept of right and wrong, so the disciple repented and forthwith followed the teachings of Jmmanuel."
>
> *TJ* 14:7, "When he returned to the city, he distributed all his possessions and collections among the poor and became a trusted disciple of Jmmanuel."
>
> *TJ* 14:8 "However, at the same time it happened that the writings in which Judas Iscariot had reported on the teachings of Jmmanuel were stolen from him, so he told Jmmanuel about it."
>
> *TJ* 14:11, "Jmmanuel said, 'But his son Juda Ihariot is the real culprit: like his father, Simeon Ihariot, he is a Pharisee who is seeking after my life.'"
>
> *TJ* 14:12, "It is he who stole the writings from you and brought them to the scribe and Pharisees, so they can judge me accordingly and put me to death."
>
> *TJ* 14:13, "He received seventy pieces of silver for your writings and will receive another thirty when he makes it possible to deliver me over to the executors."
>
> *TJ* 14:15, "But write down my teachings and life story one more time, because the time will come, in 2000 years, when your writings will be revealed."
>
> *TJ* 14:16, "Until then my teachings will be falsified and will become an evil cult, for which reason much human blood will flow."
>
> *TJ* 14:17, "Because the people are still not ready to comprehend my teachings and recognize the truth."

It was Juda Ihariot who betrayed Jesus to the chief priest and elders, who afterward repented and committed suicide by hanging. Judas' name sounded so similar to that of Judas Iscariot, it is understandable that the chief priests spread the word that Judas Iscariot did the betrayal.

Surviving the Crucifixion

The *TJ* addresses the question of how Jmmanuel survived the crucifixion, suggesting there was not supernatural help.

> *TJ* 30: 27, "Then they forced him down on the cross, beating him. They nailed his hands and feet onto the

wood. They did it this way for the first time, contrary to custom, because until then the crucified were tied to the cross."

TJ 30:47, "With the tremendous thunder clap all about, Jmmanuel cried out again, but nobody understood him, because his speech was confused."

TJ 30: 48, "Then his head fell forward, he slipped into near death, and they thought he was dead."

TJ 30:49, "It happened that a soldier took his lance and stabbed Jmmanuel in his loin to ensure that he was dead."

TJ 30:50, "Blood mixed with water came from the wound, as in the case when a person is dead or near dead."

TJ 30:51 "Since the soldier thought Jmmanuel was dead, he informed the others."

TJ 30:52, "They were all astonished, because it was unusual for the crucified to die so quickly."

TJ 30:57 "Also among them was Joseph of Arimathea, a follower of Jmmanuel."

TJ 30:58, "After a little while, he noticed that Jmmanuel was only half dead, but he told no one."

TJ 30:59, "He quickly went into the city to see Pilate, and he asked for the body of Jmmanuel so that he could bury him."

TJ 30:60, "Pilate ordered Jmmanuel be turned over to Joseph."

TJ 31:62, "Joseph of Arimathea carried the body of Jmmanuel all the way to Jerusalem and placed him outside the city into his own tomb, which he had arranged to be cut into a rock for his future burial."

TJ 30:64, "Joseph of Arimathea sought out Jmmanuel's friends from India and went back with them to the tomb. They went in through a secret second entrance unknown to the henchmen and to the soldiers and nursed him for three days and three nights, so that he was soon in better health again and his strength was returned."

TJ 31:2, {On the third day} "Behold a great thunder

> arose in the air, and a radiant light came down from the sky and landed on the earth, not too far from the tomb."
>
> *TJ* 31:3, "Then a guardian angel came out of the light, and his appearance was like lightning and his garment was as white as snow."
>
> *TJ* 31:7, "Then the guardian angel stepped up to the tomb, rolled the stone away from the door and spoke to Mary, and to Mary Magdalene, who were both there."
>
> *TJ* 31:8, "Do not be afraid, I know that you are seeking Jmmanuel, the crucified."
>
> *TJ* 31:9, "But he is not here. He lives, as he said. Come here and behold the place where he hs lain."
>
> *TJ* 31:10, "Go quickly and tell the disciples that he has risen from near death."
>
> *TJ* 31:15, "The guardian angel went to the bright light and disappeared into it: Soon a great thunder came out of it again, and it rose into the air, shooting straight into the sky."

Deardorff believes the reason Jesus possessed Indian friends in Palestine may be connected to his earlier years in India before the Palestinian ministry. In *TJ* 29:23, Jesus says, "Furthermore, I traveled much to far away places and lived for many years in India. There I was taught much knowledge and many secrets by the great wise and knowledgeable men who are called masters."

Excavations of old tomb sites northeast of Jerusalem found irregular tombs that varied in size. One excavation found two cavernous tombs with separate entrances, connecting to each other by a small narrow passage. These tombs dated to the first century A.D.

Jesus Talks with the Disciples

After instructing His disciples to meet him at a certain mountain in Galilee, Jesus gave a talk to them:

> *TJ* 31:38, "Then Jmmanuel said to him (the discipleThomas), 'Reach out and place your hand on my wounds so that you of little minds may recognize the truths.'"

> *TJ* 31:39, "So Thomas did as he had been told, and he touched the wounds and said, 'Truly it is you.'"
> *TJ* 31:40, "Then Jmmanuel went away saying, 'Keep the secret of my return, so it will not become known that I am alive.'"

Jmmanuel appeared to the disciples one last time, on a mountain near Galilee:

> *TJ* 32:2, "When they gathered there, he said to them, 'Behold, I will talk to you one last time; then I will leave and never return.'"
> *TJ* 32:3, "My path leads me to India where many of this human race also dwell, because they left this land to live there."
> *TJ* 32:4, "My mission leads me to them and to the human race that was born there."
> *TJ* 32:5, "My path there will be long because I have yet to bring my old teachings, newly presented, to many countries, likewise to the shore of the great water to the north of here."
> *TJ* 32:11, "The human being has to become a universal oneness, so that he becomes one with Creation."
> *TJ* 32:23, "The greater the human being's dedication to the laws of Creation, so much the deeper shall be the peace within himself."
> *TJ* 32:24, "The human beings' happiness consists of seeking and finding the truth . . . ."
> *TJ* 32:25, "Only through the circumstances of human life can the human being develop and use his creative power in consciousness and spirit."
> *TJ* 32:32, "The human being will attain all his knowledge and wisdom, if he seriously strives for perfection."

After His talk, Jesus entered the great light which had again appeared and descended. A fog-like cloud around it started to ascend. The light or cloud then lifted off into the sky, which Deardorff believes gave rise to the ascension story of Acts 1:9. Jesus was let off in Damascus where He lived incognito for two years. He then sent for His mother, a brother, and a disciple to accompany Him to the East.

Jmmanuel and Saul

The *TJ* provides an entirely different perspective to the encounter between the risen Jesus and Saul on the road to Damascus. The New Testament describes Saul (who later became Paul) as a zealot who persecuted Christians and indicates that he was involved in stoning to death the first martyr, Stephen. According to the *TJ*, Jesus was in Damascus and learned of Saul's pursuit of His brother (Judas - Thomas). Thomas had joined Jesus in Damascus, and Saul had learned of Thomas' whereabouts and planned a journey of pursuit to Damascus. Jesus realized that if Saul continued persecuting disciples, His teachings would be suppressed, never gaining a foundation.

Jesus planned a dangerous trick against Saul. Obtaining a secret powder, salves, and bad smelling liquids, Jesus made them into a concoction. Hiding near the cliffs, a two-day journey from Damascus, Jesus spread the mixture along the road and waited for Saul's entourage to pass. At the right moment, Jesus threw a burning torch onto Saul's contrivance, resulting in the flare-up of a very bright light that temporarily blinded Saul.

> *TJ* 33:19, " . . . Huge lightning, stars and fireballs shot into the sky or fell from it . . ."
>
> *TJ* 33:21, "Then Jmmanuel called out, 'Saul, Saul, why do you persecute my disciples?'"
>
> *TJ* 33:22, "Saul however was afraid and fell onto the ground, crying out, 'Who are you who speak to me like this?'"
>
> Answering Saul's question, Jesus replied in words simlar to those in Acts 9:5-6.
>
> *TJ* 33:23, "I am Jmmanuel whom you persecute in your hatred along with my disciples."
>
> *TJ* 33:24, "Get up! Go into the city and let yourself be taught how you should live."

Acts 22 differs from Acts 9, emphasizing that the men with Saul did not hear the voice. Deardorff believes the chief purpose of Acts 22 was to inform readers that the voice must have been connected with Jesus in a spirit form that only Saul could sense, and not in the ordinary physical form. Both Acts 22 and 26 place the happening at midday. According to the *TJ*, Saul had encountered Jesus at an earlier time. If Saul had previously heard

Jesus' voice, it would explain why he immediately recognized the voice of Jesus. Deardorff believes that Saul's failure to acknowledge the teachings of Jesus did not stem from Saul's great hatred for Him, but that he wanted to remember and worship the resurrected Jesus Christ as a different person from the Jmmanuel he had been persecuting. He saw Jesus Christ as the savior of mankind, but remembered Jmmanuel as his "thorn in the flesh," according to 2 Cor. 12:7.

> *TJ* 33:34, "Jmmanuel stayed another thirty days in Damascus and leaked news that he would presently leave the country and travel to the land of India."

The *TJ* tells of Jesus, Mary, and Thomas first journeying north from Syria and back again, returning to the city of Ephesus in southwest Turkey. Jesus was recognized by a merchant who brought Him in contact with some Essenes. Jesus did not trust them and fled eastward with His entourage. Current thought suggests Jesus may have been an Essene, but the *TJ* dispels that idea implying Jmmanuel was anti-Essene.

Rebirth and Destiny

Most mystical societies and Eastern religions teach the concept of rebirth and destiny, with the purpose to perfect the soul, so it can return to the Creator, the Supreme God. Throughout the *TJ*, rebirth, destiny, and perfection are addressed through a number of teachings by Jmmanuel.

> *TJ* 23:23, "Take heed of the laws of Creation, which teach that in a new life people do not remember their former lives."
>
> *TJ* 23:24, "At this point it is only the prophets who remember former lives, since they follow the laws of creation and therefore live in wisdom."
>
> *TJ* 23:45, "So when human beings die, their spirits live on and leave the existence for the beyond, where they continue to gather wisdom of knowledge."
>
> *TJ* 23:46, "According to the amount of spiritual wisdom gained through the learning of the consciousness, they themselves determine their future return, as well as their subsequent activties."

TJ 20:28, "Jmmanuel replied (to Peter), 'Truly, I say to you: some of you who have followed me will embrace the wisdom of my teaching, so you will be spiritually great in reincarnations to come.
But some of you will not recognize the wisdom of my teaching and spread erroneous teachings about me. They shall have a difficult time finding the truth in coming incarnations'."
TJ 21:17, "Know this, humans are obligated at all times to create a will for whatever they want to attempt because that is the law of nature."
TJ 21:18, "These human beings determined the course of their lives, which is called fate."
TJ 21:25, "Each person's spirit is created individually for the task of perfecting itself and to acquire wisdom."
TJ 21:26, "This, so as to become one with Creation according to the destiny of the laws, whereby Creation grows, expanding, and perfecting itself within itself."
TJ 18:46, "'People's lives are destined for the perfection of the spirit, so that they live their lives in fulfillment thereof."
TJ 18:51, "If people live with the mission to perfect their spirits and obtain insight and knowledge through their mistakes, they lead lives for which they were destined."
TJ 26:24, "A fool who idly rests waits for fate to act without doing anything himself perishes like an unfired pot in water."
TJ 5:47, "You should train your spirit in the course of incarnation and let it become perfect, so that you become one with Creation."
TJ 34:15, "Thus the human being perfects himself so extensively that he unfolds his creativity and in the end becomes one with Creation, as was destined from the beginning."
TJ 34:16, "Thus Creation has brought forth a new spirit, allowing it to be perfected independently in the human body, and the perfected spirit returns to

> Creation to become one with it; in this way Creation perfects itself, because within it is the knowledge and wisdom that enables it to do so."

Again, the concept of reincarnation is mentioned, thus reinforcing the evidence about the similarity in the teachings of Jesus and Buddha.

Creation and Unity

Jmmanuel tries to clarify the concept of creation.

> *TJ* 34:15, "Thus the human perfects himself so extensively that he unfolds his creativity and in the end becomes one with the Creator, as was destined from the beginning."
>
> *TJ* 34:22, "The material life is limited, but the life of the spirit lasts forever and knows no end."
>
> *TJ* 34:27, "Thus the wise understand that the secret of original Creation lies in the calculations based upon the number seven, and they will obtain and possess the knowledge that Creation has a time for work or rest that is also counted by the number seven."
>
> *TJ* 34:39, "Since the spirit in a person is part of Creation, it is one with Creation; consequently, it is not two."
>
> *TJ* 34:46, "Since everything is unity and everything emanates from it, no duality or trinity whatsoever exists because it would violate the laws of Creation."
>
> *TJ* 34:57, "A unity always consists of two parts, the spirit is a unity in two parts, but both one in themselves and one together."
>
> *TJ* 34:61, "The two parts of the spirit are wisdom and power."
>
> *TJ* 34:66, "So when the scribes teach that a person lives in trinity, this teaching is erroneous and falsified, because it is not taught according to the laws of Creation."

Wise words, no matter where they originated.

THE SCIENTIFIC ANALYSIS

Deardorff performed a detailed analysis of the *TJ*, comparing it with the Gospel of Matthew. Over the last two centuries, biblical scholars have scrutinized the Gospels, developing many criticisms suggesting they were heavily edited and copied from a proto-type. Deardorff addressed these criticisms directed toward Matthew and determined in his research that the *TJ* could hold up to the scholarly criticisms leveled against the Gospel of Matthew. To his surprise, the *TJ* withstood the test, leading Deardorff to conclude that the *TJ* was genuine and in all likelihood was the Matthew proto-type.

Deardorff expected a number of divergences from the *TJ*, that might occur whether or not the *TJ* was a hoax. He wrote, "If the *TJ* is genuine and related to Matthew, we should expect it to be free of a large share of criticisms that biblical scholars have directed against Matthew." Many of these criticisms address aspects of Matthew that appeared to be non-genuine teachings of Jesus added later by editors. Deardorff claimed that if the *TJ* was indeed a hoax, it would be expected that the hoaxers would have a scholarly background enabling them to write the *TJ* to satisfy scholarly criticism.

Deardorff expected the differences between the *TJ* and Gospel of Matthew to be a lack of any Christology and trinity in the *TJ*, which are both absent in the *TJ*. While the *TJ* does not address the concept of heaven and hell, reincarnation is addressed in the *TJ*, perhaps being the reason heaven and hell are not mentioned.

Another difference Deardorff found is the seven instances where the first person "I" was used by Jmmanuel in verses having cognates (parallels) with Matthew where "I" does not occur. In six of those cases, it reads "son of man" in Matthew, and the seventh reads "the son." In many other instances in the *TJ*, "I" appears, but has no cognate in Matthew. It also appears in Matthew with no cognate in the *TJ*.

In yet another difference in the *TJ*, Jmmanuel is called the son of Gabriel, where in Matthew the cognate is the son of God.

Deardorff believes any reference to Jmmanuel as being the son of Gabriel or of a human-like celestial son would have been heretical. In the times of gods, angels were often synonymous with the gods. Perhaps the early editor understood this and called Jesus the Son of God, rather than the son of god spelled with a lower case "g." The Gnostics also believed in two levels of gods, with the Supreme God being called Creation by Jmmanuel. Jews mistook the Supreme God for Yahweh, whom the Gnostics considered evil. Some researchers believe Yahweh was similar to the gods of Sumer, Egypt, or Greece. Yahweh was not the Creation or Supreme God. The original meaning of Elohim in the Hebrew form of the Old Testament is "gods," the plural form. In the biblical interpretation, it means singular God. Sumerian researcher, Zecharia Sitchin, believes the Elohim were the Nefilim or the Anunnaki from Nibiru. He believes these were the gods to whom the Old Testament referred. The *TJ* substantiates this belief when Jmmanuel states, "But god is a human being, like all the celestial sons and the human races except that he is vastly greater in conscious than they (TJ 4: 40)." The Bible teaches that we are created in God's image, perhaps explaining the ancient Sumerian writings which say the gods (Anunnaki, Nefilim, Pleiadians) created man with their genes.

Deardorff made a detailed comparison of the TJ verses with the Matthew verse criticisms by Francis Wright Beare, who was a Christian scholar and professor emeritus (now deceased) from Trinity College at the University of Toronto. His book, *The Gospel According to Matthew,* was published in 1981, three years after the German version of the *TJ*. It disclosed verses in Matthew that were likely redactions (editorial changes relative to Matthew's source) of which a possible hoaxer would not have known. Deardorff used only the criticisms by Beare that appeared valid and logical from the *TJ* viewpoint that he presents. Deardorff found 194 such criticisms. Not included in his analysis were other criticisms by Beare, who believed spiritual powers and miracles could not exist and represent fictitious events, as most contemporary scholars believe.

The following is a format used by Deardorff addressing 157 of Beare's criticisms:

Quotations: Matt 1:23, "Behold, a virgin shall conceive and bear a son and his name shall be called Emmanuel, which means, 'God with us.'"

> *TJ* 1:86-87 (cognate), "Behold, a virgin will be impregnated by a celestial son before she is married to man before the people. They will name the first of her womb, Jmmanuel, which translated means 'god with.'"

Criticism (Beare): "This Matthew verse is the quotation from Isaiah that has been often criticized because it more easily applies to a short range prophecy within Isaiah's own time than to a long-range prophecy for a Messiah seven centuries later."
Discussion (Deardorff): "Here we see that the *TJ* version, supposedly the correct version that should have been in Isaiah, is still a long-range prophecy that scholars will find just as distasteful for that reason as the Matthew version. To speak about an alien (angelic) impregnation within sacred Jewish scripture was surely as taboo up to seven centuries B.C. as it is today and could not have survived."

Deardorff found 194 verses validating Beare's criticism for the Gospel of Matthew. However, the matching *TJ* verses or cognates do not suffer from the same criticism. As a result, concludes Deardorff, the *TJ* is part of the proto-Matthew. He found approximately 134 other criticisms where Beare was in error, if the *TJ* represented the truth. Of these 134 criticisms, 62 were based only upon the fact that Matthew deviated from what is written in Mark or Luke. This group was not included in the 194 points. There were 51 instances where Deardorff thought Beare to be incorrect because he was just flatly wrong, compared with the 194 cases where the *TJ* indicates Beare was correct for a valid reason. Deardorff considered this error rate very good. He believes it impossible that a hoaxer could have foreseen the criticisms of Beare and acted upon them accordingly in drafting a fake, proto-Matthean text. He believes that if the Gospel of Matthew is analyzed with an open mind to the *TJ*, the *TJ* is much more genuine.

Only 17 percent of the Matthean verses (180 of 1071) perfectly correlate with the *TJ*. Deardorff considers this 17 percent figure quite high because of all the copying the text has undergone over the centuries. A perfect cognate is found to occur at the beginning of a Matthew chapter 32 percent of the time, nine chapters out of 28. Deardorff found 37 Matthew inserts relative to the *TJ*, including the beginning and ends of some chapters. Beare's research picked up on 73 percent of them, a remarkably high percentage. Verse substitutions represent similarly redacted material, and these redactions should be as detectable as the insertions, asserts Deardorff. Of the 191 verses that comprise these substitutions, Beare raised a valid concern with 60 percent of them.

Definite correlations with *TJ* verses are found in 721 Matthew verses that do not appear to have been inserted or substituted. The more Matthew deviated from the *TJ*, the more often Beare identified problems with Matthew. If the *TJ* is genuine, this should be expected, thus supporting Deardorff's hypothesis that the *TJ* was proto-Matthew.

Summary of Matthew Verses Validly Criticized by Beare:

"Perfectly" Correlated Verses	1 percent of 180
Highly Correlated Verses	11 percent of 157
Moderately Correlated Verses	24 percent of 205
Poorly Correlated Verses	37 percent of 179
Substitution Verses	60 percent of 191
Inserted Verse	73 percent of 150
Total Verses	1071

Deardorff's comprehensive analysis indicates the *TJ* is, in all likelihood, the first section of the proto-Matthew text. He considered it a masterpiece that was far too heretical to be accepted. Redactions had redesigned it to make it accepted to the proto-orthodoxy view, resulting in a multitude of inconsistencies. Deardorff states, "The *TJ* portrays Jmmanuel compared with Jesus in the Gospels, as much more of a teacher, more logical, much more of a prophet, and more provocative. Above all, he emphasized and demonstrated the existence and power of the individual spirit."

EPILOGUE OF THE TALMUD OF JMMANUEL

Most of Jmmanuel's teachings were considered too heretical by the compiler of Matthew, writes Deardorff, and he had no apprehension to radically alter them to fit the emerging Christianity. Part of the reason may have been that Judas Iscariot was the author of the *TJ*. Deardorff believes that studying the *TJ* openly is impossible for Christian scholars, and those who would study it would open themselves up to ridicule by their peers and respectful institutions.

Deardorff also recognizes a number of valid problems with the *TJ*. One serious problem is that the prophetic ability of Jmmanuel seems almost too good. A hoaxer would know the events and be able to incorporate them easily. However, states Deardorff, it could represent the full range of paranormal abilities that Jesus is reported to have to a smaller extent in the Gospels.

Another serious concern in the *TJ* is the existence of strong anti-Judaism message, much more prevalent than in Matthew. Jmmanuel put a curse on Israel, reminiscent of the curse placed upon Israelites found in Deuteronomy 28:58-59, 64-65. If the compiler was Jewish, much of this would have been edited out if the attempt was to recruit converts from the Pharisees. In the *TJ*, Jmmanuel exhibited much more anger toward the Jews than one would expect from the Prince of Peace. This seeming antisemitism remains a sore point for the *TJ* advocate, writes Deardorff.

One needs to ask other questions about *The Talmud of Jmmanuel* scenario. Are there any photos of the papyrus rolls? Rashid was an intelligent person, and it would be common sense to photograph the scrolls and have plenty of copies if the Church was in pursuit. Why was this not done? This would have allowed more qualified translators to analyze the Aramaic writings. Additionally, Rashid brought Meier to the tomb on several occasions under the cover of dark. Meier later claimed to have forgotten the location. Is he protecting himself and family because of the assassination attempts? One surely could understand his dilemma. Hopefully, sometime in the future, if photos exist and if the tomb location is found, that information will be released to the public by someone who may have additional knowledge of this intriguing mystery.

The accuracy of the original translation is also in question. Rashid had translated the Aramaic scrolls into German. How accurate was this translation, as he apparently was not an Aramaic scholar? Being of Lebanese background, one could understand Rashid having an antisemitic bias that may have leaked through in the translations.

Another interest in the *TJ* are the prophecies. The *TJ* tells of Jmmanuel's prophecies regarding the prophet Muhammed.

> *TJ* 30:11, "A new man will rise up in this land as a prophet and will legally and rightfully condemn and persecute you (the Jews) and you will have to pay with your blood."
>
> *TJ* 30:12, "This man will create a forceful new cult especially for preserving the truthful teaching and have himself recognized as a prophet and in so doing persecute you through all times."
>
> *TJ* 30:13, "Even though, according to your claim, he will be a false prophet and you will revile him as you do me, and he will bring you new teachings that will seem false to you; he will nevertheless be a true prophet, and he will have your race persecuted throughout all time in the future."
>
> *TJ* 30:14, "His name will be Mohammed, and his name will bring horror, misery and death to your kind, which you deserve."

Deardorff suggests that Jesus was prophesying the bad karma Jews had created by distorting His teachings that resulted in anguish for Jews and humanity for thousands of years.

Additionally, Eduard Meier, the *TJ* editor, portrays much anger toward organized religion and the Roman Catholic Church, as seen in the book's foreword. Meier assisted in formulating the *TJ* into its German format. Could some of Meier's bias have leached into the translation? As we have seen, biblical scribes have played an important role in setting the tone for religious documents.

Another concern relating to the validity of the *TJ* is how the *TJ* scrolls got into the tomb of Jmmanuel? According to what Rashid initially learned from reading through the *TJ*, when 45 years old, Jmmanuel married a young and pretty woman who bore Him many children. After the death of Judas Iscariot, who was buried in Srinagor at the age of 90, Joseph, the oldest son of Jmmanuel, continued writing his father's story. After Jmmanuel died of natural causes between the ages of 110 and 115 and was buried in

Sringagar, His son Joseph undertook a three-year journey to Palestine and lived in Jerusalem where he later died. Joseph hid the original scrolls in the burial cave where Jmmanuel had been placed, considering that location to be the safest. Deardorff believes he gave a copy (transcription) to some early Christians, which soon formed the proto-Matthew.

Is *The Talmud of Jmmanuel* a hoax, or is it genuine as Deardorff believes? Or was it deposited by the "gods" to correct history as a few believe? The author of this book personally has too many questions to make a conclusion. The *TJ* has undergone excellent research by Dr. Deardorff, which merited inclusion in this book. As we will see, many of the *TJ*'s teachings have substance to support them. The most important is the survival of Jesus following the crucifixion.

Chapter Six

THE EARLY LIFE OF JESUS

Miracles At A Young Age

Christianity knows very little about the early life of Jesus, the only information coming from the minimal writings found in the scripture. Fortunately, there are some early Christian writings not included in the Bible that tell of Jesus' infancy and youth. A few stories can be found in the apocrypha, which originally meant "too sacred and secret to be in everyone's possession," perhaps explaining why some of these texts were not included in the New Testament. Muhammed, according to tradition, was in possession of stories about Jesus' infancy and youth, some included in the Koran. Author Glenn Kimball spent years gathering these little known stories about Jesus and included them in his book, *Hidden Stories of the Childhood of Jesus*. Many of his findings are quite surprising and will be discussed here. We still have to remember that any story from ancient writings may have been subjected to biased editing by the early scribes.

The Parents of Jesus

According to Kimball's findings, Jesus' great-grandfather David, a descendant of King David, was given a vision that the prophecy of his fathers would be fulfilled through him. He and his wife, Sarah, had a son named Joachim, Jesus' grandfather. Joachim's cousin, Anna of Bethlehem, became Joachim's wife. After their marriage, they moved to Nazareth, taking their sheep and shepherds with them. For about twenty years, Anna and Joachim were without child.

In their prayers, Anna and Joachim promised God that if He blessed them with a child, they would dedicate the child to His service. They made a vow with God that they would send the infant child to serve in the temple. On the day of the Feast of

Dedication, however, they were told by the high priest that it was unlawful to offer alms at the temple because they were childless. Depressed and ashamed, Joachim retreated into the countryside where he fasted and prayed for many days. An angel appeared, telling Joachim that he and Anna would have a child to be named Mary. From the time of her birth, she would be filled with the Holy Spirit. The angel instructed Joachim that Mary was not to eat or drink anything unclean nor was she to converse with people in the street. She was to live inside the temple. Mary would bring forth a son of the most high God even though she would be a virgin. The child would be called Jesus, who would be the savior of all nations.

Anna was also blessed with the angel's appearance, who informed her that she would give birth to a baby daughter to be named Mary. Mary was not to leave the temple until she reached the age of discretion. The angel also told Anna that Mary would have a son who would save the world. Shortly thereafter, Anna conceived and gave birth to a daughter they called Mary.

Born in Nazareth, Mary was brought to Jerusalem by her parents at the age of three. She resided at the temple where she was to serve the Lord, with the priest Zacharias responsible for her upbringing. Zacharias would come daily into Mary's room at the temple and find food and drink brought to Mary by an angel.

When Mary was approaching puberty, the priest Abiathan offered many gifts to Mary, hoping she would marry his son, but Mary declined saying she had vowed virginity. When Mary was 14 years old, the high priest declared that all virgins in the temple who had come of age were to return home. Because they were now grown, the priest told the virgins they should marry. All virgins obeyed the priest's demands except Mary, who would not comply because of her vow of virginity.

This situation put the high priest in a dilemma, and he tried to find an answer by praying to God in the temple's Holy of Holies. A voice came to the priest that advised him to read the prophecy of Isaiah regarding the virgin birth. Isaiah had said, "There shall come forth a rod out of the stem of Jesse, and a flower shall spring out of its root, and the Spirit of the Lord shall rest upon him in the form of a dove." After reading Isaiah, the high priest ordered all eligible bachelors of the House of David to bring their rods to the altar. He declared that whoever's rod grew a flower, and on whom the spirit of God in the form of a dove should light upon, would be the one to betroth Mary. This is when Joseph appeared on the scene.

Joseph appeared with the other eligible bachelors called forward by the priest. The rod demonstration took place at the altar, and everyone presented their rods except Joseph, who withdrew his. None of the rods sprouted a flower. The concerned priest retreated and consulted God, reappearing with the announcement that Mary was to be betrothed to the person whose rod was not present. When Joseph returned his rod to the temple, it sprouted a flower and a dove perched upon him, fulfilling the prophecy. Joseph returned home to prepare for the upcoming marriage, and Mary returned to Galilee.

Joseph, who was much older than Mary, was a widower with four children. James and Simon, well-known brothers of Jesus, were actually older than Jesus and were Joseph's sons from his first marriage. Lydia and Lysia were Joseph's daughters, sisters who later played an important role in Jesus' life and ministry. When Jesus was born, the sisters had already been married and left home. James was the youngest of Joseph's children, still a young child when Mary and Joseph were married. Mary and James later formed a very special relationship.

While in Nazareth, the angel Gabriel visited Mary. A tremendous light filled her bedroom chamber, and amidst the light, Gabriel said, "Hail Mary! Full of Grace. The Lord is with you. You are blessed above all women." He told Mary not to be afraid as she was to conceive and bring forth a son, to be called Jesus. Gabriel said the Lord would give Jesus the throne of His father David, and He would reign over the House of Jacob forever. "The Holy Spirit was to come upon Mary," said Gabriel, "Who shall be born of you, shall be holy and will be called the son of God. Mary then stretched forth her hand, lifted her eyes and said, "Behold the handmaid of the Lord. Let it be unto me according to your word."

When Mary became pregnant, she stayed with her sister Elisabeth for three months until Elisabeth gave birth to a son who became John the Baptist. Joseph had returned from a trip building houses to find Mary six months pregnant. Becoming quite angry, Joseph demanded an explanation of her condition. Mary began to cry saying that she had not been with another man. Shortly afterward, an angel appeared to Joseph explaining that the Holy Ghost had come onto Mary, and Joseph became very supportive.

The Birth of Jesus

In *Hidden Stories of the Childhood of Jesus,* Kimball reveals more detail about the birth of Jesus than do the stories of the Bible.

Following a decree from Caesar Augustus that all Jews should be taxed, Joseph seated Mary on his donkey and departed for Bethlehem along with his two sons. They had almost reached Bethlehem when Mary said to Joseph, "Take me down from the donkey because the child within me is ready to be born." Taking her down, Joseph discovered a nearby cave where he led Mary inside. He then hurried off to find a Hebrew midwife.

Joseph met a midwife named Solome who asked, "Is she your wife?" Joseph told her that the mother-to-be was Mary, who was educated in the House of the Lord, and that he was chosen to be her husband, but she was not yet his wife. After telling Solome that Mary conceived by the power of the Holy Ghost, Joseph returned to the cave with Solome. A bright cloud came over the cave, and Solome said, "This day my soul is magnified, for mine eyes have seen surprising things and salvation is brought to Israel." The cloud became so bright that it became almost unbearable. Gradually it disappeared, and they saw an infant in the arms of Mary, who was feeding the newborn Baby Jesus. Joseph and Mary left the cave after the birth of Jesus and continued on to the inn at Bethlehem. Because there were no vacancies due to the tax pilgrims, they stayed in the stable.

Solome had a withered arm that an angel of the Lord healed following Jesus' birth, saying, "The Lord God hath heard your prayer. Reach forth your hand to the child and carry him and by doing so your hand shall be restored." Solome picked up the newborn Jesus and said, "This is a great King which is born in Israel." From that moment Solome was made whole. A voice came to Solome saying, "Do not talk about the strange things which you have seen until the child returns to Jerusalem."

Solome later accompanied Jesus' family to Egypt and helped care for Him throughout his life, becoming a disciple of Jesus.

According to the law of Moses, it was required that the newborn be presented before the temple of the Lord with offerings. The law states that every firstborn male be set apart as holy. Great pleasure filled the old priest Simeon when he saw Jesus in the arms of Mary, shining as a pillar of light. He said, "Now, O my Lord, I shall die in peace, according to the promise which has been made to me. For mine eyes have seen the vessel of the salvation of all nations . . . A light to all people and glory of Israel."

As Joseph was preparing to go home, a great commotion arose in Bethlehem as wise men from the East had come to Palestine asking, "Where has the King of the Jews been born?" They arrived in Jerusalem at the temple where the servants of Herod had dismissed the priests. Herod's servants asked the wise men, "What sign were you told to look for at the coming of the Baby King and what signs did you see?" They answered, "We saw a large star shining among the other stars of heaven, and it so outshined all the other stars, that it made the stars around it no longer visible. We therefore knew that the great King was born in Israel and have come to worship him."

Herod sent a message to the wise men instructing them to find the Baby King and bring him word so that he might worship Him also. The wise men continued to follow the star to Bethlehem where Baby Jesus remained with his mother. They offered Jesus gold, frankincense, and myrrh, and Mary took an article of Jesus' swaddling clothes and gave it to them. That night, an angel warned the wise men in a dream that they should not return to Herod, so they returned to their own country by a different route. An angel also appeared to Joseph in his sleep, saying, "Arise, take the child and his mother and go into Egypt as soon as the cock crows." Early the next morning, Joseph departed south to Egypt with his family.

After hearing that the wise men mocked him, Herod became angry and ordered certain men to kill all the children under two years of age in Bethlehem and the surrounding region. When Elisabeth, the mother of John the Baptist, heard the decree to kill babies, she escaped into the mountains with baby John. Herod thought the most logical baby to become king of Israel was John. He sent his servants to the temple to talk to Zacharias, John's father, about the baby's whereabouts. Zacharias replied to them, "I am a martyr for God and if Herod shed my blood, the Lord will receive my soul. Let it be known that you shed innocent blood." Herod's servants proceeded to murder Zacharias in the temple. Later, some of Zacharias's blood was carried to the mountain and spilled on a rock in fulfillment of the prophecy of Ezekiel (Ezekiel 24:6-8) that God would take vengeance on those who killed priests and the children.

The Egyptian Journey

On their journey to Egypt, Mary and Joseph stayed overnight at an inn. (Some nonbiblical writings suggest that Jesus' family was well off financially as they had been descendants of the Hebrew royal family. During Jesus' early life they received valuable gifts from the Magi and later from the rulers of Egypt when Jesus healed their sick children. These writings tell of Mary and Joseph staying at inns during the Egyptian exile.) The city's priest had a son possessed by an evil spirit. Mary had washed the swaddling clothes of Jesus and hung them out to dry upon a post. The possessed boy happened to take an article of clothing from the post and placed it on his head. From that moment on, the boy was healed. The boy sang praises to the Lord and told his father who responded, "My son, perhaps this baby is the son of the living God who made the heaven and earth. For as soon as he came amongst us, the idol where I stood to administer was broken. All the gods fell down and were destroyed by a greater power."

Mary and Joseph heard about the broken idols and feared the Egyptians would be angry. They quickly departed the city traveling through a secret place where thieves robbed travelers. As Joseph and his family approached, the thieves heard a great noise like a king and his great army of riding horses. Afraid of this great noise, the robbers departed and left behind all their precious booty and prisoners, who escaped with their possessions.

The family entered another city where Mary encountered a possessed woman whom she pitied. Mary caused the evil spirit to withdraw, relieving the woman of her torment. The woman said, "Woe to me because of Mary and her son." The woman, being from an affluent family, was grateful for the miracle, and the family entertained Mary and Joseph with great respect.

Continuing their journey into Egypt, Jesus' family entered another town in the early evening where a marriage was about to take place. The bride was deaf and without speech. She encountered Mary and stretched out her hand to Baby Jesus. She hugged and kissed Him with great love. Immediately the bride could talk and hear, and she sang praises to God for restoring her health.

The next day a woman brought perfumed water to wash the Baby Jesus. After washing Jesus, the woman saved the water and happened to sprinkle some upon a girl with leprosy. Shortly afterwards, the girl was healed. This caused the town's people to say, "Without a doubt Mary and the Boy are gods." The healed girl asked if she could join them, and Mary and Joseph consented. After arriving in another city, the girl met the prince's wife and told what happened to her. It so happened the prince and his wife had a child who had contracted leprosy. This upset the prince, who threatened to kill the baby or send him away. The prince and princess invited Joseph and Mary to a great feast, and the next day the princess took perfumed water to wash Jesus. Afterwards, she poured the water upon her son, whom she brought along, and immediately her son was healed from leprosy. She sang with great praise and offered large gifts to Mary before she continued her travels.

In Egypt they came to a place with a sycamore tree, now called Matarea. Here Jesus caused a well to spring forth and Mary washed her coat. The journey proceeded to Memphis where they saw the Pharaoh and took up residence. During His time in Egypt, Jesus performed many miracles, but it came time to return to Judea.

The Return to Judea

Kimball relates a string of anecdotes about Jesus after His return to Judea. The family returned after hearing about Herod's death. Joseph was afraid to enter the country after hearing that Archelaus, Herod's son, was the new king. An angel appeared to Joseph who told him, "Fear not to go to Nazareth and live there." Upon coming to Bethlehem, they were told about several types of distemper that were killing the infected children.

While Mary was bathing Jesus, a woman brought her son infected with distemper. Mary told the woman to sprinkle some bath water onto her son. After the mother's son awoke from his nap, he was perfectly healed.

Another woman in Bethlehem had two sick sons, one died and the other near death. She approached Mary with her problems, and Mary took pity on her. She instructed the woman to place the sick boy, Batholomew, in Jesus' bed and to cover him in Jesus' clothes. As soon as Bartholomew touched the bedding of Baby Jesus, he was cured.

Another instance of Jesus' special power happened when Mary and Jesus had gone to the home of a neighbor, who was a dyer of cloth. Jesus wandered into the room containing the dye vats and clothes that were to be dyed. Jesus dropped all the clothes in the black dye vessel. Once the shopmaster discovered what happened, he became quite upset and demanded Mary pay for the clothes before she left the shop. Mary gave Jesus a stern lecture saying, "Look at all the damage you have done." Jesus walked over to the vat and pulled the clothes out. They came out the color they were intended to be. As the man heaped praises on Jesus, Mary took Jesus in her arms and kissed Him.

Another mother had a son possessed by an evil spirit. When possessed by Satan, the boy Judas was inclined to bite those in his presence and even himself. The woman brought her son to Mary, and the boy sat down on the right side of Jesus. He tried to bite Jesus but could not. Frustrated, the boy lashed out and struck Jesus on the right side causing Him to cry out. At that moment, the evil spirit left Judas, whose last name was Iscariot.

Another anecdote Kimball discusses regards Joseph. Joseph was summoned by the king of Jerusalem, who said, "I would have you make me a throne to occupy the place where I commonly sit." Joseph worked on the throne for two years before he finally finished it. Jesus accompanied Joseph for its installation, but then Joseph realized he had made it the wrong size. The king became very angry causing Joseph great anxiety. Jesus asked him, "What are you afraid of?" Joseph responded, "I am afraid that I have lost my labor in the work which I have been about these two years." Jesus then said, "Do not be afraid or sad. Lay hold on one side of the throne and I will take hold of the other and we will bring it to its dimensions." Then both of them pulled their respective sides. The throne obeyed and was brought to its proper dimension. Both were astonished and praised God.

Another story tells of a friend of Jesus who was chopping wood and struck his foot. Jesus kneeled down and put His hands on the injured foot, which immediately healed, allowing the boy to return to work. A crowd had gathered and saw what Jesus had done, and they worshiped Him, saying, "We believe that you are the son of God."

In yet another example, Jesus was playing with neighbor boys when a group of people passed Jesus carrying a boy bitten by a poisonous snake. Seeing the boy was near death, Jesus asked what happened, and then instructed the people to return the boy to the serpent. Jesus called out the viper, instructing the serpent to suck out all the poison. Slithering onto the boy, the snake took away all its poison. Jesus then touched the boy, who was immediately restored to health. The boy began to cry, and Jesus said, "Cease crying, for hearafter thou shalt be my disciple." The boy was Simon the Canaanite.

Another serpent incident occurred when Joseph sent his son James to gather wood with Jesus. A poisonous snake bit James, who began to cry. Jesus blew upon the wound, instantly healing it.

Later, Jesus and some boys were playing on the housetops when one of the boys fell off and died. After the others fled, Jesus was left alone. The boy's family accused Jesus of killing their son by throwing him off the housetop. Jesus denied the accusations and replied, "Do not charge me with a crime of which you are not able to convict me. Let us go ask the boy himself. He will tell the truth." Jesus stood over the head of the dead boy and said, "Zeinunus, who threw you down from the housetop?" The dead boy answered, "You did not throw me down, but someone else did." All who were present praised the Lord.

Another miraculous incident occurred when Mary told Jesus to fetch some water, which He did. When the water pitcher broke, Jesus spread His mantle on the ground and gathered up the water into His cloak. He brought it to His mother who was astonished.

One day when Jesus and His friends were playing by the river, Jesus had sculptured 12 sparrows out of clay in small pools on the river bank. It so happened that it was the Sabbath, and Hanani the Jew passed by them and said, "Why do you make figures of clay on the Sabbath?" Hanani hurried to destroy the small pools where the clay sparrows were sitting. Jesus clapped His hands over the clay sparrows, and the birds flew away chirping.

Another time, a schoolmaster named Zaccheus lived in Jerusalem and asked Joseph, "Joseph, why don't you send Jesus to me?" Joseph agreed and told Mary about the encounter. They brought Jesus to the schoolmaster, who as soon as he saw Jesus, wrote out an alphabet for him. The teacher asked Jesus to say "aleph." When Jesus had said "aleph," the master asked him to pronounce "beth." Jesus said to him, "Tell me first the meaning of the letter aleph, and then I will pronounce beth." The master became angry and threatened to give Jesus a whipping, but then Jesus proceeded to explain the meanings of the letters aleph and beth. He told the schoolmaster why one letter went before another, and many other things about the Hebrew alphabet. The surprised master said, "I believe this boy was born before Noah." He told Joseph, "You have brought a boy to me to be taught who is more learned than any master." Then he told Mary, "This, your son, has no need for learning."

When Jesus was 12, Mary and Joseph brought Him to Jerusalem to the feast of the Passover. Unknowingly to Mary and Joseph, Jesus stayed behind in the temple among the elders and the learned men of Israel. A certain rabbi asked Jesus, "Have you read books?" Jesus answered and said He had read books. He went on to explain to the scholars about the books that described the laws, precepts, and statutes. Jesus explained to them about the mysteries contained in the books of the prophets. The rabbi said, "I never yet have seen or heard of such knowledge!" All that heard Jesus were astonished at His understanding and His answers.

A certain astronomer was present at the gathering and asked Jesus whether He studied astronomy. Jesus responded by telling him the number of heavenly bodies, and the trines, squares, and sextile aspects of the planets. Jesus told him about the progressions and retrograde motion of planets, their size and several prognostications associated with them. Essentially, Jesus gave the astronomer a mini course in astronomy and astrology. Jesus also talked about philosophy, physics, and metaphysics to the elders. He explained the principles of the physical body and how the soul operated within the body. A philosopher arose and worshiped Jesus saying, "O Lord Jesus, from henceforth I will be your disciple and servant."

After walking for three days and realizing Jesus was missing, Mary and Joseph returned to Jerusalem seeking Jesus. They found Jesus among the doctors in the temple, and Mary asked Jesus, "My son, why have you done this to us? Behold, your father and I have been worried and have been looking for you." Jesus answered Mary, "Why were you looking for me? Didn't you know that I ought to be about my Father's business?" Jesus returned with Mary and Joseph to Nazareth and obeyed them in all things.

Kimball later describes an anecdote found in the nonbiblical text, *History of Joseph, the Carpenter, or Death of Joseph,* which describes the death of Joseph. He had become ill and went to the temple to pray, so he would be delivered from the terrors of death. After returning home, Joseph became ill and weak. Jesus said,

> "I wept. My mother asked if Joseph must die and I told her that it must be so. I sat at his head, Mary at his feet. Mary felt his legs and found them cold as ice. My brothers and sisters were summoned. Lydia, my oldest sister, lamented. So did all. I looked at the south of the door and saw the angel appointed to take him at his death and other angels. Joseph saw them and feared. I rebuked them and the angels fled, except the one who was behind the door. I prayed for protection for the soul of Joseph. When I had said amen, my mother answered me, in the language of the inhabitants of the heavens of Michael and of Gabriel. The choir of the angels came. Numbing and panting seized Joseph. The angel, appointed to take him at his death, was timid. I arose and went outside and bade him and go and do his appointed work. Joseph died at sunrise.
>
> The people of Nazareth came and mourned till the ninth hour. Then I put forth, anointed and washed

> the body, angels came and shrouded the body, and the body was laid beside Jacob his father."

Later the apostles asked Jesus why Joseph should not have been exempt from death like Enoch and Elias. Jesus told them that death was inevitable and that both Enoch and Elias will have to die as well. They will be in trouble until their death is over. Jesus said at the end of the world the Antichrist will shed the blood of two men because of the reproaches the two men will heap upon Him. Then the apostles asked, "Who are these two men?" Jesus told them that they were Enoch and Elias.

Some of these stories collected by Kimball came from *The Gospel of the Birth of Mary* written by Matthew in the fourth century. Jesus' brother James, the first apsotle in Jerusalem, was credited with writing the *Proevangelion,* a historical account of the birth of Christ and the perpetual Virgin Mary. Another source of Jesus' early life was a Gnostic writing entitled *The First Gospel of the Infancy of Jesus Christ,* a text used in Africa and Asia. Some scholars believe Muhammed used this book in compiling the Koran. Other sources were *The Thomas Gospel of the Infancy of Jesus Christ,* originally connected with the *Gospel of Mary* and *History of Joseph, the Carpenter, or Death of Joseph,* often associated with the infancy gospels listed above.

These are but a few anecdotes that Kimball collected in his book. They all illustrate that even at a young age, Jesus had miraculous powers. Still missing is the mystery of Jesus' life during the lost years. The following chapter sheds light on this intriguing period of Jesus' earthly journey.

Chapter Seven

JESUS IN INDIA

Explaining The Lost Years

Scholars have long puzzled how the teachings of Jesus could have so closely paralleled Buddha's teachings. Also frustrating to them has been the lack of information regarding the 17 years prior to Jesus' baptism by John the Baptist. In 1894, Nicolas Notovitch, a Russian author, shed light on both dilemmas by publishing a book titled *The Unknown Life of Jesus Christ.* He reported his discovery in India that challenged the Church doctrine that Jesus was in Nazareth during the lost 17 years. The book caused a media uproar among scholars and theologians, but as we will see, the findings of Notovitch proved to be true.

Very little is known about the early life of Jesus. No record of any kind has described the life of Jesus between the ages of 12 and 30, referred to as the "lost years of Jesus." Theologians have insisted that Jesus lived in Palestine during those years, in or around Nazareth, but have no facts to support this claim. Because His father, Joseph, was a carpenter, theologians assumed Jesus was also a carpenter, again with nothing to back the assertion. In fact, Origen, in the early 3rd century, objected to the entire idea that Jesus was a carpenter because "Jesus himself is not described anywhere in the gospels accepted by the church."

Only four of the 89 gospel chapters describe the life of Jesus prior to His ministry. Two chapters each in Matthew and Luke describe the genealogy, conception, birth, and familiar anecdotes such as the annunciation. They also describe the escape into Egypt where Jesus and His family remained until the death of Herod in 4 B.C., when they returned to Nazareth. After returning, the Gospel of Luke records only two events about Jesus' youth. One tells about His physical and spiritual growth, and the other about His Passover visit to the temple at the age of 12.

After attending the Passover feast in Jerusalem, Joseph and Mary were returning to Nazareth. Suddenly they realized Jesus was missing from their company. Returning to the city, they found Jesus in the temple sitting among doctors, both listening and asking questions. After Mary reproached Jesus, He replied, "Wist ye not, that I must be about my Father's business?" The family then departed from Nazareth, and for the next 17 years there is no knowledge about the life of Jesus.

The apocryphal writings tell that when Jesus was growing up in Egypt and Palestine, He performed many healings and miracles. They recount how Jesus healed a boy's foot; how He carried water in His cloak; when He shortened a wide beam while assisting Joseph with carpentry; and the miracle of fashioning 12 sparrows out of clay and bringing them to life with a clap of His hands. All have been discussed earlier.

The early Christians were not interested in history. Some scholars conjecture that the early Christians expected Jesus to return after the crucifixion, and found it unnecessary to record anything. Even early Christian scholars were more interested in the ministry of Jesus than the lost years. A breakthrough came, however, in the last part of the 19th century.

THE SAGA OF NICOLAS NOTOVITCH

Nicolas Notovitch was born in Crimea in 1858, of the Russian Orthodox faith. Some believe he may have been converted to Judaism because his brother Osip was born Jewish. Little biographical information is available about Notovitch, but he is known to have written 11 books, with *The Unknown Life of Jesus Christ* being the first on a religious subject. Following the Russo-Turkish wars of 1877 - 78, Notovitvh began a series of travels in the East. On October 14, 1887, he left Lahore for Rawalpindi with plans to visit Kashmir and then Ladakh.

While at Mulbekh, he visited a Buddhist monastary called a "gompa," which means a solitary place often built on a mountain top as Mulbekh or on the face of a cliff. Mulbekh remains the gateway to the world of Tibetan Buddhism. A lama greeted Notovitch and during their conversation told him that in the archives of Lhasa, the capital of Tibet, there were several thousand ancient scrolls that discussed the life of the prophet Issa, the Eastern name for Jesus. Confiding to Notovitch, the lama said some of the monasteries had copies, but not Mulbekh.

This astounding revelation intrigued Notovitch, and he was determined to find the records concerning Issa. After leaving Mulbekh, he visited several monasteries where the resident monks knew of the documents but were not in possession of them. His travels led him to Himis, 25 miles from Leh, the capital of Ladakh. Located in a hidden Himalayan valley 11,000 feet above sea level, Himis is the most celebrated monastery in Ladakh.

Due to its primitive location, Himis was one of the few gompas that escaped destruction by invading Asiatic aggressors. Because of this isolated position, treasures and books were brought from other monasteries for safekeeping. Notovitch asked the chief lama if he had heard of Issa. Responding, the lama said the Buddhists greatly respected Issa, but few knew much about Him except for the chief lama, who read the records of Issa's life. During their conversation, the lama talked about the many scrolls at Himis, and among them "are to be found descriptions of the life and acts of the Buddha Issa, who preached the holy doctrine in India and among the children of Israel."

The lama told Notovitch that the scrolls had been brought from India to Nepal and then to Tibet. They were originally written in Pali, the religious language of the Buddhists. The copy at Himis had been translated into Tibetan. Very excited about this discovery, Notovitch asked if the lama could recite the copies to him. The lama said he was unsure of their exact location, but if Notovitch ever returned he would find them and be glad to show them.

Dejected that he had come so close, Notovitch departed Himis. But as fate would have it, Notovitch fell from his horse, fracturing his leg near the gompa of Pintak. Using this as an excuse, he returned to Himis, only a half day's journey away.

During Notovitch's convalescence at Himis, the chief lama produced two bound volumes with yellowed pages. The lama read aloud sections concerning Issa, with Notovitch's interpreter translating the readings, and Notovitch meticulously recording them in his journal. The story of Issa found in the manuscript was composed of scattered, untitled verses that were out of sequence.

Notovitch put the verses in order and published his discovery several years later, including the account of his saga.

THE LIFE OF SAINT ISSA

Notovitch titled his text *The Life of Saint Issa: Best of the Sons of Men,* which contained 244 verses arranged into 14 chapters with the longest containing 27 verses. The text includes many similarities with both the Old and New Testaments. Included is the deliverance of the Israelites by Mossa (Moses); the wayward actions of Jews; the foreign invasion and subjugation by Rome; and finally, the incarnation of a divine child born to poor but pious parents. Additionally, the text describes God speaking through the mouth of the infant, and claims people came from all over to hear Him. Quickly, though, the narrative jumps to Issa's thirteenth year, the first of the lost years.

At this age, Israelite boys generally took a wife. Issa's home was very humble, according to the text, but it became a meeting place for the rich and noble.They all desired to have him as a son-in-law because he was "already famous for his edifying discourse in the name of the almighty." However, Issa had other plans. He secretly left his parents' home and departed from Jerusalem with a caravan of merchants. Issa traveled to the East to study the laws of the great Buddha in order to perfect himself in the "Divine Word."

At the age of 14, Issa crossed the Sind, a region of the lower Indus River Valley in Southeastern Pakistan. The text describes His establishment of Himself among the "Aryas," thought to be a reference to the Aryans who migrated into the Indus Valley during the second millennium B.C. It did not take long for Issa's fame to spread, and the Jains invited Issa to stay with them. Instead, Issa decided to travel to Juggernaut where He was welcomed by the Brahmin priests. They taught Him to read and understand the Vedas, to heal, to perform exorcisms, and the art of teaching.

According to Notovitch, Issa spent six years studying and teaching at Juggernaut, Rajaginha, Benares, and other Holy cities. He began teaching the holy scriptures to the lower castes, resulting in a conflict with the Brahmins and the Kshatriyas, the priestly and warrior castes, respectively. The lower castes included the Vaisyas, consisting of farmers and merchants, and the Sudras, the peasants and laborers. The priestly class of the Brahmins insisted that the Vaisyas were only to hear the Vedas read aloud during festivals. Sudras were not allowed to hear them read nor were they allowed to even look at these teachings. Issa was unwilling to abide by these injunctions, and He began to preach to the Vaisyas and Sudras against the wishes of the Brahmins and Kshatriyas. Aware of Issa's criticism against them, the priests and warrios plotted to kill Issa.

Alerted to the diabolical plot, the Sudras warned Issa, who quickly left Juggernaut under the cover of night. His journey took Him to the foothills of the Himalayas in southern Nepal, where five centuries earlier the great Buddha (Guatama) was born, a prince born of the Sakya clan. Studying for another six years, Notovitch states that Issa "had become a perfect expositer of the sacred writings." Leaving the Himalayas, Issa journeyed west and preached against idolatry along the way. At the age of 29, Issa returned to Palestine.

The *Life of Saint Issa* deals with three main topics. (1) Chapters 1 through 4 are concerned with the conditions that led to the incarnation, His birth, and early life. (2) Chapters 4 through 8 explain the lost years, from age 13 to 29. (3) Finally, chapters 9 through 19 unfold the events during the Palestine mission. The account of what took place in Palestine after Issa's return parallels the gospels, except for three major differences. (1) John the Baptist does not appear in the story of Issa. (2) The resurrection is omitted but is not completely denied. (3) Pilate is the antagonist who tries through a series of events to trap Issa and condemn Him, while the Jewish priests and elders found no fault with Him.

As the story goes, Pilate had become fearful of Issa's popularity and the chance that Issa might be chosen king. After three years of Issa's teaching in Palestine, Pilate ordered a spy to accuse Issa. Arrested by Roman soldiers, Issa was tortured and thus confessed to treason. After hearing about His sufferings, the chief priests and elders plead with Pilate to release Issa on the occasion of a great feast. Pilate rejected the plea, and the priests then asked Pilate to let Issa appear before the tribunal of elders so that He could be acquitted or condemned prior to the feast. Issa was tried with two thieves. During the trial, Pilate interrogated Issa and produced false witnesses to testify against Him. Issa in turn forgave the witnesses but rebuked Pilate, who became infuriated. The enraged Pilate condemned Issa to death. The judges objected and told Pilate, "We will not (have) upon our heads the great sin of condemning an innocent man and acquitting thieves." They washed their hands in a sacred vessel proclaiming, "We are innocent of the death of the just man."

Pilate ordered Issa and the two thieves to be nailed to the crosses. At sunset, Issa lost consciousness and His soul left the body "to become absorbed in the divinity." Concerned about the reaction of the people, Pilate released Issa's body to His parents, who brought it to a tomb near the place of execution.

Crowds gathered to pray at Issa's tomb. Three days after the crucifixion, Pilate feared an insurrection and instructed his soldiers to remove Issa's body and bury it elsewhere. The following day, the people found Issa's tomb open and empty. This caused the immediate spread of a rumor "that the Supreme Judge had sent his angels to carry away the mortal remains of the saint in whom dwelt on earth a part of the Divine Spirit."

Notovitch claims the story of Issa's crucifixion in Palestine was allegedly written down three to four years after the crucifixion. It was based on eyewitness accounts brought to India by merchants who had witnessed the events. The merchants were not Jewish, but Indian merchants who witnessed the crucifixion prior to their return to India.

THE AFTERMATH

Notovitch thought Christian scholars and theologians would be elated to have additional information about the life and times of Jesus. To Notovitch's dismay, his discovery was not well received among this elite group. As happens too often in academic and religious settings, these guardians of knowledge seem to preserve the status quo.

For the public, *The Unknown Life of Jesus Christ* was an immediate success. Eight editions of the book were published in France during 1894, and three separate English editions appeared in the United States. The next year found another English edition published in London, followed by translations into German, Spanish, Swedish, and Italian.

It didn't take long for the book to become very controversial, however. Some critics denied the authenticity of the text and claimed that Notovitch had not actually traveled to Ladakh. Others called Himis a "mythical convent," even questioning its existence. Professor F. Max Mueller of Oxford University, a noted Orientalist with a worldwide reputation and editor of the *Rig Veda* and *The Sacred Books of the East,* called *The Life of Saint Issa* an outright fraud. He inferred the hoax was possibly carried out by the lamas of Himis, but most likely perpetuated by the Russian writer. This criticism did not help with Notovitch's original goal of sharing his discovery with the Church.

Notovitch wanted to share his information with the Roman Catholic Church before publication. He brought the manuscript to Cardinal Rotelli in Paris and to an unnamed cardinal close to the Pope. The latter allegedly told Notovitch that he would make many enemies if he published the manuscript, saying, "If it be a question of money which interests you, I might ask that a reward should be made to you for your notes, which should indemnify you for your expenses you incurred and the time you have lost." To some, this sounded like a bribe. Cardinal Rotelli also opposed the publication believing that it would aid the enemies of the "evangelical doctrine."

When Notovitch was at Himis, the lama initially refused to show him the manuscript, telling him he would show it to him on a return trip. Notovitch did not press the issue, but critics later challenged Notovitch on this, not believing the scenario. The Russian journalist explained the initial refusal as a distrust of Orientals towards Westerners. He claimed Orientals tended to see Westerners as thieves and would interpret inquiries about a manuscript equivalent to an admission they wished to steal it. Because of his Eastern diplomacy, which was an indirect approach, Notovitch was able to veil his real interest and put to rest the lama's fear.

Critics also claimed the manuscripts about Issa did not exist because they were not listed in the *Tanjur* nor *Kanjur*, the standard catalogues of translated Buddhist texts and commentaries. Notovitch responded by saying there were more than 100,000 scrolls at the monastery of Lhasa, and the catalogues only contained 2000 manuscripts.

As years passed, verification of Notovitch's find came from several reputable sources. Elizabeth Prophet, in her book *The Lost Years of Jesus,* did an excellent study on the Notovitch saga and aftermath that followed. One verification came from Swami Abhedananda, a scholar and good friend of Professor Max Mueller. He claimed to have seen the Himis scrolls, thus confirming Notovitch's story.

In 1922, at the age of 56, Swami Abhedananda journeyed to Himis. Arriving at the monastary, he was received by a lama who proceeded to show him the historical Issa document. "The lama who was showing Swamji around took a manuscript (about Issa) off the shelf and showed it to Swamji. He said that it was a copy and the original was at a monastery at Marbour near Lhasa. The original was written in Pali, but this was a translation into Tibetan." This story was consistent with that reported by Notovitch. Abhedananda then requested a lama to assist him in translating the text into English. Abhedananda's copy was later translated into Bengali and published. A few discrepancies were found between this version and Notovitch's, probably the result of multiple translations. Included in Abhedananda's version was a footnote that described how Jesus halted at a wayside pond near Kabul to wash His hands and feet, and rested there for a while. That pond still exists and is known as "Issa Pond."

Additional confirmation came from Nicholas Roerich, who wrote extensively about Saint Issa's travels throughout the East. Leading an expedition through Central Asia, he recorded the living history of Issa's life in the East as embodied in legends that were cherished by Asian people of different nations and religions. Roerich also discovered several manuscripts on the subject.

Roerich was a Russian-born painter, poet, archeologist, photographer, and mystic. In 1890, he was appointed to a professorship at the Imperial Archaeological Institute at St. Petersburg, and by 1920 he was an internationally acclaimed artist. Nicholas, his wife Helena, and son George were the key figures of the Central Asian expedition between 1924 - 1928. During the journey, he painted 500 pictures. His son George was a noted archaeologist and Orientalist, trained at Harvard and the School of Oriental Languages. On his trek through Asia, Nicholas collected stories of Solomon and his flying carpet, the coming of Maitreya, legends about Shamballa, and the legend of Issa.

While in Srinagar, Roerich first encountered the legend of Christ's visit. After returning home, he reported how widely spread in India, in Ladakh, and in Central Asia was the legend of Christ's life during the lost years. These legends were widespread, and only the lamas knew the significance of these traditions. While in the heart of Asia, Roerich heard several variations of the legends, but he noted that "all versions agree on one point, that during the time of his absence, Christ was in India and Asia." While in Ladakh, Roerich wrote, "The writings of the lamas recall how Christ extolled woman - the mother of the world. And lamas pointed out how Christ regarded the so-called miracles." Writing in the Himalayas, he said, "Let us hearken to the way in which, in the mountains of Tibet, they speak of Christ. In the documents that have an antiquity of about 1,500 years, one may read: Issa secretly left his parents and together with the merchants of Jerusalem turned towards India to become perfected in the Divine Word, and for the study of the laws of the Great Buddha." This story is very similar to Notovitch's.

On his visit to Himis, Roerich was disappointed as he was told the manuscripts of Christ did not exist. After further inquiry in the area, the old people in Ladakh admitted they knew about the ancient scrolls. Further evidence that the lamas were very selective about who saw the manuscript.

Throughout Asia, Roerich discovered the legends of Issa's (Jesus') sojourn to the East, these legends preserved among people of varying religions and regions. Roerich's books often refer to the writings and manuscripts about the Issa legends, some of which he saw and some of which he heard. He published much material about Issa that had not been included in Notovitch's book. His three books, *Himalaya, Altai-Himalaya,* and *Heart of Asia,* discuss at length Issa's life in the East. Fortunately for Roerich, he was not viciously attacked by the press as Notovitch had been.

In 1939, additional evidence substantiated the Notovitch discovery. During that summer, Madame Casperi traveled to mount Kailar, located in Tibet. She was a Swiss musician and professor of music pedagogy who had no previous knowledge of Notovitch and his book. Her route, by happenstance, followed that of Notovitch, bringing her to Himis.

Casperi's traveling party arrived just after a three-day festival, and they had just missed a mystery play that they had hoped to see. In honor of their visit, however, the lamas agreed to perform it a second time. Several days later, she and a traveling companion, Mrs. Gasque, were approached by the monastery librarian along with two other monks. In their possession were three manuscripts with ornate coverings, one of which the librarian ceremoniously unwrapped. He presented Mrs. Gasque the parchment paper and in great reverence said, "These books say your Jesus was here." The manuscripts were written in Tibetan. Neither woman asked for a translation, but Madam Caspri did take a picture of the lama proudly displaying the scrolls.

In 1950, Tibet was overthrown by the Chinese communists. Following the Chinese suppression of a 1959 uprising, virtually all the monasteries were destroyed or converted to secular use. The lamas were forced out of their religion practices! Some believe that if the original Pali manuscript was still in Lhasa during 1959, it was probably confiscated or destroyed. Fortunately, the Himis monastery escaped destruction by the invading forces, becoming a repository for paintings, books, costumes, and valued property of other monasteries.

Other evidence of the manuscript is supplied by Elizabeth Prophet who writes that former Supreme Court justice, William Douglas, had traveled to Himis in 1951. She quotes him, "One of the apocryphal tales concerns Jesus. There are those who to this day believe that Jesus visited the place, that he came here when he was fourteen and left when he was twenty-eight, heading west to be heard of no more. The legend fills in the details, saying that Jesus traveled to Himis under the name of Issa."

The Roman Catholic Church is certainly aware of this legend and has done nothing to investigate it. The Vatican library has 63 complete or incomplete manuscripts, in various Oriental languages, referring to the legends of Issa. Most of them were brought to Rome by missionaries from India, China, Egypt, and Arabia.

EARLY CHRISTIANITY IN INDIA

Following the crucifixion, the disciples' mission was to spread the word of Jesus. One of the first countries to receive the teachings was India. Notovitch wrote that the verses quoted to him by the lama at Himis "may have been actually spoken by Saint

Thomas - historical sketches traced by his own hand or under his direction." Besides Saint Thomas, traditions state other early evangelists, such as Saint Bartholomew and Saint Matthias, preached the gospel in India, Tibet, and China.

Historians now believe that Christianity reached southern India immediately after the crucifixion. The disciple Thomas is said to have brought the gospel to Muziris, India in 52 A.D. Various legends tell how Thomas arrived there. One version in the Apocryphal Acts of Thomas was written around 225 A.D. at Edessa in Syrian Mesopotamia. In this version, after the Ascension, the apostles drew lots to decide in which country they should preach the gospel. Thomas drew India. Thomas arrived by ship to Muziris where he was greeted by a flute-playing, Jewish girl. During his mission he baptized Brahmins and Jewish merchants and founded seven churches before moving to the East. Twenty years after his arrival, Thomas became a martyred victim to a plot engineered by envious Brahmin priests.

Another version, also found in the Acts of Thomas, tells how the apostles, while in Jerusalem, divided the world by lot where to preach the gospel. India fell to Thomas, who initially did not want to go. Jesus attempted to persuade Thomas to go to India, and according to this story, Jesus sold Thomas as a slave to an Indian merchant. Thomas sailed to India where the king gave him money to build a palace. Instead, Thomas spent the money on the poor and preached the gospel in Christ's name. After a precarious confrontation with the king who found out what he had done, the king eventually freed Thomas.

Supporting information about the early Christians in India is provided by the British scholar of Buddhism, Edward Conze, who asserted that the Buddhist tradition influenced Christian Gnosticism. The Gnostic philosophy was very similar to both Greek philosophy and Buddha tradition. He points out that "Buddhists were in constant contact with the Thomas Christians (that is, Christians who knew and used such writings as the Gospel of Thomas) in southern India. Trade routes between Greco-Roman and Far East were opening up at the time Gnosticism flourished for generations."

Around the time of Christ, Buddhist missionaries had been proselytizing for generations in Alexandria, leading some scholars such as Gruber and Kersten to hypothesize that Jesus was first introduced to Buddhism during His exile to Egypt in the early years. Because of this connection between East and West, Elaine Pagels also raises the question whether early Christianity was influenced by Indian tradition.

Evidence that Christianity arrived in southern India came from Pantainos of Alexandria when he found an Aramic copy of the Gospel of Saint Matthew while on a missionary trip to Kerah. Scholars have debated for years whether this text actually existed because for centuries theologians believed that the Gospel of Matthew was the first of the gospels. Only recently have scholars believed that the Gospel of Mark was the first. The important point is that an Aramic copy existed, as we saw in chapters four and five. Perhaps modern day scholars are erroneous about the Gospel of Mark being the prototype of Matthew.

THE DALAI LAMA AND THE WISE MEN

When Notovitch arrived at the Buddhist monastery, he was afforded a very cordial reception. He asked the lama why he was favored in this way. The lama replied, "Now the Europeans are altogether different. Not only do they profess the essential principal of monotheism, they have almost as much title to be considered worshipers of Buddha as the lamas of Tibet themselves." The lama continued, "The spirit of Buddha was indeed incarnate in the sacred person of Issa, who without aid from fire or sword, has spread knowledge of our great and true religion throughout the world."

Notovitch asked the lama, "You tell me that as son of Buddha, Issa spread your religion over the earth. Who is he then?"

The lama explained, "Issa is a great prophet, one of the first after the 22 Buddhas. He is greater than any of the Dalai Lamas, for he constitutes part of the spiritual essence of our Lord. It is he who has enlightened you, who has brought back within the fold of religion the souls of erring, and who allows every human being to distinguish between good and evil. His names and deeds are recorded in our sacred writings."

After further research and pondering Notovitch's conversation with the lama, Holger and Kersten came to the conclusion that the arrival of the wise men to visit Baby Jesus parallels that of the Buddhists' search for the Dalai Lama's newborn reincarnation. Kersten believes that by the time the wise men arrived to see Jesus, He was almost two years old. Correspondents between the methods for the search of Jesus and the Dalai Lama are very similar, even to this day. Before the present day Dalai Lama was born in 1933, he had left clues to the place and time of his next reincarnation shortly before his death. Several years following the death of the Dalai Lama, the head lama, after three days of preparatory meditation, had a vision where the Dalai Lama had reincarnated. Preparations were made for the search. First, they needed a pronouncement by an astrologer, without whose calculation no significant search could be made. In 1937, various expeditions were sent out to seek the holy child, according to heavenly signs. Included in each search group was a wise lama. Each group took costly gifts with them, including previous possessions of the deceased Dalai Lama. The possessions were to serve as a test: if the child could recognize them, it would help in verifying if he was indeed the Dalai Lama. Several candidates were found, but none matched the details of the vision nor the astrological pronouncement.

Finally, the searchers came to a place described in the vision. Two lamas disguised themselves as servants when they met a two-year-old boy in his parent's farmhouse, and a servant had disguised himself as a lama. They presented the young child with the deceased Dalai Lama's possessions along with other objects that were similar, serving as a control for their testing. In each instance, the boy chose the possession over the control objects. The monks were astonished when the child recognized the lama as a servant and knew he had come from Sera. He also identified the disguised servant by name. The young boy had known the servant from his previous life as the Dalai Lama. Another delegation of lamas came later to retest the boy. Again, he passed the test by identifying personal belongings of the previous Dalai Lama. Years later, it was decided that the thirteenth Dalai Lama had visited the area and gazed at the farmhouse, remarking how beautiful the place was.

Similarily, the followers of Jesus knew that Jesus was the reincarnation of somebody, but could not identify the previous incarnation. Jesus confirmed the disciple's ideas indirectly, by encouraging their inquiry, "But who do you say I am?" Several New Testament verses (Matt 14:1-2, 16:13-14, Mark 6:14-16, and Luke 9:2-9) tell of various people, including Herod, conjecturing who Jesus might have been in a previous life.

The search for the Dalai Lama has many parallels to the story of the three wise men and Jesus. Many costly gifts were brought to Jesus by the magi from the East. Even if the wise men started their journey at the time of Jesus' birth, it would have taken months to arrive in Bethlehem. If this parallel holds, a child must be two years old to pass the possession test. What is known is that the wise men came on a long journey from the East; they were magicians; they were well versed in astronomy; and they were rich.

Kersten also explains the Star of Bethlehem. Matthew 2:1-2 states, "Now when Jesus was born in Bethlehem of Judea in the days of Herod the king, behold, there came wise men from the East to Jerusalem. Saying, where is he that is born King of Israel? For we have seen his star in the East, and are come to worship him."

Kersten believes it was an alignment of planets that was the Star of Bethlehem. A conjunction of Saturn and Jupiter occurred three times in the constellation of Pisces during 7 B.C. This configuration occurs once every 794 years, and the conjunction took place at an altitude of two degrees, separated by a delineation of one degree, with precisely the azimuth. This occurred on May 7, October 3, and December 5. Both planets are visible from dusk until dawn, and they reach their maximums around midnight. Most scholars believe December 25 was not the birthday of Jesus. Christianity chose that day because it corresponded to a Roman pagan holiday. As we will see, some evidence suggests Jesus was born in the spring.

Matthew mentioned the star three times. The wise men said, "We have seen the star in the East . . ." Matthew 2:7 reads, "Then Herod, when he privily called the wise men, inquired of them diligently what time the star appeared." This implies Jesus' birth occurred a good time before. When the wise men arrived in Jerusalem, the conjunction between Jupiter and Saturn would have been well into the second year, suggesting the birth may have been 7 B.C. This may have been the reason Herod ordered the massacre of all children below the age of two in certain communities.

If Jesus had an Eastern connection as evidence shows, this could explain many of the unanswered questions about the unknown life of Jesus. It would account for the "lost years," the similarity to Buddha's teachings, the subtleties about reincarnation, and even the role of the wise men. As we will discover shortly, there is other evidence that Jesus had a life in the East.

Chapter Eight

THE TURIN SHROUD
A Church Conspiracy?

Protected within a modest cathedral in Turin, Italy lay the most sacred relic of Christianity, the Turin Shroud. For centuries religious authorities believed the Shroud may have been the burial cloth of Jesus. Beginning in 1898, science played an important role in determining the authenticity of the Shroud. Photography, textile analysis, cloth pollens, image analysis, blood testing, and historical data all supported the hypothesis that the Shroud may have been the burial linen of a man who suffered on a cross two millennia ago. Only one scientific test remained that could determine the age of the Shroud, radiocarbon dating. Methodology for carbon dating became more sophisticated over the years, requiring smaller samples. In 1988, this factor allowed the Roman Catholic Church to consent that the Shroud to be carbon dated. On October 13 of that year, experts from three laboratories, who specialized in dating of old material, issued statements. The results of their testing showed that the Turin cloth actually originated in the Middle Ages.

This discovery came as a complete surprise to sindologists, or scientists researching the Shroud, as their research suggested the Shroud was much older. Many were suspect of the carbon-dating results, but could not publicly acknowledge their suspicions and did not know the motive for deception. Two researchers, Holger Kersten and Elmar Gruber, did not believe the carbon-dating results either. Through meticulous detective work, they discovered that the Turin cloth samples had been switched with a fourteenth century cloth during the sampling process, so that the results would be from the Middle Ages. But why? To many, it would seem the Church would want the Shroud to be dated at the time of Christ. However, scientists discovered that the body wrapped in the Shroud had been alive. If true, this would be devastating to Church doctrine, which claimed Jesus died on the cross, with the Resurrection being the cornerstone of the Christian faith. Kersten and Gruber believed this was the Church's motive for switching the cloth samples, calling it the "fraud of the century."

The Turin Shroud is 4.36 meters long and 1.1 meters wide, showing the impression of a male body. Half the Shroud imprints the back view of the person, and the other half shows the front view of a crucified male. Above the head of the man, the cloth is folded in the middle. One can easily recognize the head, face, arms, legs, and feet of the man. Various shades of brown with some areas of gray comprise the image. Visible traces of blood are also found on the Shroud.

Two darkened stripes run the length of the fabric, these being burn marks from a 1532 fire. The cloth had been folded into 48 sections and was lying within a silver shrine in the castle chapel of Chanbery, France. The Shroud was nearly lost in a fire that year, but was saved at the last minute only after one side of the container began to melt in the heat of the flames. Fire and molten silver left their burn marks, clearly seen today.

For aesthetic reasons, a strip of cloth was sewn on one side, shifting the image to the center of the cloth to give it symmetry. This cloth strip is made of the same fabric with the same weave, leading investigators to believe it was sewn on soon after the main cloth was produced. The cloth is linen with a herringbone weave that uses a three-to-one pattern. Here, each weft thread is passed under three warp threads, then over one, and so forth. Woof threads run across the weave, and warp threads pass lengthwise. This type of weave was used at the time of Christ, with scientists placing its origin in Syria.

THE SHROUD'S HISTORY

The history of the Turin Shroud can be verified since the mid-fourteenth century with little debate among scholars. Prior to that time, the whereabouts of the Shroud are somewhat in question, but enough clues have been left to follow its journey through the first 13 centuries. Following the crucifixion of Jesus, the gospels report at least two or more burial clothes having been left behind in the tomb. In the apocryphal Gospel of the Hebrew, it reports that after the Resurrection, Jesus Himself gave the Sindon (Shroud) to the "servant of the priest." Scholars have no idea who the servant was. Another story from St. Nino (died c335) states the burial cloth was in the possession of Pilate's wife for a while. The legend says it then passed into the possession of St. Luke, who hid it in a safe place. Another tradition says that Peter had found the sudarium, the face cloth. Bishop Braulio of Saragossa (631 - 651) wrote centuries later that the linen and face cloth had been found, but there were no clues as to their whereabouts. The Bishop said he did not think "that the apostles neglected these and such like relics for future times." Often these sacred relics were used as magic talismans for healing and protection.

Perhaps the journey can be picked up with King Abgar V of Edessa (15 - 50), who after hearing about the miracles of Jesus, sent a messenger to Jerusalem. Edessa lay between the Greek and Oriental worlds in present day Turkey. King Abgar invited Jesus to visit Edessa to heal the king of health problems. Jesus sent a handwritten letter telling King Abgar that He had important tasks to perform in Palestine and could not come Himself. Jesus promised to send a disciple who would heal the king. This anecdote is mentioned by Eusebius, the early Christian historian. Aethsia, a Christian pilgrim from Aquitaine, knew about this letter and journeyed to Edessa around 383. After making inquiries about its location, Aethsia found it in the church archives. She brought a copy of the letter back with her, because the one in the West was not complete.

Another tradition came to light at the end of the 6th century when Evagrius Scholasticus (527 - 600) claimed that Jesus sent not only a letter but also a picture of Himself that had been miraculously formed. Eusebius recorded the oldest portrait story version in the *Doctrina Addai* at the end of the 4th century in Syria. In the 1840s, this early version of the portrait was confirmed by the discovery of ancient manuscripts in the Natron Valley in lower Egypt. These manuscripts tell of a sermon given on August 16, 945 by Archdeacon Gregory entitled *The Story of the Edessa Portrait.* The picture of Jesus once served as a symbol of protection for the community of Edessa. In August of 944, according to the sermon, a picture of Christ not made by human hands, called the Mandylion, was brought to Constantinople from Edessa. The sermon, in honor of the portrait arriving in Constantinople, tells the history of the Edessa picture.

The miraculous portrait of the Savior, not made by human hands, was presented to King Abgar by a disciple following the crucifixion. Greek writings claim this emissary to Edessa was Thaddaeus, the Syrian *addai*. He was not the apostle Thaddaeus, but "one of the seventy" (Luke 10:1) whom Jesus chose and sent out ahead of Him in pairs. Thaddaeus was healing the sick in Edessa before he met with King Abgar. A meeting was arranged between the two where Thaddaeus placed the portrait of Jesus on the king's forehead, and King Abgar was overwhelmed by the radiant glow from the picture of Jesus. After seeing the picture of Jesus, the King's paralyzed limbs and leprosy were healed, and he immediately confessed that Christ was the true God. Shortly after the king received the portrait, it vanished, only to be rediscovered centuries later.

Five centuries later, Evagrius Scholasticus reported the reappearance of the Mandylion. He said the portrait had been used as a protective palladium when Edessa was under siege by the Persian King Chrosroes I Anushirran. The Mandylion was hidden above the gates of Edessa, as revealed to Bishop Eulalios in 544 by a female apparition. Convinced that the vision was real, the Bishop pushed aside the stone above the archway and discovered the Mandylion, where it had been positioned to turn back the invading Persians.

Scholars believe the picture had been concealed many years before the establishment of the early Christian community. The sermon text claims King Abgar had removed the statue of a Greek deity from the gateway arch and replaced it with the Mandylion, mounted on a gold decorated panel. All who passed through the gateway into Edessa were meant to honor the new Christian faith, symbolized by the acheiropoieton of Christ, the Mandylion. Fearful that the picture would be destroyed by Abgar's pagan nephew, the bishop of the diocese hid the picture and placed it in a semicircular cylinder hollow, concealing it with a stone. He then sealed the entrance from the outside with brick and mortar until it was discovered a half millennium later.

Shroud researcher Ian Wilson believes the Mandylion of Edessa is the Turin Shroud that was folded, so only the face of Jesus was visible. Many agree with this hypothesis; others do not. Supporting evidence that this was the Shroud can be inferred that after the discovery of the Edessa portrait in the 6th century, many copies of it were made. These copies circulated throughout Asia Minor and again were copied, and the Mandylion from Edessa became represented in numerous churches and monasteries. After its discovery, the portrayal of Jesus' face by artists became somewhat standardized. Until that time, there was no clear consensus what Jesus looked like.

The portrayal of Jesus around the time of Constantine (306 - 337) showed how unsure artists were of His appearance. In the early period, Jesus was portrayed as a clean-shaven youth in portraits uncovered in the Roman catacombs. In the sixth century, all the unbearded, rounded, and feminine images of Jesus disappeared suddenly, as did Roman and Hellenized images. The new Jesus portraits showed Him having larger eyes, a long face, distinctive eyebrows, a long nose, a chin beard often parted in two, and long, wavy hair parted in the middle. The new image corresponded to the Turin Shroud. This hypothesis claims the Mandylion of Edessa was the Turin Shroud, and when discovered in the sixth century it became the prototype of the true picture of Jesus.

Several researchers compared the artist's image of Jesus with those on the Shroud. Researcher Paul Vignon compared the Shroud's face with artists' images during the eighth century Justinian period. Vignon and Edward Wuenschel identified 20 unique features on the Shroud, which a Byzantine artist could have copied for the true likeness of Jesus. Some of these features include a V shape at the bridge of the nose; a raised right eyebrow; an enlarged left nostril; a U form on the forehead; the fork in the beard; a hairless area between the lip and beard; and two loose strands of hair falling from the center of the forehead. Many of these Shroud distinctions were found on surviving icons of sixth and seventh centuries. This image of Christ was also found on coins struck by Justinians II at the end of the seventh century. These images closely matched the distinguishing marks designated by Vignon and Wuenschel. Another researcher, Dr.

Alan Whanger, discovered 145 points between the face on a Justinian coin and the Shroud. A picture, titled *Christ Pantocratol*, painted at the end of the 11th century, was found in the monastery church cupula at Daphni near Athens. Thirteen of the 20 Shroud characteristics were identified on it. Following their studies of early Jesus paintings, Werner Bulst and Joachim Pfeiffer concluded that the Turin Shroud did have a lasting influence on the image in portraits. They believed artists must have had the chance to study the Edessa portrait at leisure. The researchers found that on post-Justinian Jesus portraits, the nose appears correspondingly long and narrow as found on the Turin Shroud. During the eighth century, the new image of Christ progressed westward.

A movement to abolish the veneration (worshiping) of icons developed within the Byzantine Empire during the eighth and ninth centuries. Iconoclasts did not believe it possible to portray Jesus, as it was contrary to the hope of Resurrection. Few images of Christ survived this mass destruction by the iconoclasts, who tried to portray the artists as greedy money swindlers. In 726, Emperor Leo III banned the worship of images in the whole of the Eastern Roman Empire. Everywhere Christian zealots destroyed religious icons, and within a few years, a priceless treasure of artwork was reduced to ruins. Fortunately, icon art at St. Catherine's monastery on the Sinai escaped the destruction. Also a few of the oldest surviving pictures of Jesus from the third and fourth centuries did survive and were found in the catacombs of Rome and Naples. Finally, at the Seventh Ecumenical Council at Nicaea an attempt was made to halt the destructive efforts of the iconoclasts.

In Edessa, where the Mandylion was greatly revered, the portrait was first kept in the Hagia Sophia, especially built to house it. Monophysite nobles then took possession of the portrait, believing there is only one nature, the divine, which is the person of Christ. They protected it from the iconoclasts. After the iconoclast fanatacism subsided, an effort was then made to bring the Mandylion to Constantinople.

In 942, this effort to obtain the Shroud for Constantinople occurred when Emperor Romanus Lacenus sent a most trusted soldier, Curcuas, to the now Arab town of Edessa to fetch the image of Jesus. Leading a Byzantine force to the city, Curcuas made an offer to the town of Edessa. In exchange for the portrait, he would forego taking Edessa, release all Muslim prisoners, and pay the city 12,000 silver crowns. Christians living in Edessa objected to the offer, as they did not want to lose their most sacred relic. Finally, however, the Archbishop Abramius of Samosata interceded and handed over the Mandylion along with two copies. Upon Curcuas' return to Constantinople with the sacred portrait, a triumphant reception was held. The Mandylion was displayed at the famous church, Our Lady at Blachernal, and Archdeacon Gregory gave the now famous commemorative sermon about the Edessa portrait. Professor Zanninolto discovered the original text of the sermon and published the most important parts.

Archdeacon Gregory declared the image could be traced back to Jesus at Gethsamane. He said about the cloth, "The splendor was derived solely from the drops of sweat at the agony of the garden, which emerged from the countenance, which is the source of life, flowing down like drops of blood and imprinting with divine fingers." He continued, "There are truly the beauties which the color of imprint of Christ has brought forth, which finally improved (colored) by the drops of blood flowing from his own side . . . I say it is there (blood and water) which have been imprinted on the cloth." The side wound appears to be the key, as it strongly suggests that the Mandylion and the Turin Shroud are one and the same because the Shroud has an image of the side wound where the soldier thrust a lance into Jesus' side. It could not have been a face towel if the lance wound was visible, but would have been formed after the crucifixion. The final destination of the Mandylion became the Pharos Chapel where it remained for many years.

It wasn't until the twelfth century that the secret of the Mandylion was unveiled. Church historian Ordericus Vitalis (c1141) wrote that Jesus had a precious cloth sent to Abgar "on which the image of the Savior appears portrayed in a miraculous manner, which allows the viewer to see the body form and proportion of the Lord." Between the 12th and 13th centuries, statements like this were made, suggesting the Mandylion was indeed the Turin Shroud, as the statements referred to a full length cloth. Scholars speculate that the old picture frame of the Edessa portrait (Mandylion) was worn out after a millennium and needed to be replaced. At this time they may have discovered the folded cloth. Ian Wilson and other sindologists speculate that when the discovery was made, the sacred relic had to be preserved and a copy needed to replace the genuine Mandylion in the Pharos chapel. After the secret of the Edessa portrait was discovered, Wilson speculated the church patriots played down the importance of the Mandylion. Gruber hypothesizes that the new Mandylion copy had to remain in the chapel at Pharos, and the original was moved to the Blachernae Church, which already housed Mary's robe.

Following the Fourth Crusade invasion of Constantinople on April 13, 1204, the Shroud again disappeared. Crusaders hoped to reconcile the schism between the East and West factions of the Catholic Church. During that time, soldiers looted and plundered the city for three days, the time when the Mandylion disappeared. It resurfaced 150 years later in a provincial church in France.

The crusaders knew about the Mandylion as Crusader Robert de Clair said that in August of 1203, before the invasion of Constantinople, he saw in a city church "which they call My Lady St. Mary of Blachernae, where was kept the syndoine in which our Lord was wrapped, which stood up straight every Friday so that the (figure) of our Lord could be plainly seen there." He adds, "No one, either Greek or French, ever knew what became of this syndoine after the city was taken." The Image of Edessa disappeared, as did the image-bearing syndoine described by deClair. The consensus during that period was that the Edessa portrait was an image of Jesus before the crucifixion. People had no idea that they could be looking at a burial shroud folded and mounted with only the face visible. Ian Wilson claims every description of the Image of Edessa during this time is compatible with the Shroud. A 10th century historical description states the cloth was mounted on a board, embellished with gold. A 6th century text describes the Image of Edessa doubled in four. If the Shroud was folded in this manner, the face alone would appear. Wilson also believes the Byzantines may have kept it for centuries without realizing it was a burial shroud. At any rate, both the Edessa Image and syndoine were missing, believed to be one and the same, with possibly a copy of the Edessa Image in the Pharos Chapel.

Wilson believes the most likely person to remove the Shroud during the invasion was Mary Margaret, the Hungarian-born Empress. She is described as a colorful woman who married the older Emperor Isaac II Angelus at the age of ten. Isaac died during the crusade invasion of the city. Crusade leader Boniface de Montferrat took charge of the imperial palace and found the just-widowed Mary Margaret, still attractive at the age of 29. He immediately proposed and within a month, they were married. Mary Margaret founded the Church of the Acheiropoitos (of the Image of Edessa), today known as the Eski Cuma Cami or Ancient Friday Church. Wilson believes this church had housed the Edessa portrait.

De Montferret died in 1207, and Mary Margaret again married; this time to Nicholas de Saint-Omer, and they had a son, William, who became a member of the Order of Knights Templar (thought to be the precursor of the Freemasons). It is certain that by the end of the 13th century, the Templars secretly had the Shroud, and it is not known if William played a role in passing the cloth to the Order. During that time, most of Europe was buzzing with rumors that the Templars were worshiping some form of bearded, reddish-colored male head. Some references described it displayed on a plaque at secret chapter meetings. In 1307, these and other rumors gave King Philip of France, blessed by the Pope, an excuse to arrest the Templars and confiscate their wealth. The original image of the male head was never found, but a copy of it was found on the site of a former Templar building at Templecombe in Somerset, England. The image was a bearded, Christ-like face painted on a wooden panel, an image very similar to the Shroud in its folded position.

Following the Templar demise by King Philip, Templar Geoffroy de Charnay, the Master of Normandy, and Jacque de Molay, the Order leader, were burned at the stake in 1314 because of their Templar association. One generation later, it was discovered that Geoffroy de Charny was the first certain owner of the present Shroud. Researchers found that "Charnay the Templar" spelled his name slightly different from the owner of the cloth, and an incomplete genealogy search did not find a relationship between him and Geoffroy de Charnay. The son, Geoffroy II de Charny, claimed his father had received the cloth as a generous gift. Wilson conjectures that if the cloth were a gift to Charny, it would have been unthinkable to discuss from where the Shroud came. During a court date in 1443, Geoffroy's granddaughter suggested the cloth had come from loot obtained in a military campaign. These conflicting statements suggest uncertainty as to origination of the cloth. Historian Dorothy Crispino believed that Charny came into possession of the cloth between 1349 and 1353, as he wanted to build a church to house it. Unfortunately, no public statement was ever made by Geoffroy de Charny when he had possession of it. Bishop of Troyes, Pierre d'Arcis, wanted to prevent Geoffroy II's exhibition of the cloth in the small church of Lirey because he believed the cloth was a forgery, a claim that did not hold. Ironically, for centuries the Church of Rome tried to gain its possession.

In 1443, the patron of Lirey made a claim for it, but Margaret, the last of the Charnys, was granted custody of the Shroud by the courts. She publicly exhibited it in 1452, then Margaret searched for a family to whom she could pass on the Shroud, finally deciding in favor of Louis, the Duke of Savoy, who in return gave her a castle in Geneva. Louis of Savoy paid the canons of Lirey 50 gold francs in lieu of their claim on the cloth. For over 400 years until 1983, the Shroud remained in possession of the Savoy family.

At the beginning of the 16th century, the Shroud was festively displayed in the chapel of the Savoy residence at Chambrey. Pope Julius II, in 1506, declared May 4 the Feast Day of the Holy Shroud, and it was displayed frequently in the following years. In 1532, it narrowly escaped the chapel fire. Duke Emmanuel Philbert of Savoy transferred the cloth to Turin on September 17, 1578. The cloth was put on display for eight days in May of 1898 to celebrate the fiftieth anniversary of Italy. At that time, Secondo Pia took the first photo of the Shroud. From May 2 to May 23, 1931, the sacred relic was exhibited again, this time honoring the wedding of Prince Umberto. More photos were taken.

For the next 50 years, the Shroud's history leads up to the declaration of its forgery. At the outbreak of WWII in 1939, the

Shroud was brought to the abbey of Monte Verquine in Avellino for safekeeping and remained there until war's end. The first scientific commission was allowed to examine the cloth under Cardinal Pellegrino's discretion in June of 1969. An unknown person forced entry into the chapel on October 1, 1972 and tried to set the linen on fire, but an asbestos lining inside the altar saved it. In November of 1973, threads were removed for scientific examination, and testing again was done on October 8, 1978, the final day of a six-week exposition. In 1983, King Umberto II bequeathed the Shroud to the Holy See in response to Pope John Paul II's request. Finally in October of 1988, scientists declared the Turin Shroud a medieval forgery.

THE SCIENCE OF THE SHROUD

Is the Shroud the burial cloth of Jesus, or is it a fraud perpetuated by an unknown artist? Over centuries, an excessive demand for sacred relics has produced a flourishing market, including forgeries of many kinds by unscrupulous artisans. Even as late as the 16th and 17th centuries, the Vatican traded in catacomb skeletons unearthed in the bowels of Rome. In the 19th century, Ulysse Chevalier, a Catholic priest, wrote a scholarly work about the Middle Ages after discovering evidence that the Shroud was definitely a fake painted by an artist around 1350. Chevalier was the first to publish a critical study of the cloth's authenticity. His opinion was accepted by historians around the first of this century, greatly diminishing interest in the cloth.

In 1902, however, Yves Delage, a professor at the Sorbonne in Paris and director of the Museum of Natural History, disagreed with Chevalier's theory, concluding that it would have been impossible for a medieval artist to paint the picture of the Shroud as Chevalier had claimed. Delage claimed that over 1,000 verifiable details could be identified on the cloth itself. In fact, all attempts by artists over the centuries to replicate the cloth image have met with failure.

Photography was one of the surprising mediums that shed clues about the Shroud. When Secondo Pia took the first Shroud photo in 1898 during an eight-day expedition, something unusual happened. When Pia developed the film, the photographic negative seemed to be a true-to-life photograph of Jesus with natural-looking, shaded tones. The negative plate displayed a positive image of Jesus. To many, the negative proved the authenticity of the relic. Only two of Pia's official photographs remained for research. In the meantime, Pia was accused of retouching the plates, and it was not until 1931, when the Shroud was again photographed, that Pia was vindicated. Scientists believed that with the aid of precise scientific methods, deciding its authenticity should be easy.

Paul Vignon, who was on staff of a biology journal published by Professor Delage, traveled to Turin during the early 1900's and secured the two plates with negative copies of the Shroud. Vignon also found two unofficial photos that confirmed Pia had not doctored the originals. He discovered that only when the photographic technique reversed the tonal values of light and dark that a body could be recognized on the negative with natural proportions and contours. His conclusion was that the cloth could not be the work of a fourteenth century artist. He asked, "How could a painter have an idea of a negative before the invention of photography, and how could he have portrayed a picture in such perfection?" Photography, he believed, provided the key to the cloth's secret.

Vignon found the intensity of the image shading varied in proportion to the distance of the sheet from the bodily extremities. The image color was more intense where the cloth lay directly on the skin, and brighter with increasing distance above the depression in the surface. Those areas of the body touching the cloth or less than a centimeter from it left coloring. Thus Vignon came to three conclusions: (1) The picture was produced by direct contact, but it also involved some kind of projection. (2) Vapor from the body must have formed the image. (3) Warmth of the body had transferred the vapors onto the fabric, in an emanation following the principle that warm air rises. Finally, after many centuries, a scientific hypothesis was developed on the formation of the Shroud image.

The Gospel of John indicates large quantities of aloe and myrrh were used in Jesus' entombment. Vignon was able to authenticate this claim. After experimenting in the lab, Vignon replicated the image color of the Shroud. He found that humid vapors that bore ammonia from urea secretions were found abundantly in sweat as a result of the mixture of aloe and myrrh. This caused an oxidation process in the cellulose of the linen fibers, producing a change in the surface color. The color change was caused by the reaction of the aloe/myrrh solution absorbed by the cloth, forming ammonium carbonate. The vapors from this chemical reaction produced the color of the fibers. Vignon's experiments found the color was darker where the cloth touched the body, and it became fainter as the distance between the body and cloth increased, as on the Shroud. This explained why the image was similar to a photographic negative. In 1933, scientists strongly criticized Vignon's experiments stating that body warmth, which caused the evaporation process, could not occur in sufficient amounts from a corpse. These scientists, of course, believed the body was dead. Based on Vignon's research, Gruber and Kersten concluded that the body was still alive! In fact, Gruber and Kersten experimented on themselves with various combinations of aloe and myrrh on a linen cloth, producing an image somewhat similar to that on the Shroud.

Shroud photography was again done in the 1930's by Giuseppe, who showed the body was naked. Historians knew criminals were executed and beaten while naked under Roman law. Giuseppe's photographs also showed the body had been crucified. The victim's hands had been nailed to a cross beam and his feet to a vertical post. This type of capital punishment was abolished by Emperor Constantine I (306 - 377), leading investigators to conclude the body had lain in the burial Shroud before 330 when this decree was ordered. Scientific evidence was mounting that the body wrapped in the Shroud could have been Jesus.

More photography produced more evidence. Details from the positive photo images show evidence of six cross stations and details of the crucifixion as reported in the gospels:

1. Severe swelling under the right eye suggests blows by Roman soldiers.
2. Many conspicuous dumbbell-shaped marks were found on the front and rear of the body, especially numerous on the shoulders and back. They are clustered in groups of three at fixed

angels to the body. Scholars believe they were made by the Roman flagrum, a Roman whip with three leather thongs whose ends had small lead dumbbells. Ninety of these wounds have been counted.

3. In the shoulder region of the Shroud image, there are blood-smeared wounds corresponding to the carrying of the cross beam, which was the custom then.
4. An irregular course of a bloodstream on the forehead and back of the head infers a crowning with thorns.
5. Nail wounds in the hand area are very noticeable. The course of the larger streams of blood indicates the arms were stretched on the cross at an angle of 55 to 65 degrees. Blood flow on the cloth shows where the nails were driven through the wrists. This fact is supported by later crucifixion research identifying the nail location. In art, only the palms are nailed.
6. An oval wound is found on the right side, 45 centimeters in length, located between the fifth and sixth rib. Much blood flowed from this wound.
7. No injuries to the legs were discovered. The gospels state that Jesus' legs were not broken.

In addition, photos showed precise anatomical representation of the body. This, along with the seven details corresponding to the gospel stories of the Passion, have convinced many scholars to believe the Shroud is not a forgery.

The medical profession next became involved in an attempt to prove or disapprove authenticity of the Shroud. British physician, Dr. David Willis, who studied the blood marks on the side wound, observed an inhomogeneous dispersion, broken by clear areas, suggesting the mixture of a clear fluid with blood. John 19:33 states "blood and water" flowed from the side wound. Another opinion by Dr. Herman Modder, a Cologne, Germany physician, hypothesizes the clear fluid was from the pleural sac that had increased by the whipping.

Dr. Pierre Barbet, chief surgeon at St. Joseph's hospital in Paris, experimented with amputated forearms. His research on the cloth wounds showed the nails went through the "space of Destot" at the base of the hands. This space was large enough to allow a thick nail to be easily driven through. The ring arrangement of bones at the hand base provides stability to support the body weight, but with great pain. He also studied the nail placement on the image's feet, concluding that a person hung from the cross in this manner could support himself by his feet, and the body weight would not tear through the hands. Nails could easily be pushed through the wound areas found on the Shroud. A victim could last for days, supporting and pulling up his torso; this is the principle underlying crucifixion.

Scientists also investigated residual changes of the Shroud expected to occur by long-term storage. While in Edessa, the portrait was kept in an upright chest with shutters opened for brief intervals during annual festivals. This would explain why there is no perceptible darkening of the facial area, as darkening occurs as a result of long periods of light exposure. Additionally, if the Shroud was folded in the same position for 1,000 years, one would expect to see crease lines. Dr. John Jackson published a scientific paper titled *Foldmarks as a Historical Record of the Turin Shroud,* in which he claims he pinpointed at least four of the old Image of Edessa fold marks, and another two of which he was reasonably certain. The remainder were there by implication. One fold mark measured precisely one-eighth the length of the Shroud's natural halfway fold line, corresponding to the Edessa portrait's fold location. This provided additional evidence that the Shroud could have been the Edessa portrait.

Turin Cardinal Pellegrino, on June 16, 1969, convened a commission of experts to examine the cloth itself, with six of the eleven observers being scientists. Kersten believes the wrong kind of scientists were chosen for this study, as very little knowledge came from this poorly designed investigation. In 1973, a more qualified group of scientists convened, which including Gilbert Raes, the first person to be given a sizable fragment of the Shroud to study. Raes, a professor at the Institute of Textile Technology in Ghent, determined the complex weaving of the Shroud was from the first century, but at that time the weave was used almost exclusively with silk fabric. Textile experts postulated a Syrian origin of the cloth, rather than Egyptian.

On the cloth, Raes found traces of cotton that adhered to the fabric by chance, possibly from the workshop where it was manufactured. Various types of cotton can be distinguished by characteristic twists. Cotton grows in two phases: an exterior coat develops during the first 30 days, and during the second stage, twists develop that help distinguish one of the three species. Raes found the Shroud cotton had eight to nine twists per centimeter, suggesting a particular species cultivated in the Near East.

In another experiment attempting to uncover the authenticity of the Shroud, Dr. Max Frei, head of the Zurich police laboratory, noticed the cloth was covered with small dust particles, including pollen grains, not detected by normal vision. Frei removed samples from 12 different Shroud areas with an adhesive tape, finding one to four pollen grains per square centimeter. Frei believed that by identifying the type of pollen, it would help identify its origin and geographic location. Fortunately, outer shells of pollen grains are extremely resistant, allowing pollen to survive for millions of years. In his research, Frei identified 49 different species of plant pollens on the Shroud. Many of these plants have been identified in regions where the cloth is presumed to have been. He discovered pollen from the cedars of Lebanon, and he found 11 kinds of plants that do not grow in Central Europe. They were halophytes from the Middle East, meaning they lived in soil with extremely high salt content, such as near the Dead Sea. Traveling to destinations where the Shroud was thought to have been, Frei collected pollen samples from these locations and compared them with the Shroud samples. Forty-four plant species were found in the immediate geographical vicinity of Jerusalem, 23 plant species were found around Urfa, the former Edessa, and 14 species were found around Istanbul. Since some pollen grains were present in the sedimentary layers of the Sea of Galilee during Jesus' time, Frei concluded that the concentration of Jerusalem flora showed the cloth had been in Palestine, most likely landing on the fiber during manufacture of the cloth. This provided evidence that the Shroud could have been in Jeusalem.

A next generation of experiments occurred on October 8, 1978, on the last day of a 42-day exhibition, when the cloth was removed from its bulletproof container and placed on an adjustable board to be examined by scientists. Computers, cameras, and x-ray equipment were used by an international team of researchers to reconstruct the "man of the Shroud" in three dimensions. The relief image showed the body to be 1.82 meters (almost six feet) and to weigh 79 kilograms (about 174 pounds).

Scientists next wanted to test the blood sample on the Shroud, and fluorescein X-ray spectrum testing was done on the blood marks. By using X-rays of certain energies, every atom can be made to emit its corresponding radiation. This testing proved the blood marks on the Shroud contained high concentrations of iron, a constituent of blood. Detailed spectrographic analysis by Sam Pellicori of the Santa Barbara Research Center did show the cloth marks, in fact, to be blood. He proved the marks to be denatured methemoglobin, resulting from the oxidation of hemoglobin iron in the blood.

However, not everyone accepted the findings of the Shroud research. Some sindologists hypothesized the cloth image originated by some kind of unexplained radiation emanated by the body of Jesus at the time of Resurrection. This radiation, they conjecture, burned the image of the entire body into the fabric. Pellicori tested this and similar hypotheses by comparing the fluorescence spectrum of the cloth with artificially-produced images on the linen. He discovered that a superficial singeing on the cloth produced an image similar to that of the Shroud. However, the Shroud body image of the cloth did not fluoresce under ultraviolet radiation. If the body image had been formed by heat radiation, it should have fluoresced a reddish-brown color in the same way as in the singed cloth experiment, thus debunking the radiation hypothesis.

Other scientists also tried to determine how the image was formed. They found the brown-colored shading of the image was caused by a change in the chemical structure of the linen cellulose. These color variations were produced in the laboratory by decomposing the linen cellulose with various oxidizing substances, as these oxidative images became more distinct as time passed. Scientists applied aloe, myrrh, sweat, olive oil, and skin oil to the test cloth, and each, individually applied, made the cloth darker. A combination of myrrh, sweat, and skin oils made the test cloth even more red. These investigators discounted the Vignon hypothesis of a vapor process, not considering the body to have been alive.

Another scientist came up with evidence debunking Vignon's hypothesis. Pellicori discovered the chemical process of image formation was not affected by different pressures on the front and rear sides of the body on the cloth. His experiments showed that aloe and myrrh imprints do not fluoresce with ultraviolet light, similar to the nonfluoerscent Turin cloth. The Institute of Forensic Medicine used aloe and myrrh to test about 80 pieces of cloth bearing the imprints of body faces. None of these were close to the quality of the Turin image, but no testing was done with live bodies.

Another high level scientist got involved. American chemist Walter McCrone, in 1981, claimed from his research that the iron in the marks appearing to be blood was a clear indication of iron oxide pigments used by painters since the fourteenth century. He also found stray particles of mercuric sulfide used in artists' vermilion and ultramarine, the artists' yellow pigment. He concluded the Shroud had been in an artists' studio, but acknowledged that he could not prove the cloth was the work of an artist. No artist in the Middle Ages was known to have worked in that medium format. Some scholars conjecture if the image was made by an artist, it was made by Leonardo da Vinci himself or one of his students. However, an entirely nude Jesus would have been unthinkable in the mid-fourteenth century.

Hoping to solve the Shroud mystery was a team of scientists known as the Shroud of Turin Research Project (STURP). In 1978, the team showed by X-ray fluorescent testing that iron, calcium and strontium were present in trace quantities all over the Shroud. The blood image showed a stronger iron signal consistent with blood containing one percent iron. Their findings showed the signal for iron in the image was no different from the non-image areas, leading to the conclusion that iron oxide was not involved in any of the Shroud body image colorization. The Shroud iron oxide was chemically pure to a level over 99 percent, in contrast to artists' pigment, which is contaminated with elements such as manganese, nickel and cobalt. Pure iron oxide results from a natural process when making linen from flax, thus explaining McCrone's abundant iron oxide theory.

In yet another experiment, John Heller, M.D., a former professor at Yale Medical School, found that samples taken from the blood region of the Shroud were indeed blood. His tests determined the samples consisted of hemoglobin in the acid methemoglobin form. Heller also found excessive amounts of bilirubin, which occurs when blood is broken down. Such high bile pigments indicate the person was severely jaundiced or had been in a severe accident, which would be consistent with severe beatings and scourging that the man in the Shroud had undergone. Heller concluded this would have hemolyzed and disrupted many red blood cells. When the released hemoglobin reaches the liver, it produces bilirubin which is responsible for the reddish-orange pigment in bile. Also, Professor Alan Adler, working with Heller and STURP, tested the blood marks positively for blood protein. His findings suggested that the Shroud blood went into the cloth before whatever process was responsible for the body image, which would have been the reverse of how an artist would be expected to work. Overall, Heller and Adler determined 12 signs that indicated genuine blood, with a blood type AB. Both Heller and Adler believe the other pigments identified by McCrone were stray particles that did not contribute to the Shroud image. In all likelihood they came from an artist's studio where the Shroud image may have been reproduced on a canvas.

Another finding that concluded the Shroud could not have been produced by an artist is that researchers determined the thickness of an artist's brush could not have been more than one fibril wide, less than the thickness of a human hair in order to produce part of the Shroud image. An artist would have had to keep track of the number of fibrils he discolored per unit to produce the reverse image. The overall conclusion by investigators was that the image was not derived from paint or dye, but from something of the linen's own substance having been taken away. It could have been oxidation or degradation of the cloth, or an aging of the linen cellulose.

Interestingly, a similar image has been seen in botany departments around the world from aged collections of pressed plants. The heavy paper covering these plants is commonly imprinted with a striking image of the specimen involved. These images are said to parallel the Shroud. Flowers, leaves, stems, and roots all leave their image with the same degree of completeness. Inverse relief characteristics are found, the fainter image having the greater distance from the paper. Similar to the Shroud, they become lifelike when seen in a photographic negative.

The next phase of research was to create a three-dimensional figure using a VP8 three- dimensional tester. Drs. John Jackson and Eric Jumper of the STURP team thought they could discern small, button-like objects laying on the image's eyelids. If coins, high magnification photography might reveal the inscription on the coin. Chicago theology Professor Francis Filas discovered on a large negative print what seemed to be four letters, UCAI. Among the coins during the time of Jesus was a tiny lepton or mite of Pontius Pilate bearing an astrologer's staff, accompanied by an inscription TIBERIOU KAISAROS. Filas conjectured the Shroud image of UCAI might be the central letters of TIBERIOU KAISAROS with a C substituted for the Greek letter K. In fact, two actual examples of Pontius Pilate leptons have been found with this mispelling. Robert Haralick, Director of the Virginia Polytechnic Institute and State University Data Analysis, supports the Filas hypothesis, but cautions that it may be random quirks of the Shroud's weave. Additionally, there is little evidence that Jews used coins to close eyelids of their dead.

A number of scientists have come to the conclusion that the man in the Shroud was still alive. New York pathologist, Dr. Michael M. Baden, doubts the Shroud ever contained a corpse. He draws his conclusion from the suspicious blood flow and other signs. Professor W. Bonte, M.D., from the University of Dusseldorf and Director of the Institute for Court Medicine, wrote, "The posture visible on the Shroud could in my opinion also be assumed by a living person, that is to say a person only appears dead."

Also, the man of the Shroud gives the impression of lying in a relaxed state, as there are no signs of stiffening, such as would be found from a corpse. Different temperatures in different regions of the body occur in corpses. With the Shroud, there was an even distribution of markings, indicating a functioning circulatory system. If the body were dead, scientists expected a strong impression on the buttocks and shoulder blades because gravity would sink the blood to the lowest point. This impression was not found on the Shroud. Scientists from the East Midline Forensic Laboratory thus concluded that a living person, not a corpse, was wrapped in the cloth.

Rigor mortis, which is a peculiar stiffening of muscles, sets in 30 minutes after death. Depending on the environmental temperature, rigor mortis becomes complete after three to six hours. A biochemical process causes rigor mortis, with the lowering of ATP (adenosine triphosphate) levels after the heart stops beating. The entire skeletal muscle system stiffens in the posture assumed by the dying person. Rigor mortis disappears spontaneously 36 to 90 hours after death, remaining longer in healthy people.

If Jesus had died on the cross, His body would have stiffened in the three or four hours He hung on the cross after "death." As one observes the impression on the back of the body cloth image, the back of the head, thighs, and shanks of the "corpse" lay flat on the cloth. If Jesus had been dead, His rigor mortis body would not have been erect, His legs would be folded at the knees, and His head would be tipped forward. This was not the image on the cloth, thus concluding the body was not dead.

According to the gospels, Joseph of Arimathea and Nicodemus did not wash the body of Jesus, as was the custom following a Jewish death. The Shroud shows that fresh blood flowed when Jesus was lying horizontally on the cloth. Resinous aloe saturated the fabric and prevented blood from being absorbed into the cloth, causing it to spread over the surface. This would explain why blood marks cannot be seen on the reverse sides, even though the material is quite thin.

Additional research proved that the body in the Shroud was alive instead of dead. Sharp points from the thorns on the head left small, penetrating stab wounds in the skin of the head. When the crown of thorns was on the head, the thorns sealed one- to two-millimeter sized wounds. Small amounts of blood flowed out from the wound and coagulated in the hair. At the back of the head, the linen image shows larger bloodstreams running in all directions. This caused scientists to believe blood trickled onto the cloth when the body was laid on the Shroud immediately after removing the crown of thorns. Blood also collected in the cavity between the back and buttocks, and could have flowed to that position only if the body were horizontal. After the body was laid out, the open wounds to the feet started to bleed again, and the blood spread out in all directions. Researchers have found a total of 28 wounds that continued to bleed after removal from the cross. Scientists claim blood can never flow like this from a corpse that has been dead for several hours. Thus the evidence concludes that the body could not have been dead when it was placed in the tomb!

THE CHURCH CONSPIRACY

Kersten and Gruber speculated that the Catholic Church came to realize that the man in the Shroud may have been still alive. This knowledge, they assert, resulted in the secret testing of the Shroud beginning on June 16, 1969, when the Turin chapel was closed to the public for three days. Cardinal Pellegrini laid out the Shroud on a long table covered with a white sheet. For the first time scientists could perform a direct examination.

Hans Naber, a German sindonologist, was informed of this secret meeting by a Vatican official "mole" who told Naber, "They go to work like thieves in the night." Naber had been the first to go public with what many already knew, that the blood marks on the Shroud proved that Jesus was still living when He was removed from the cross. Of course, the public found the claim ridiculous, as the Vatican officially denied Naber's accusations. Although many authors before Naber suggested that Jesus did not die on the cross, Naber's assertion became a sensation for the press. Naber visited the Vatican on June 28, 1969, providing documents that Jesus did not die on the cross. He then received a secret message from the Vatican stating that it would not tolerate a controversy regarding the death of Jesus. Believing the Vatican was going to destroy the Shroud, Naber immediately called the London news agency, Reuters, reporting his fears. Both Reuters and UPI ran a similar account of the story. Pellegrino responded to the news releases saying the charges were "unfounded and irresponsible." He admitted the Church had examined the Shroud, but only for the purpose of improving its preservation. From that time on, the Church had no choice but to be open about future examinations. In 1976, the report of the 1969 investigation was made public. The Vatican then attempted to influence scientists to verify that the body in the Shroud was dead, but evidence found in 1978 did not support this claim.

Most scientists in the early 1970's believed the Shroud was a forgery. Radio carbon-dating was a scientific procedure that would settle the controversy once and for all. If the dating could show the Shroud was from the Middle Ages, the Vatican's dilemma would be solved. The Vatican needed to gain ownership of the Shroud, and this was done when the Pope convinced exiled King Umberto to transfer ownership to the Vatican. Two weeks later, on March 18, 1983, Umberto died.

Kersten asserts the Vatican was trying to break the flow of scientific evidence that supported the Shroud's authenticity and survival of Jesus. The Vatican had long agreed on a radio carbon-dating protocol, but then began to make a series of mistakes, as we will see. A conclave of scientists convened in 1981 to decide the protocol for testing. They agreed on the following:

1. Seven laboratories were to be involved in the radio carbon testing, with five using the AMS technique and two using other methods.
2. The British Museum would supply the control sample.
3. Samples of the control and Shroud were to be handed over to the individual laboratories after being unthreaded to be unrecognizable.
4. Three institutions were to serve as supervisors: Pontifical Academy of Science, and British Museum, and Archiepiscopal Ordinariat of Turin.
5. On a certain date, the labs were to pass on the data to the three institutions for statistical analysis.

In early 1987, Professor Luigi Gonelli shocked the scientific community by announcing only two or three labs were to be used in the testing. Those ended up being in Tucson, Oxford University, and Zurich. Another shocking development was the exclusion of two supervisory institutions, leaving only Dr. Michael Tite of the British Museum to supervise the protocol. Scientists were outraged by the change in protocol, with many saying it was better to do nothing at all. Protest letters were sent to the Pope, British Museum, and the scientific journal *Nature*. Rumors were spreading that the Vatican restricted the tests to three laboratories hoping for contradictory results.

The testing began when Giovanni Riggi, on April 21, 1988, cut off a small portion of the Shroud and gave it to Professor Testore, who divided and weighed the cloth samples to be given to the laboratories. In attendance at the sampling ceremony were representatives from each of the three laboratories. Accompanied by Cardinal Ballestrero, Dr. Tite took the samples into the adjoining sacristy and put them into metal containers. The two emerged from the sacristy with nine cylinders, three for each laboratory including the Turin sample and two controls. Nearly six months later the test results were announced that the Turin Shroud was dated to the Middle Ages. For religion and science, as Kersten puts it, it was the end of a legend and the end of a myth.

At the time of the announcement, Holger Kersten had been studying the Shroud for over 10 years. When he heard the test results, he became quite skeptical but was determined to find out if the proper scientific protocol had been followed by all participants. Kersten visited Professor Gilbert Raes, who had previously been the only person to possess a fragment of the Shroud for study. Raes admitted that he did not use the entire sample in his testing in the 1970's, but returned the remaining fragment to Church officials in Turin. Nobody knew what happened to the leftover sample. Raes was also quite disappointed with the protocol and wondered why the three laboratory representatives were present during the sampling. The weave of the Turin Shroud could be easily recognized, thereby negating a blind test. He was suspicious that the labs had been in contact during the testing period.

Kersten acquired a BBC video tape regarding the sampling procedure. Cardinal Ballestrero spoke on the tape, stating that if the cloth was not genuine, it would present no problem for him or the Church. At that time, no serious sindonologist doubted the authenticity of the Shroud, leading Kersten to believe the statement by the Cardinal was strange. When the Cardinal suggested the possibility that the cloth might be a religious painting, Kersten felt the Cardinal had everything settled in advance; that is, the cloth was from the Middle Ages.

Next to be interviewed by Kersten was Professor Wolfi, who was in charge of testing at the Zurich laboratory. Wolfi admitted that recognizing the cloth sample from a 1978 fabric photograph was easy. He said the labs agreed not to perform a blind test, but wanted the public to believe that it was. After some persuasion, Wolfi agreed to show the weighing results recorded in his diary. The two blind specimens matched the Turin weight exactly, but the Shroud specimen given to Zurich differed appreciably from the Turin weight, which Wolfi could not explain. Before leaving, Kersten acquired a photograph of the sample that he later compared with the original Turin photograph. The sample measured precisely 18x14 millimeters, which was one-third of the original that measured 54x14 millimeters. However, the BBC documentary tape said the original measured 70x10 millimeters, convincing Kersten that the Shroud specimens had, in fact, been exchanged for another cloth similar in appearance. After receiving the sample photos from Kersten, Professor Raes agreed the Zurich fabric was different from the Turin original, meaning the labs were not given a piece of the original Shroud.

The next stop on Kersten's investigation was London, where he met with Susan Brown, Secretary of the British Society for the Turin Shroud. She provided evidence that the Shroud had been secretly dated by a team of Americans in 1982. The American team was thought to have used the missing Raes fragment that he returned to Turin in 1973. A single thread was divided into halves and tested at the University of California, dating the fabric at either 1000 A.D. or 200 A.D. This information never reached the public.

Brown warned Kersten to be careful for his life, as she told him of the death of Roberto Calvi, who was involved in a Vatican scandal. Brown said only the Cardinal of Turin and Dr. Tite were in a position to switch the samples. Kersten asked if Tite could be bribed, but Brown did not know. Being the head of the textile department at the British Museum, Tite did have access to Middle Age textiles. Brown believed the British Museum had a piece of material similar to the Turin Shroud.

Tite had told the British Society that the sample taken from the Shroud was cut into three pieces from the original 10x70 millimeter piece. Later it was learned it had been cut into four pieces. Tite also claimed the sample was 10x70 millimeters, when in fact it was almost twice as long. After first denying the laboratories did not have contact with each other, Tite changed his story and said they had been in contact and conceded the test was not blind.

Kersten next wrote to Professor Hall, who was in charge of the Oxford University testing. Hall claimed all the samples weighed about 43 milligrams, not very precise or scientific, and definitely not correct for the Shroud sample. Hall sent along a poor photograph of the cloth samples.

On September 7, 1989, the International Scientific Symposium on the Turin Shroud was held in Paris. Outside the Symposium facilities, members of the Catholic Counter Reformation distributed pamphlets titled the Carbon 14 Affair, accusing Dr. Tite of fraud, claiming he had switched Shroud fragments in the sacristy. During the conference, scientists presented data showing the Shroud existed centuries before the carbon 14 test date. Riggi met Kersten there and handed over photographic prints of the Turin samples that were later compared with the original Turin cloth. Scientists found a number of differences between the two: (1) A difference in optical impressions was found between the sample and original, due to a looser structure in the Oxford sample. (2) A difference in thread thickness was discovered. (3) The two sections compared had a six-degree difference in the angle of herringbone structure. (4) The strip of fabric used for testing was much wider than the sample taken from the Shroud. According to Kersten, the data for the weights and sizes of the cloth samples began to look like a comedy of errors. Riggi claimed the strip of cloth removed was 10x70 millimeters. At the Paris Symposium, he gave the weight as 497 milligrams and then changed it to 540 mg. Kersten read the weight off the balance on the BBC video, and the figure was 478.1 mg. When confronted with these inconsistencies, Riggi changed his version. Cameras had not been allowed in the sacristy when the samples were measured and put in the metal containers. Later it was discovered by Kersten that the cloth samples Tite put in the cylinders for the Turin cloth had actually come from the Plurial of St. Louis, confirming Raes analysis that the samples were not from the original Turin cloth.

Dr. Michael Tite from the British Museum was the key person remaining to assure proper scientific protocol in testing. Kersten claimed that Bruno Bonnet-Eyman and his colleagues accused Tite of manipulating the results. They claim it was Tite, on Vatican orders, who was to date the relic in the Middle Ages. Interestingly, Tite was a good friend of Professor Hall at Oxford University. And Hall belonged to the British Museum team of advisors, which in itself is a conflict of interest. Following the announcement of the test results, Tite became director of Hall's laboratory. He came to his new job with one million pounds in financial reserves, which an anonymous wealthy friend and other donors had given Hall on Good Friday 1989 to secure the position. The players were identified to explain this monumental hoax.

The Vatican had achieved its purpose, having to explain why the body covered by the Shroud was still alive. A "neutral party" had dated the Shroud to the Middle Ages, and this has now put a stop to the discussion that Jesus survived the crucifixion, despite Kersten's proof otherwise.

Chapter Nine

THE CRUCIFIXION
How Jesus Survived

When one reads the Gospel of John carefully, it appears the author is trying to communicate the mysterious events of the crucifixion and burial of Jesus in a hidden way. The crucifixion story is told in the three synoptic gospels (Matthew, Mark, and Luke), the Gospel of John, and several apocryphal texts. As one parallels the gospel books, a series of contradictions make it difficult to grasp a consistent scenario. For example, the synoptic gospels state the crucifixion took place on the day after the Passover, but John states it occurred the day before. John, the last gospel, was completed toward the end of the first century in Ephesus, showing the greatest independence of the four gospels. Thus, many scholars consider John the most authentic of the gospels. It includes stories not found in the others, such as the wedding at Cana, the talk with Nicodemus, and the resurrection of Lazarus. Detailed historical knowledge of geographical locations strongly suggest that "John" himself, or the writer behind the name, was present at these places during the time of Jesus. The Passion scenario is written from an eyewitness viewpoint. To many, John is the best witness for the events surrounding Jesus and is considered the most reliable in describing the crucifixion and burial of Jesus.

Research by Holger Kersten and Elmar Gruber has carefully examined the gospel evidence, which strongly suggests how Jesus survived the crucifixion. Results of their independent investigation came to the same conclusion as found in the *Talmud of Jmmanuel*, unbeknownst to them, that Jesus was indeed rescued from the crucifixion.

DEATH ON THE CROSS

Romans considered death on the cross to be the most demeaning and frightful form of execution. Cicero referred to it as "the most horrible and repulsive punishment." Crucifixion in the Roman Empire was used as a terrifying deterrent to keep order among the people. As today, Palestine in Jesus' time was a place of nationalistic unrest. Between 167 B.C. and 134 A.D., 62 rebellions, wars, and uprisings occurred against the Greek and later Roman imperialists, with 61 disturbances originating from Galilee, Jesus' homeland. Crucifixion had become very common in this unrestful land as a means of punishment. It was foreign to Jews, however, as their method of capital punishment included stoning, burning, decapitation, and strangling. Mosaic law allowed a criminal already executed to be publicly hung on wood, as an additional punishment and humilation.

If the Roman death sentence by crucifixion was ordered, great care was taken to complete the execution before the Sabbath. Jesus' crucifixion took place on the day of preparation, so an urgency arose as it had to be over before the onset of evening. This was difficult to arrange, however, because the special suffering caused by crucifixion was the prolonged and agonizing torture. The agony usually extended over days until the victim finally expired.

Various methods were used to secure the person to the cross. If the body weight was supported entirely from the wrists, death would occur within five to six hours due to gradual suffocation. In this position, breathing is severely hindered, and the body dies from a lack of oxygen. Unconsciousness results, and the head droops further, reducing breath intake.

To prevent a quick death, a small wooden cross piece was often fixed to the vertical post, allowing the victim to prop himself as long as his strength allowed. Called a *suppedaneum,* it was a small, horizontal beam on which the victim could stand. The feet and hands during the crucifixion were either bound with thongs or nailed to the cross. Death could be delayed by the victim if he supported himself at the point of attachment (the nails, thongs, or footbeam), by pushing the body upwards.

According to the gospels, Jesus was nailed on the cross at the sixth hour (noon) and died at the ninth hour (3:00 P.M.).

Toward evening He was taken for dead and then removed from the cross. Pilate was surprised at how rapidly Jesus had died and consulted with the head centurion to see if everything was in order (Mark 15:44). Physicians have tried to explain the rapid death of Jesus, blaming it on the mistreatment before the crucifixion, since He appeared to be quite healthy otherwise. Jesus was a strong man, crucified during the prime of life. The night before, He was of clear mind when He talked to the court. Simon of Cyrene even relieved Jesus of carrying the cross beam for a good part of the way, about 550 to 650 meters from Pilate's praetorium to the site of execution. Everyone who was crucified suffered whiplashes, and by Hebrew law only 39 lashes could be given. Priests often carried out the punishment in the synagogue with a three-thronged clafskin whip. In summary, it is difficult to explain why Jesus supposedly departed the body so rapidly, as it seemed He suffered no differently than other victims.

Additional insight is given by the Gospel of Peter as it describes Jesus after He was nailed on the cross: "But he kept silent, as if he felt no pain." Gruber hypothesizes that during Jesus' training, He learned to master pain by meditation or with the mind, similar to Indian yogis. In those times, many religious sects throughout the East knew how to control pain. Gruber suggests that Jesus may have been in a deep meditative state while on the cross.

The journey to the crucifixion site was frequently part of the punishment. Often the victim's arms were first fixed to the cross beam, weighing between 40 and 65 pounds, which he had to carry on his shoulders to the place of execution. Great strength was needed to transport the heavy load, but in Jesus' case He was helped by Simon. According to the gospels, Jesus was nailed to the cross at the site of the execution. He laid nakedly when His wrists were nailed to the beam. Then He was raised with the cross beam to the upright post of the cross.

Scholars find it is difficult to understand why Jesus supposedly departed from His body, following a loud cry, so early in the crucifixion process. The two criminals crucified alongside Jesus were still alive. Their legs were broken, preventing them from straightening up, and resulting in painful suffocation within a few hours. "But when they came to Jesus, and said that he was dead already, they brake not his legs" (John 19:23). Again, scholars were puzzled at the decision by the Roman soldiers not to break Jesus' legs. The Romans had doubts, according to the gospels, whether He was dead and viewed His unconsciousness with skepticism. Otherwise, they would not have thrust the lance into Jesus' thorax. John 19:33-35 states that blood and water flowed out after the lance was driven into Jesus' side. All these circumstances surrounding the crucifixion give insight to how Jesus may have survived the crucifixion.

THE DRINK AND SIDE WOUND

Just before the alleged death of Jesus, something interesting happened. "Now there was set a vessel full of vinegar: and they filled a sponge with vinegar, and put it upon hyssop (a plant used for ritual sprinkling) and put it to his mouth. When Jesus therefore had received the vinegar, he said, 'It is finished.' and he bowed his head, and gave up the ghost" (John 19:29-30). Hence remains the question, why did Jesus die immediately after He had taken the bitter drink? Gruber wonders if it was really vinegar. It was common in Jewish custom to offer a person sentenced to death wine spiked with myrrh or incense, which helped alleviate pain. No mention of wine is reported in the gospels, but only a brew with a very bitter taste. One Roman soldier even helped Jesus take the drink (Matt 27:48, Mark 15:36, Luke 23:36, John 19:29).

John's narrative suggests the vinegar drink was brought to the crucifixion for a special purpose. Gruber believes it was part of the plan developed by Joseph and Nicodemus to save Jesus, suggesting the drink consisted of wine laced with opium. It was well known during those days of the anesthetic and narcotic properties of opium, which comes from an unripened seed head of a particular poppy plant widespread in Palestine. In fact, the effect is so strong that it can lead to a stupor state in which the person is without sensation.

Morphine, the active ingredient in opium, produces a narcotic, sedative effect that reduces breathing and relaxes cramps. Gruber believes the dose given Jesus killed the pain and was designed to make Him lose consciousness in a short time, making

Him appear dead when hanging on the cross. Opium lowers the heart rate, calms breathing to an extraordinary degree, and makes the body completely limp. Gruber conjectures Essene therapeuts had knowledge of the correct dosage, possibly assisting in the plan. Interestingly, medical opinion claims that if Jesus was close to death because of suffocation, it would be impossible to cry out loud as the gospels report. However, if drugged, Jesus could say a few words before the narcotic effect took hold and before losing consciousness.

The procedure of thrusting a lance into a crucified victim served as a confirmation of death. If the body did not react to the stabbing, one could assume the person was dead. The term used in the original Greek text for the thrust of the soldier's lance is *nyssein*, meaning a light scratch or puncture to the skin. It does not mean a thrust with full force, let alone a deep penetration. The stabbing was not meant to be a death procedure, and probably the centurion had performed the test in previous crucifixions. A special emphasis in John, writes Gruber, was given to the testimony of "blood and water," which flowed from the side of Jesus, suggesting that Jesus was still alive. Even at the time of Jesus, it was known that corpses do not bleed. Origin (185 - 254), an early Church Father, wrote that corpses do not bleed, but he still believed Jesus was dead. The eyewitness in John's account was so surprised to see so much blood pouring out of a dead body that he appropriately expressed his astonishment.

THE CENTURION

Pilate was surprised that Jesus had died so early in the crucifixion and summoned his centurion to confirm the death before releasing the body (Mark 15:44-45). This is the same centurion who was so moved by the events that he called Jesus the true son of God (Mark 15:39, Mark 27:54, Luke 23:47). In the apocryphal *Acta Pilata*, the centurion is called Longinus, the captain in charge of the crucifixion. Longinus later became a bishop in his homeland of Cappadocian, according to Gregory of Nyssa. Gruber suggests there may have been an association between Longinus, Jesus, and His followers before the crucifixion, hypothesizing that Longinus was a Jesus follower. If so, this would answer many questions about the crucifixion.

If Longinus, Joseph, and Nicodemus were all Jesus' secret followers, they were all in influential positions that enabled them to be informed well in advance about the outcome of Jesus' trial. Joseph was a well-respected member of the Sanhedrin, the supreme Jewish council existing since the second century B.C. that decided affairs of state, law, and religion. Membership totaled 71 under the leadership of a high priest. Gruber believes that Joseph and Nicodemus were kept well informed of the time and place of the execution and were able to make plans to rescue Jesus. In fact, Nicodemus sent Mary Magdalene a letter warning Jesus about the attacks by the Jews when he was in Ephraim (John 11:53f).

Joseph and Nicodemus knew the crucifixion could not be avoided, conjectures Gruber. If they could take Jesus down from the cross early enough, keeping Him alive might be possible if everything went according to plan. This would enable Jesus to continue His mission elsewhere. The disciples could not be involved in the rescue plan, as most had gone into hiding in fear of prosecution. To save Jesus, Joseph, Nicodemus, and Longinus had to have worked in concert.

RESCUE FROM THE CROSS

Joseph of Arimathea had purchased a garden site near Golgotha, close to the crucifixion site. He had a new family tomb cut from the rock on the estate, a sanctuary where the "dead body" could be quickly brought for safety. Having an unused tomb ready was important. According to the gospels, Joseph brought the body of Jesus to this new family grave. Gruber found it strange that Joseph, who came from Arimathea near the Samarian border, built a family tomb in Jerusalem. In Jewish tradition, having the family tomb in one's home town is normal. And it appeared that Joseph had no intention to move there, as the Pilate texts state Jews came to visit him in his hometown of Arimathea, to which he returned. Gruber believes the new tomb near Golgotha was not meant for the dead, but was instead used as an excuse not to move Jesus far if they were able to get Him off the cross in time. The crucifixion took place on the day of preparation, which was an advantage, meaning Joseph of Arimathea and Nicodemus could speed up the burial process without arousing suspicion. Of course, they had to make it appear that Jesus appeared dead.

Shortly after Jesus became unconscious, Joseph hurried to secure the release of the body from Pilate. Some believe he exerted influence on Pilate to accelerate the process, with some speculation a bribe was paid by the wealthy Joseph. Once Pilate released the corpse, Joseph and Nicodemus took Jesus from the cross and moved Him to the rock tomb. The opium drink would have made Him oblivious to the pain, and the medical herbs of aloe and myrrh hastened the healing process.

Joseph and Nicodemus knew they could not leave Jesus in the tomb long, speculates Gruber. The Jews were quite suspicious that Jesus followers would steal the body and pretend there had been a miraculous resurrection, so they asked someone to guard the tomb (Matt 27:62- 66). The Sabbath prevented the Jews from forming a watch themselves, and only Matthew tells of a Roman guard being assigned to the tomb. Rescuers only had until the Sabbath to care for Jesus before they could move Him. Once He regained strength, they needed to move Him out of the tomb quickly.

LAZARUS

The Lazarus story precisely describes the Jewish burial custom during the time of Jesus. This is very important when we compare the burial of Lazarus with Jesus. The resurrection of Lazarus is found in John 11:1-45, claiming Lazarus was dead. He was bound hand and feet in grave clothes described by the Greek word *keiriai,* which denotes long bands of linen wrapped around the body. From this passage, one assumes the whole body was wrapped in linen bands, including hands and feet. According to the Gospel John, Jesus was wrapped in the tomb by *othonia,* referring simply to clothes.

A cloth called a *sudarium* was "bound about" (*peridedemenos*) the head of Lazarus. This term suggests a chin band, used to bind the head of a Jewish corpse to prevent the lower jaw from falling down. However, different words are used to describe the burial of Jesus. His head was not bound with a *sudarium* but covered (*entetyligmenon*) by it. John says quite clearly the cloth was placed "on the head" or "over the head" (*epi tes kephales*). Gruber believes the author purposely tried to distinguish between the burial of Lazarus and that of Jesus, using different words that seemed similar but meant something entirely different. Lazarus was raised after the burial of a dead body, but in Jesus' case, it was not an ordinary burial. Lazarus came forth without any help (*exelthen*) and ascended from the grave. He was released from his linen wrappings, so he could move about freely. Scholars have a difficult time explaining the strange burial of Jesus that was hurried and incomplete. The Lazarus story has provided more evidence through the Gospel of John that Jesus could still have been alive after the crucifixion.

THE TOMB

The most common Jewish tomb at the time of Jesus consisted of a chamber cut into the rock. Within the chamber, oven-like cavities (*kokim*) were cut, measuring 50 cm wide x 80 cm high x 200 cm deep. Bodies were inserted lengthwise into these cavities.

Jesus' burial, however, was described quite differently in John. He was placed on a bench within the tomb, not pushed into a tomb cavity. On the morning of the resurrection, Mary Magdalene saw the angels, as they are called, "The one at the head, and the other at the feet, where the body had lain" (John 20:12). It is theorized that Jesus had not been pushed into a cavity (*kok*, which is singular), because no one could have sat at the head end.

Kokim tombs were reached through an entrance below ground level, often closed by a rolling stone. The tomb consisted of a large inner chamber, with a number of *kokims* cut out in the sides. A square hollow was found at the center of the inner chamber, serving as a drainage area. On the side of the pit, the body was laid out for washing and oiling. Lamps were often placed in niches of the tomb, as these cave-like structures required illumination, even during the day. John 20:5 states the favorite disciple "ran to the grave and stooping down, looked into the sepulcher and saw two 'angels' at the place where Jesus had lain." Light passing through the very low doorway can only reach the middle of the tomb chamber. Gruber believes the body of Jesus could only have been lying on the edge around the central hollow, certainly not in one of the cavities. The Gospel of John again provides evidence that Jesus could have been alive after the crucifixion.

ALOE AND MYRRH

The Gospel of John refers to Nicodemus bringing 100 pounds of aloe and myrrh to Jesus' tomb after the crucifixion. Scholars are puzzled at the reason for this if Jesus was dead. John 19:30 reads, "And there came also Nicodemus, which at first came to Jesus by night, and brought a mixture of myrrh and aloe, about a hundred-pound weight." The Greek text of John 19:40 states, "Then took they the body of Jesus, and wound (*edesan*) it in linen clothes (*othoniois*) with the spices (*meta ton aromaton*) as the manner of the Jews is to bury." Gruber claims if the aloe and myrrh were in a dried, powdered form, a row of sacks was probably necessary to make up this weight. Some theologians believe these herbs were used for embalming, but embalming was never part of the Jewish custom. Rabbinical writings only refer to an oiling of dead bodies. Some speculate John chose his words carefully for those who could read between the lines, as John clearly differentiated between the burials of Lazarus and Jesus.

Jewish custom required the body be washed and oiled, the hair cut and tidied, and the corpse be dressed again, covering the face with a cloth. Washing the body was very important, even if it was the Sabbath. However, the gospels make no mention of washing. Instead, the gospels say on Easter morning the women came to the tomb to oil the body. One may conclude that Joseph and Nicodemus were involved in something having nothing to do with Jewish burial rites. John clearly states that they buried Jesus in the way customary for the Jews, but then goes on to describe a burial that contradicts the Jewish custom. But why? The question remains: why would Nicodemus bring such a large quantity of aloe and myrrh to the tomb of Jesus if

He were dead? Perhaps exploring the uses for aloe and myrrh will answer these questions.

Aloe vera, a plant found in southwestern Arabia and on the island of Socotra, grows close to the classical trade routes that lead to the Mediterranean. Aloe has been used as a medicine and incense since the third millennium B.C. Used mainly for healing wounds, skin inflammation, and burns, the sticky gel is a compound rich in phenols, especially aloin.

Myrrh, on the other hand, is a gum resin harvested from the shrub commiphora and has an aromatic fragrance used in Indian and Oriental rituals. Israelites also used myrrh as an herbal perfume in their sacred anointing oil. Since early times, myrrh was used for healing wounds, and Hippocrates even found it to be a great disinfectant. During the Middle Ages, it played an important role for treatment of infectious diseases and epidemics. Although myrrh was used for Egyptian embalming, Jewish burial rites did not include its use.

Combined, aloe and myrrh were used to treat large, injured areas. At the time of Jesus, the mixture was considered the most specific means for the rapid and effective healing of wounds, with the greatest efficacy against infection. One might easily conclude that Nicodemus procured this great quantity of aloe and myrrh for the sole purpose of treating Jesus' wounds.

Gruber believes John's secret style of writing revealed a tremendous event to the attentive reader, yet concealing it from the eyes of the ignorant. It appears that John claimed Jesus was not meant to be buried as He did not die on the cross, and John was a witness well informed by Joseph and Nicodemus. All of the evidence strongly suggests that Jesus did not survive because of a miracle, but from medicinal healing.

THE OPEN TOMB

When the women came to Jesus' tomb with the anointing oils on the first weekday, they discovered the stone rolled away and the tomb empty of Jesus' body. Two men stood by them in shining garments and bowed down their faces to the earth and said unto them, "Why seek ye the living among the dead?" (Luke 24:1-5). Additionally, Mark 16:4-6 states, "They entered into the sepulcher and saw a young man sitting on the right side, clothed in a long, white garment. And he saith unto them, 'Be not affrightened: Ye seek Jesus of Nazareth, which was crucified: he is risen; he is not here; behold the place where they laid him.'"

If Jesus was resurrected, Gruber asks why would the massive stone be rolled aside from the tomb? The open tomb suggests that someone acted quickly to get Jesus out. Friends were still in the tomb, and Gruber believes those wearing shining white robes were Essenes who wore white garb. Luke's comment about seeking the living among the dead suggests Jesus was still alive.

One additional statement leads us to believe that Jesus did indeed live through the crucifixion. In the apocryphal Gospel of Peter, the guard saw three men emerge from the tomb, two of them supporting the other one. Gruber asks if a resurrected person needs support. Of course not, but an injured person coming out of a coma does.

MARY MAGDALENE

According to John 20:1-18, Mary Magdalene had come to the tomb early in the darkess of the morning and saw the stone rolled away. This frightened her, and she ran to fetch Peter and John, lamenting that someone had taken the Lord out of the sepulcher. When Peter and John arrived at the tomb, they saw only the linen clothes with no sign of Jesus anywhere. Mary Magdalene stood weeping before the tomb and asked the gardener if he had carried the body away. The gardener addressed Mary by her name, and she realized it was Jesus. Gruber believes Jesus, disguised as a gardener, had just exited the tomb before Mary arrived. It is possible that Mary may not have recognized the person as Jesus because of His swollen face and brown colorization, resulting from the aloe-myrrh solution. Mary fell to her knees before Jesus and wanted to touch His feet, and Jesus replied, "Touch me not" (John 20:17). Perhaps Jesus did not want her touching His sensitive wounds.

THE DISCIPLES

The gospels tell of Jesus meeting with His disciples after the "Resurrection," but they give no time. Most meetings were around Galilee and perhaps one in Jerusalem. These secret meetings were of short duration because Jesus needed to keep out of public sight to avoid arrest.

Scholars conclude the entire twenty-first chapter of John was written by a different author, who describes the appearance of Jesus to the disciples at the Sea of Tiberias. After the crucifixion, most of the disciples had gone back to their original occupations. Thomas, Nathaniel of Cana, and the Zebedee sons all went back to fishing (John 21:2). Jesus' appearances to the disciples are described as apparitions because He entered through locked doors. However, Jesus emphasized His physical reality.

Shortly before His departure from Palestine, the gospels report that Jesus made it clear to the disciples that He had survived the crucifixion and had recovered. Initially, the disciples considered Jesus to be in spirit form. Jesus worked to convince the disciples of His physical state: "And he said unto them, 'why are ye troubled? And why do thoughts arise in your hearts? Behold my hands and my feet that it is I myself: handle me and see; for a spirit hath not flesh and bones, as you see me have.' And when he had spoken, he showed them his hands and feet. And while they yet believed not for joy, and wondered, he said unto them, 'Have ye here any meat?' And they gave him a piece of broiled fish, and of a honey comb. And he took it, and did eat before them" (Luke 24:38-43). Jesus was determined to convince His disciples that His body was physical, just as was before the crucifixion. He emphasized His bodily presence by encouraging the apostles to touch Him, He ate food, and told them He was not just a spirit.

Jesus wanted to prove to the disciples that His body had not been transformed, so He showed them His wound marks and asked the doubting Thomas to touch His side wound. He criticized the disciples for not believing those who had seen Him after His rising (Mark 16:14). His message was that He had not been transfigured, and He was not a ghost.

THE LINEN CLOTH

The gospels refer several times to the burial cloth. John 20:4-7 reads, "So they ran both together [Peter and John], and the other disciple did outrun Peter, and came first to the sepulcher. And he, stooping down and looking in, saw the linen clothes lying; yet went he not in. Then cometh Peter following him, and went into the sepulcher, and seeth the linen clothes lie. And the napkin that was about the head, not lying with the linen clothes, but wrapped in a place by itself."

The linen cloth was left unused: its only function was for burial purposes. Was John trying to tell his readers something, by saying it lay untouched and folded up there the next day? The gospels say that the favorite disciple suddenly believed upon seeing it; that is, John believed in the Resurrection, according to theologians.

All the synoptic gospels use the word *sindon*, referring to a linen in the most general way. In Mark, a *sindon* was used as a cloth for wrapping around the body. Greek texts refer to a *sindon* as a precious cloth used to make robes and linen sheets.

The *sudarium* was the most important cloth left behind, unexpectedly mentioned by John. *Sudarium* means a towel or napkin. It lay to one side in the tomb, and sight of it gave faith to the favorite disciple. The length of linen placed around Jesus was a special kind of towel; it was the healing cloth speculates Gruber. It not only absorbed perspiration, but with herbs it was used as a therapeutic cloth. When Jesus was removed from the tomb in the early morning, the healing cloth was the first thing removed. Laid to one side was the folded cloth, while the other cloths had served as a mattress and were left crumpled up. Gruber believes because the long strip of linen was expensive, they wanted to take care of the healing cloth and folded it up. Good linen fabrics were valued, comparable to gold, silver, and silk, and were often used in sacred functions.

The Shroud used by Jesus, described as an unworked strip of fabric, matches the description of the Turin cloth exactly. Measurements of the Turin Shroud matched the unit of measurement used in Palestine during the time of Jesus. A philetaric cubit is about 53 cm, while the Turin cloth size is two philetaric cubits wide by eight cubits long.

On the ledge of the central pit in the tomb chamber were spread out a number of cloths (*othonia*) made of undyed (*kathara*) pieces of linen (*sinden*). Over these cloths lay another strip of linen (*soudarion*). A solution of healing herbs consisting of aloe and myrrh was applied to the naked body of the unconscious Jesus. The body was placed on the length of the linen, and because the whole body was covered, it achieved the function of a *sudarium*. Because of the great quantity of aromatic substances in the cloth, the weight of the cloth provided a definite pressure- packing effect on the body. This was the scene reconstructed by Gruber following his research. The biblical description of the Shroud matches the science underlying the Turin Shroud, which covered a body that was alive.

THE RESURRECTION

After discovering that Jesus was not in the tomb, Mary said to Peter and John, "They have taken away the Lord out of the sepulcher. . . ." Gruber interprets this as if she knew who "they" were. He believes that Joseph and Nicodemus confided with Mary, Peter, and John about the rescue plan for Jesus. In this case, "they" would refer to Joseph, Nicodemus, and their helpers. When John, the favorite disciple, said, "I believe," Gruber interprets this as not being that he believed in the Resurrection, but that he believed in the rescue of Jesus.

The biblical Resurrection has been given a different interpretation, following the research by Father Dr. Gunther Schwarz, a philologist and theologist. The terms "rise" and "coming back to life" found in the Bible translation were originally derived from the Aramaic verb meaning "resuscitate." He claims the evidence is conclusive that these Aramaic words mean "resuscitation" and not "resurrection." Schwarz refers to the synonymous words, *achaguta* and *techijjuta,* that the Bible refers to as resurrection, Aramaic words he said that Jesus would have used. Both nouns are derived from the verb *chaja,* meaning "life," and consequently mean "resuscitation," emphasizes Schwarz.

Even the Greek interpretation disagrees with the Christian

translation given to the Aramaic words. The Greek word used in the early New Testament manuscript, *antihistemi,* means to "awaken" or "get up." Only later did Christians interpret *antihistemi* to mean "raise from the dead" and "resurrect." The Greek word *anastasis* is the word that actually means "resurrection."

In addition to the evidence that the literal translation provides, Luke 24:5 strongly suggests that Jesus was alive when the white-robed men asked why they, the women, were seeking a living person among the dead. This statement infers that Jesus was rescued and had no reason to be in the tomb. He was living among the living.

Jesus had gone ahead to Galilee where He was going to meet with His disciples. Most of the disciples had not been informed of the rescue plan. When seeing Jesus, they believed they were seeing the spirit of a dead person. Jesus had a difficult time convincing them that He was still alive in the flesh. Thus, theologians perpetuated the resurrection myth following the crucifixion of the human Jesus, providing the dogma for Christianity.

THE TALMUD OF JMMANUEL

Biblical evidence has been provided of how Jesus may have survived the crucifixion. The Talmud Jmmanuel also explains the rescue of Jesus, providing additional insight as to how it was accomplished. Assisting Joseph of Arimathea during the post crucifixion were friends of Jesus from India, not Essenes. A crucial piece of information explains how the helpers got in and out of the tomb without detection. The Talmud describes Joseph's tomb as having two entrances, allowing passage out of the guard's sight. The following is the Talmud's version of the rescue.

> 30:58 "After a little while, he [Joseph of Arimathea] noticed that Jmmanuel was only half dead, but he told no one."
>
> 30:59 "He quickly went into the city to see Pilate, and he asked for the body of Jmmanuel so that he could bury him."
>
> 30:60 "Pilate ordered Jmmanuel be turned over to Joseph."
>
> 30:61 "Many people went with him and they took

Jmmanuel off the cross. Joseph wrapped the body in pure linen that he had previously painted so as to form an image of Jmmanuel." [Could this have something to do with the Shroud?]
30:62 "Joseph of Arimathea carried the body of Jmmanuel all the way to Jerusalem and placed him outside the city in his own tomb, which he had cut into a rock for his own future burial."
30:63 "He rolled a big stone in front of the tomb and went to obtain some medicine in order to nurse Jmmanuel."
30:64 "The entrance of the tomb was guarded by soldiers and Jmmanuel's mother so no one could enter and steal the body."
30:65 "Joseph of Arimathea sought out Jmmanuel's friends from India and went back to the tomb. They went through a secret second entrance unknown to the henchmen and to the soldiers and nursed him for three days and three nights, so that he was soon in better health again and his strength restored."
30: 31 "They went away, watched the tomb, and sealed the stone in front of the door."
30:32 "But they did not know the secret of the grave, namely that it had two exits and entrances, so that Jmmanuel's helpers could, without being seen, go to him to apply healing salves and herbs, so that on the third day he was again strong enough to walk."
30:66 "The tomb was guarded on the other side by the soldiers, because the chief priests and Pharisees had gone to Pilate, saying:
30:67 'Sir, we considered that when this crazy man was still alive, he said to the people, I shall return after three days and three nights and rise, because I will be only half dead.'"
30:68 "But since it was established through a soldier that he was really dead, his tomb should be guarded so that no one can come, steal the body and say, 'Behold, he has risen from the dead after all!'"
30:70 "Pilate said to them: 'Take my soldiers as

guardians. Go and watch the tomb as well as you can.'"

31:1 "When the first day of the week had come after the Passover, the three days and nights had passed following which Jmmanuel would live again after near-death, as he had foretold."

31:2 "Behold, a great thunder arose in the air, and a radiant light came down from the sky and landed on the earth, not far from the tomb."

31:3 "Then a guardian angel came out of the light, and his appearance was like lightning and his garment was as white as snow."

31:4 "He went to the tomb, and the soldiers got out of his way because they feared him."

31:5 "He lifted his hand from which came bright lighting that hit the soldiers one after the other."

31:6 "And they fell to the ground and did not stir for a long time."

31:7 "Then the guardian angel stepped up to the tomb, rolled the stone away from the door and spoke to Mary, the mother of Jmmanuel, and to Mary Magdalene, who were both there."

31:8 "Do not be afraid. I know that you are seeking Jmmanuel the crucified."

31:9 "But he is not here. He lives as he said. Come here and behold the place where he lay."

31:10 "Go quickly and tell his disciples that he has risen from near-death."

31:11 "Also tell them he will walk ahead of you to Galilee and there you will see him. Behold I have told you."

31:12 "But Mary asked, 'Yet he was dead and lay here dead, how can he rise?'"

31:13 "The guardian angel answered, 'Why are you seeking someone alive among the dead?'"

31:14 "Go now and spread the news among his disciples, but beware, and do not tell anyone else."

31:30 "Peter also came, went into the tomb and found everything just as the other disciple had."

> 31:31 "The bandages had been carefully folded and placed on the ground, and the sweat cloth that had been on Jmmanuel's head had been placed on a particular spot, together with the salves and herbs, and peculiar figures of clay as he had never seen before, and so they were strange to him."

A scenario has been provided in this chapter, using scripture and the *Talmud of Jmmanuel,* that demonstrated how Jesus may have survived the crucifixion. The Gospel of John provides the most logical scripture scenario, as the author seems to have first-hand information of the Passion. One can provide a logical scenario, but is there any evidence of Jesus' life on earth following the biblical ascension? As we will see, there is!

Chapter Ten

THE POST-CRUCIFIXION

Jesus Returns To The East

Holger Kersten's excellent research of Jesus' life following the crucifixion gives us insight as to what happened to the resuscitated Jesus. Legends about Jesus between Israel and India along the Silk Road provide clues regarding his journey to Kashmir. Numerous geographic sites along this route have been named after Jesus, who made a great impression on the people in His "second life." Legends tell of Jesus taking His mother Mary along with Him on His return trip to India. The scenario described by Kersten's research greatly parallels the story told in the *Talmud of Jmmanuel.* As we will see, Kashmir had an ancient Jewish legacy, perhaps dating back to the biblical patriarchs.

THE JOURNEY EAST

Following His recovery from the crucifixion, Jesus remained in hiding and could no longer teach in public. If caught, there was little likelihood Jesus could survive a second crucifixion. His first destination was Galilee, with His departure from Jerusalem being described in Luke 24:50-52 by the ascension story. "And he led them out as far as to Bethany, and he lifted up his hands, and blessed them, he was parted from them, and carried up into heaven. And they worshiped him, and returned to Jerusalem with great joy." Kersten conjectures that from outside the city of Jerusalem, Jesus took the path to Bethany that climbs over the southernmost foothills of the range that includes the Mount of Olives, up to the "Peak of Ascension." When Jesus walked over the summit and down the other side, He was quickly lost to sight.

After meeting with His disciples in Galilee, Jesus proceeded to Damascus, located in mid-Syria, 180 miles northeast of Jerusalem.

Approximately three miles outside Damascus is a place that is still called Mayuam-i-Isa, "the place where Jesus lived." An eyewitness account by Paul tells us that Jesus did not permanently disappear following the so-called "ascension." Jesus had learned of Paul's trip to Damascus presumably in pursuit of Christians. When Jesus was in Damascus, He made his appearance to Paul on the road to Damascus as described by Acts 9:3-6:

> "And as he [Paul] journeyed, he came near Damascus: and suddenly there shined round him a light from heaven.
> And he fell to the earth, and heard a voice saying unto him, Saul, Saul, why persecutest thou me?
> And he said, 'who art thou?'
> And the Lord said, 'I am Jesus whom thou persecutest: it is hard for thee to kick against pricks.'
> And he trembling and astonished said, 'Lord, what wilt thou have me do?'
> And the Lord said unto him, 'Arise, and go into the city, and it shall be told thee what thou must do.'"

Some scholars believe this encounter between Jesus and Paul occurred about two years after the crucifixion.

Following that experience, Paul became the most zealous supporter of Jesus and seeded the Christian church as we know it today. Acts 9 says that Jesus later asked Ananias, who was living in Damascus, to visit Saul. Understandably, Ananias was quite reluctant because of Paul's reputation for persecuting Christians. Jesus told Ananias, "Go thy way: for he is a chosen vessel unto me, to bear my name before the Gentiles, and Kings, and my children of Israel: For I will show him how great things he must suffer for my name's sake" (Acts 9:15-16). Following these instructions by Jesus, Ananias baptized Paul and introduced him to the teachings of Jesus.

Jesus lived and taught in Damascus following the crucifixion, according to Persian historian Mir Kawand. During His stay in Damascus, Jesus received a letter from the King of Nisibis in Asia Minor requesting Jesus to cure him of an illness. Jesus sent his disciple Thomas ahead with the message that He would soon follow. The Persian scholar Fakir Muhammad writes that Jesus took His mother and others to Nisibis, but upon their arrival they discovered the King had already been healed by Thomas. Confirmation of Jesus' stay at Nisibis comes from Iman Abu Jafar Muhammad, who wrote in the text *Tafsir-Ibn-i-Jarir-at-Tabir* that Jesus was in danger while at Nisibis, and He had risked His life by appearing in public. Jesus needed to leave quickly, and His next destination was to the northwest.

The Apocryphal Acts of Thomas tell that Jesus then visited the King of Andrapa's royal court, where He appeared suddenly during the wedding festivities of the princess. Andrapolis was located in the extreme northern part of Antolia, in present-day Turkey, and had been in the Roman province of Galatia since 7 B.C. At the wedding, a reunion took place between Jesus and the Apostle Thomas, as they had traveled there separately. Jesus wanted Thomas to go to India, but Thomas refused. "But he did not want to go there, and said he could not travel because of weakness of the flesh. 'How can I, a Hebrew, travel and preach the truth to the people of India?' And as he reflected and spoke this, the Savior appeared to him in the night and spoke to him: 'Do not be afraid, Thomas. Go to India and preach the word there, for my Grace is with you.' But he would not obey, and said, 'Send me anywhere you want, but somewhere else! For I shall not go to India'" (Actae Thomae I).

The Acts of Thomas then tell of Jesus selling the reluctant Thomas as a slave to the Indian merchant Abban, who had been instructed by King Gundafor to find a carpenter. History confirms Parthean King Gundafor was on the throne during the first century. Jesus and Abban signed a contract for a sum of three pounds of unstamped silver, presumably the fare to India, assuring that Thomas got there.

According to the Acts of Thomas, Thomas was afforded the deepest secrets of Jesus. In Chapter 29, Thomas is given a special title: "Twin brother of Christ, Apostle of the highest, and initiate, sharer in the knowledge of the hidden word of Christ, who receiveth his secret pronouncements." Scholars are somewhat puzzled why Thomas was called Jesus' twin, as some believe that Thomas had a similar outward appearance, or perhaps a very close relationship. Another version states that Thomas received "the hidden mysteries of the Son of God," and he was considered the keeper of Jesus' secret words.

After Thomas arrived in India, descriptions of his ministry were written.The Acts of Thomas quotes Indian King Misdai saying, "That oil, water, and bread were elements in the apostle's magic." Thomas was called a servant or handmaid of God who shared in God's power and was considered a member of the inner group. His becoming a servant in the power of God helps explain the terminology describing him as being sold as a slave. Thomas did establish a Christian church in India, and its parishioners were called "Thomas Christians." During the fourth century, long after Thomas died near Madras in southern India, his remains were brought back to Edessa. Both texts, the Apocryphal Gospel of Thomas and Acts of Thomas, are of Syrian origin, traced back to the missionary activity of Thomas in Edessa. They are esoteric works of the Gnostics written in Syriac Aramaic used at the beginning of the third century by the Gnostic group called the Manicheans.

Continuing with Jesus' journey back to India, we find many site names along the old Silk Road that show a connection with Jesus or Mary, many thought to be stopover stations. Near Ephesus, on today's west coast of Turkey, stands the House of Mary.

Legends continue today among the various people who were on the route of Jesus' journey to the East. Scholars have studied the Kurdish people of eastern Antolia who have many legends about Jesus living in the region of southeast Turkey after the crucifixion. Persian folklore claims Jesus lived in the town of Nisibis, near Edessa, presently called Nusabin, on the Turkish border with Syria. Tradition among the Alawites of Antolia claims Jesus survived the crucifixion and was nursed back to health by His disciples, leaving the territories under Roman rule and migrating east.

These remote communities might have preserved the original Christian doctrine in a less distorted form than the Church of Rome. Many scholars believe these communities are desert descendants of the Essenes and Nazarenes, who after the time of Christ merged with the Jewish Christians to oppose Paul's dominant Hellenistic groups. In order to survive, they had to assume the guise of an Islamic sect. The Alawites of Turkey occupy the ancient home of the Galations, who Paul once addressed. All these groups celebrate Christian festivals, especially Easter. They give great esteem to John the Baptist and Peter, but have little regard for Paul.

Historical documents found in Persia (present-day Iran) suggest that Persia was the next destination for Jesus on His 16 year journey to Kashmir. Jesus was known as Yuz Asaf, a name that followed him to Kashmir. Various manuscripts, still preserved today, tell how Yuz Asaf preached all over Persia. In Persia, Jesus resided in Mashag, where it is written that He visited the grave of Shem, the son of Noah. The prophet entered the land from the West, with teachings identical to Jesus, allowing scholars to conclude these men were one and the same. The meaning of Yuz Asaf is found in an ancient Persian historical text called *Farhang-i-Asafia*, which tells how Jesus (Hazrat Issa) healed some lepers, who were thereafter called *asaf* (the purified), having been cured of their illness. Yuz means "leader," so Yuz Asaf means "leader of the healed," a common epitaph for Jesus, whose mission was to cleanse impure spirits.

The journey next led to modern Afghanistan and Pakistan. Geographic names commemorate the activity of Jesus in these locales. There are two plains that bear the name of Yuz Asaf in eastern Afghanistan near the towns of Ghazni and Jalalabad, where tradition tells of Jesus visiting.

The Acts of Thomas then put both Jesus and Thomas in Taxila in present-day Pakistan. This occurred at the court of King Gundafor in 47 A.D., during the twenty-sixth year of his reign, when Thomas was asked to build a magnificent palace for the king. Instead, Thomas distributed the money among the needy and thanked Jesus for this opportunity to render service.

"I thank thee O Lord, in every way that I can, you who died for a short while that I may live eternally in you; and for you selling me, in order to liberate many others through me. And he never ceased to teach and give relief to the troubled saying, 'The Lord gives this to you, and ensures that everyone receives nourishment. For he is the nourisher of orphans and provider for widows, and offers the gift of tranquility and peace to all who are troubled'" (Actae Thomas 19).

King Gundafor was eventually converted to mark the event of receiving a "palace in heaven." Thomas baptized both King Gundafor and his brother with water, and then anointed them with oil, followed by a celebration of the Eucharist. "At the conclusion of the initiation rite, Jesus Himself appeared, and said, 'Peace be with you brothers'" (Actae Thomae 27). The writings say Jesus did not live continuously at the court, but returned there regularly. Jesus again visited Thomas, who had been expecting Him, and told him, "Thomas, rise early, bless everyone, and after prayer and worship, go along the path east for two miles, and there I shall show you my glory. Through the work that you are about to begin, many will come to seek refuge in me, and you will triumph over the world and the power of the enemy" (Actae Thomas 29). Thomas went to the designated place and found a young boy who seemed to be dead, and in the presence of a crowd, he brought the boy back to life. The boy told Thomas he had seen Jesus, "For I saw the man, as he stood next to you: 'I have many miracles to perform through you, and there are great works that I shall accomplish through you.'"

Forty miles east of Taxila is the small town of Mari, leaving us another clue to the eastward travels of Jesus. Formerly spelled Murree, it lies on the Pakistan/Kashmir border. A grave is found there that has been maintained and honored for ages. It is known as the Mai Mari da Asthan, meaning "The Final Resting Place of Mother Mary." By the time Jesus had reached this destination, His mother would have been over 70 years old, and probably quite exhausted after a long, arduous trip. The Christian community has no idea where the mother of Jesus is buried, so the grave of Mari certainly could be the Virgin Mary's. The grave is aligned in an east-west direction, common with many Kashmir graves thought to reflect a burial custom of the Jews who lived there. In contrast, Islamic graves are orientated north-south. Perhaps another mystery has been solved, the lost years of Mother Mary.

Mary's tomb is found on Pindi Point, a mountain outside the village, and revered by the Islamic population as the tomb of Jesus' mother. Today the burial site is found in a demilitarized zone on the border close to the ceasefire line. At the time of Jesus, the area around Mary's tomb was Hindu. Hindus normally cremate their dead and scatter the ashes, except for monks and saints, who are interred. Kersten hypothesizes that the buried person was regarded as a saint. During the eighth century when

Islamic invaders passed through India, they destroyed many of their enemies' places of worship, but spared the shrine of Mary's tomb. Some scholars speculate that the Moslems acknowledged it as a shrine of the Christian or Jewish faith, religions that they respected at that time.

A military watchtower was built by the British army next to the shrine in 1898. Many people continued to visit the shrine, which gave concern to British authorities. In 1917, the British decided to destroy the sacred site to prevent pilgrims getting too close to the military zone. However, destruction of the site was halted by a protesting population. Today an asphalt road runs from Mari to Srinagar, over 100 miles away, through a beautiful, wooded, mountainous area.

After sixteen years from His Palestine departure, Jesus finally arrived in Kashmir. According to tradition, Jesus lived well past 100 hundred years. Fatima, the daughter of the Prophet Muhammad, claims her father said Jesus lived until the age of 120. If Jesus lived in this region, there should be evidence confirming this tradition. About 25 miles south of Srinagar, between the towns of Naugam and Nilmag, lies the Yus-Marg, the meadow where Jesus preached. This is according to the tradition of shepherd tribes known as the Bani-Israel (children of Israel), who settled the area around 772 B.C.

The ancient Hindu writings called the *Puranas* also refer to a person whom many think was Jesus. From the fourth century B.C. until the seventeenth century A.D., the *Puranas* were continuously updated. Written in Sanskrit, the sacred language of India, the writings consist of 18 volumes. The ninth volume, *Bhavishyat Maha-Purana,* was written in the third and seventh centuries A.D. and contains a supplement that describes how Jesus came to India. It also tells about the Israelites who had come earlier to India. Verses 17 through 32 tell stories about Jesus while in the land of India.

> "One day, Shalivahana, the lord of the Shakas, came to a snowy range. There, in the land of Huna, the powerful king saw a handsome man seated on the mountain. He had a white body and wore white garments.
>
> The King asked the holy man, 'Who are you?'

> The other replied, 'Know that I am Ishaputra (Sanskrit for 'son of God') born of a virgin, proclaimer of teachings of the barbarians, which bear the truth.'
>
> The King then asked him, 'What teachings do you mean?'
>
> The other replied, 'At the end of Sata Yuga, the Golden Age, I appeared as Masiha (the Messiah) in the depraved land of the unbelievers. The goddess Ishamasi also appeared before the barbarians in a terrible form. The goddess Ishamasi is thought to be a general expression referring to evil and wicked, a name not found elsewhere in the literature. I was brought before her in the manner of unbelievers and attained the Masiha-tva (Messiah hood). Hear O King, I brought the religion unto the unbelievers. . . Thus was Ishamasi destroyed, and the form of Isha was revealed in the heart, ever pure and bestowing happiness, and I was called Isha-Masiha.'"

Many scholars believe that the teacher of the unbelievers was Jesus, who referred to Himself as Isha-Masiha. "Isha" is a Sanskrit word meaning "Lord," also used for "God." "Isha- Maasiha" thus refers to the Lord, Messiah. Professor Hassnain, from the University of Kashmir in Srinagar, from whom Kersten acquired much of his Jesus' information, said King Shalivahana ruled over Kushan around 50 A.D., and others claim his reign was around 78 A.D. Although the land of Huna has not yet been identified, the snowy mountains refer to the Himalayas.

Other evidence suggests Jesus' stay in Kashmir. Aish-Mugam lies about 36 miles southeast of Srinagar, which is a cave extending nearly 37 feet into the mountainside. A magnificent shrine has been erected at the entrance containing a reliquary of an Islamic saint named Zainuddin, who lived in the cave during the rule of Sultan Zainul Abidin Badshah (1408 - 1461). The saint had been given a staff by Sheikh Noor Din Wali, a most sacred relic still watched over today by tomb attendants. Made of olive wood, the staff measures about seven feet long and is said to have miraculous power. It is known by two names, the "Rod of Moses" and the "Rod of Jesus." Tradition indicates it first belonged to Moses when he came to India, and then it was later used by Jesus.

"Aish-Mugam" refers to Jesus, with "Aish" derived from "Isha" or "Issa," and "mugam" meaning "place of rest." The cave is believed to have been a place of meditation for Jesus.

More evidence of Jesus' presence in Kashmir is found on an inscription found on the Takhti-i-Suleiman, the Throne of Solomon near Srinagar. In 1413, a history of the throne was written by Mullah Nadiri in the *History of Kashmir,* telling of the restoration of the throne by a Persian architect, during the reign of Gopadatta. During the renovation, sayings in Old Persian were inscribed on the sides of the steps leading to the grand entrance. The entrance inscription reads,

> "The constructor of these columns is the most humble Bihishti Zargar, in the year fifty and four. Khwaja Rukan, son of Murjan, had these columns built. At this time, Yuz Asaf announced his prophetic mission in the year fifty and four. He is Jesus, prophet of the sons of Israel."
>
> Nadiri continues, "At the time of Gopadapatta's reign, Yuz Asaf came from the Holy Land up into this valley, and announced that he was a prophet. He epitomized the peak of piety and of virtue, and proclaimed that he himself was his own message, that he lived in God day and night, and that he had made God accessible to the people of Kashmir. . . . I have also read a Hindu book that the prophet is really Hazrat Issa, the spirit of God, and he adopted the name of Yuz Asaf. True knowledge is with God. He spent his life in this valley.
>
> After his passing, his body was laid to rest in Mohalla Anzimarah. It is said that the light of prophecy emanates from the tomb of this prophet . . . "

King Gopadapatta ruled in Kashmir beginning in 53 A.D. and through 54 A.D.

Kersten's research has found 21 references in ancient texts confirming Jesus' stay in Kashmir, and names of Kashmir's geographic sites also confirm His presence. Twenty-four locations contain the word Issa, Yus, or Yuza.

During the time of Jesus, Kashmir was a great religious, cultural, intellectual, and political center. It was the hub of an enormous

Indo-Scythian Empire ruled by the great King Kanishka I (78 - 103 A.D.) of the Kushan dynasty. A true visionary, he tried to unite the various races with a tolerant and generous policy. His hope was to combine the harmony of Indian and Greek philosophy. The University of Taxila became the academic center of these merging cultures. King Kanishka saw the perfect umbrella for the realization of his ideas in Buddhism, and he sought advice from the Buddhist monks. However, he became disappointed after discovering that Buddha's teachings had become fragmented into so many sects and schools. Hoping to resolve and unify this fragmentation, the King assembled the various Buddhist sects at the Council of Haran. But it wasn't until 300 years later at the Fourth Buddhist Council that the Mahayana Buddhist religion was established, allowing salvation to all people.

A history of Kashmir is found in the *Rajah Tarangini,* written in Sanskrit verses by Pandit Kalhana in the twelfth century. The text tells of a holy man named Isana, who performed miracles similar to Jesus. Isana saved an influential statesman named Vazir from death and brought him back to life. Vazir later ruled Kashmir for 47 years. Kalhana wrote that Isana was the last reformer in Kashmir, who lived and worked during the first century A.D. Many scholars believe that Isana was none other than Jesus.

Additional evidence of Jesus' life in the East is provided by a mystical order of the Nath Yogis, found throughout India, which has preserved an old Hindu sutra known as the Natha-Namavali. The sutra tells of the great saint Isha Nath, who came to India at the age of 14. He returned to his homeland, spreading his teachings, but fell victim to a conspiracy and was crucified. By means of yogi power that he learned in India, Isha was able to survive the execution. With the help of the supernatural powers of his Indian teacher Chetan Nah, who was a Nath guru, Isha returned to India where he founded an ashram monastery in the foothills of the Himalayas. The Shaivite (Shiva centered) Nath Yogis are one of the oldest Hindu orders of monks, easily recognized by their large earrings, with origins long before the time of Jesus. Contrary to other Hindu orders, the Nath Yogis do not recognize the caste system and supremacy of the Brahmins. They consider all people to be as brothers and sisters and accept all God-seeking people into their order, regardless of status and background.

Legends, writings, and geographical names all suggest that Jesus lived in Kashmir under another name. As we will see, Jesus may have had a good reason to end His life journey in this region.

THE KASHMIR/JEWISH CONNECTION

Evidence has been presented that strongly suggests Jesus spent the majority of His life in Kashmir following the crucifixion. Why would Jesus choose Kashmir to live? As we shall see, Kashmir had a strong Jewish heritage, beginning with biblical patriarchs. Kersten's research about this ancient heritage answers many biblical questions that have eluded both historians and theologians.

The Semitic heritage of Kashmir may have originated with Abraham. In Genesis 24:4, "Later Abraham sent his eldest servant to Haran unto my country and to my kindred, in order to find a wife for his son Isaac." Biblical scholars have assumed Haran to be in the Mesopotamia lowlands in modern Turkey, in a city now called Harran. However, several miles north of Srinagar lies a town called Haran with ancient walls dated long before the Christian era. From Haran, the people moved to Canaan, where Abraham fathered his son Isaac, who in turn fathered Jacob and Esau. Jacob, who became patriarch of the Jewish tribes, had 12 sons. Joseph, the second youngest of Jacob's sons, was sold by his jealous brothers into bondage in Egypt. At that time, Hyskos was the Egyptian ruler whose reign allowed Joseph to rise in power, becoming second in command to the pharaoh.

Canaan was suffered a severe drought, which forced Jacob and the clan to move to Egypt, encouraged by Joseph. They settled in the province of Goshen on the northeast Nile delta, and there became known as Hebrews; their purpose was to serve the Egyptians. The ancient Egyptian historian Manetho describes this event differently, calling them the people of a peasant culture, who appeared unexpectedly in Egypt and had come from the East. About 1730 B.C., they boldly entered Egypt and forcibly took possession of the country, without meeting resistance.

The Old Testament book of Exodus describes Moses leading the Hebrew tribes out of Egypt that was ruled by an oppressive pharaoh. They were in search of the land of their fathers they called the "land of milk and honey" promised by Yahweh. Moses gave the Hebrew tribes their law in the form of the Ten Commandments. Coincidently, an archetypal pattern had developed with lawgivers of other civilizations. Manu was the lawgiver for religion and social conduct in India. Manes gave the law to Egyptians, and Minos codified the laws of ancient Greece. The Ten Commandments were a codified summary of laws known by the people of the Near East, long before Moses. The same laws were promulgated by King Hammurabi of Babylon, 500 hundred years earlier. Kersten believes they were based on the old Indian Rig Veda, millennia earlier.

Old Testament scholars have concluded that Moses was not the author of the Torah, the first five books of the Bible, traditionally thought to have been written by him. Historians say it was compiled from centuries of oral and written legends. A variety of sources was used, as determined by a lack of uniformity in vocabulary, repetitions, and theological contradictions. Recently the sixth and seventh editions of the *Book of Moses* have been discovered. They tell of Egyptian esoteric traditions that included spells, sorcery, and magical incantations. Moses was known as a great magician, a gift even recognized by the Greeks.

Perhaps the Old Testament explains how the Jews got to Kashmir. During the third month of the Exodus, the Jews arrived at Mount Sinai where they remained for eight months before leaving for the Promised Land. They wandered in the wilderness for another 40 years, a mystical number meaning a long time. When they reached the Jordan Valley, Moses sensed he was not long for the world (Deuteronomy 31:2). He gave his people final instructions and appointed administrative officers to govern the group after the Jordan had been crossed. Following his farewell speech, Moses climbed Mount Nebo to see "the land of milk and honey" before he died. There he met his end (Deuteronomy 34:5), but his burial site remained a mystery. Surprisingly, the burial site has not been found even though the Bible gives a detailed description: "And Moses went up from the plains of Moab unto the mountain of Nebo, to the top of Pisgah, that is over against Jericho . . . over against Beth-peor. . . . " Kersten believes the Israelites did not give Moses a worthy burial. In fact they did, not in Palestine but in northern India.

Five landmarks are named by the Bible in relation to Moses' burial site. They include the plains of Moab, Mount Nebo in the Abarim mountains, the peak of Mount Pisgah, Beth-peor, and Heshbon. Numbers 27:12 declares the Promised Land beyond the Jordan had been reserved for the children of Israel, but not for all the Hebrews. Beth-peor means "place that opens out." The River Jhelum (which sounds somewhat like Jordan) in north Kashmir flows into in a small town of Bandipur where the Valley of the Jhelum opens out onto the broad plain of Lake Wular, originally called Behat-poor. Located 12 miles northeast of Bandipur is the small village of Hasba or Hasbal, which is the biblical Heshbon mentioned with Beth-peor and Pisgah. Pisgah (now Pishnag) lies north of Bandipur. In the valley lies Mown, which corresponds to the plains of Moab located three miles northwest of Mount Nebo, a single mountain in the Abarim range. Mount Nebo (also called Baal Nebu or Niltrop) provides a beautiful view of Bandipur and highlands of Kashmir. These five landmarks used to describe Moses' burial are found in one location, Kashmir. Lying beneath Mount Nebo is the tombstone of Moses, which has an official guardian called the *Wali Rishi,* who also guards the tomb of an Islamic saint, Sang Bibi, a female recluse. Traditions of the rishis say they have been tending the grave for more than 2,700 years. The view of the "land of milk and honey" by Moses referred to in the Bible is Kashmir, not Palestine!

Quite a few places with biblical names are found in the locale near Moses' grave. Two sites are named Mugam-i-Mussa, meaning the "place of Moses." South of Srinagar, on a riverbend in Bijihara, is a spot referred to as "Moses' bath place." Found there is a magic stone weighing more than 150 pounds called sana-i-Musa, the "stone of Moses." Tradition indicates the stone rises by itself and remains suspended one meter above the ground if 11 people touch it with one finger, chanting "ka-ka, ka-ka." Many legends in Kashmir tell of Moses residing there.

Following the death of Moses, the 12 tribes of Israel gained control of Canaan under the leadership of Joshua. The territory was divided among the tribes in the thirteenth century B.C., with the whole division process taking 150 years. Israel needed a strong king to rule the land, and Samuel, the last of the Judges, announced Saul to be King of Israel at the end of the eleventh century B.C. Later, only under the reign of King David did Israel become a single united nation, and it remained united under David's son, King Solomon, who built the Temple in Jerusalem.

Kashmir is still known by the local Islamic population as Bugh-i-Suleiman, "the Garden of Solomon." On a mountain overlooking Srinagar is a small temple Takht-i-Suleiman, meaning the "Throne of Solomon." According to tradition, Solomon once visited the region and is credited with building the small temple. He is also credited with dividing the mountain Barehmooleh to create a channel for water that still flows into the large Lake Dal.

King Solomon died around 930 B.C., succeeded by his son Rehoboam. A rebellion led by the Ephamite broke out against the new king on the pretext of excessive taxation, resulting in the kingdom being divided into two. The ten tribes of the North formed an independent state called Israel, led by Jeroboam. The remaining two tribes in the South named their territory Judah and continued to be ruled by the House of David. For 250 years these opposing states lived beside one another. Israel then became occupied by the Assyrians led by Sargon II, who dispersed the population. The ten tribes deported by the Assyrians comprised the greater part of the Hebrew population and became known as the lost tribes of Israel. After centuries of wandering, evidence suggests these ten tribes did arrive in the Promised Land of their forebears, that being northern India. Judah had held out for another 130 years, but in 587 B.C., King Nebuchadnezzar of Babylon overtook Jerusalem and destroyed it. The people of Judah were expelled from the land, with many taken to Babylon. Fifty years later, half the population was permitted to return. However, most departed for the East and were never heard from again.

More evidence suggests an Old Testament connection with Kashmir. In fact, there is some evidence that the Garden of Eden may have been Kashmir. According to the Bible, the place where humanity was created lies to the East (Genesis 2:8). The Bible specifies the geographic location being in the land of four rivers. Genesis 2:10-11 states, "And a river went out of Eden to water the garden: And from there it parted, and became four heads." Scholars considered Mesopotamia to be the location of Eden, but it has only two rivers, the Tigris and Euphrates. Northern India has five great rivers, all tributaries to the Indus, giving the region its name, the Punjab. The flood described in the Vedas lasted forty days, the same as the biblical flood. Abraham was a direct descendant of Noah, chosen by God to survive the flood. Cush (Kush) was a grandson of Noah whose descendants were to populate the world. Kersten suggests that the "Kush" of the Bible could easily be "Kash," as every name in the Bible is subject to phonetic modification. Was this the root of the name Kashmir?

Going back to the ten tribes, reports from Western explorers in the nineteenth century told of their great surprise that all over northwest India were people of Jewish descent. Even some people in Afghanistan claimed to be of Jewish descent, saying their lineage goes back to King Saul of Israel. In the eleventh century, Arab historian Biruni wrote that two centuries earlier, no foreigners were allowed into Kashmir, except Hebrews. Over 30 authors have given evidence that Kashmir's population is of Israelite descent. More than 300 Old Testament names of geographical features of towns, regions, estates, clans, families, and individuals can be matched linguistically with similar names in Kashmir and surroundings.

Many similarities exist between the inhabitants of Kashmir and the Jewish people, but surprisingly, Kashmir's customs differ greatly from the rest of India. Their way of life, behavior, morals, character, clothing, and language all have Jewish overtones. The older Kashmir women wear similar clothing as older Jewish women, and cooking and dances of the Kashmir culture bear Jewish parallels. After childbirth, a Kashmir woman observes 40 days of seclusion, similar to that of the traditional Jewish woman. With this evidence connecting Kashmir and ancient Israel, perhaps this may be the reason for Jesus choosing Kashmir as a final destination.

JESUS AND THE KORAN

Ironically, some scholars of Eastern philosophy claim the truth of Jesus and His teachings are better preserved in Islam than in Christianity. Muhammed tried to protect the original teachings of Jesus against distortion, but his message also became distorted as had Jesus'. The Koran, the Holy Book of Islam, states that Jesus did not die on the cross, but He survived the execution attempt and lived on a peaceful hillside. His survival, they believe, was of a divine nature.

Issa is the name ascribed to Jesus by the Moslems, a name derived from the Syrian name Yeshu. Kersten and others believe the reason that the accounts of the prophet Issa are so extensive (and probably correct) was to correct the distortion made by Jesus' followers. The Muslims believe that Jesus was the last great prophet before Muhammed, who prophesized the coming of the "greatest of all prophets." Jesus was welcomed into the Islamic world as the one preparing the way for Muhammed. Koran 5, 76 even states, "The Messiah, the son of Mary, was a messenger; other messengers had gone before." Muhammed considered himself to be the promised "spirit of truth," and his mission was to reinterpret the teachings of Jesus and rehabilitate the prophet's image after His shameful near-death on the cross.

The Koran describes the mission of Jesus and who He was, "And verily, to Moses we (God) gave the Book and we sent other messengers in his footsteps, and we gave Jesus, the son of man, visible signs, and strengthened him with the spirit of Holiness" (Koran 2, 88). Contrary to Christian theology, the Koran says Jesus was man, not God. "People of the Book, do not transgress the bounds of your religion. Speak nothing but the truth about Allah. Truly the Messiah, Jesus the son of Mary, was only a messenger of God and (a fulfillment of) his word which he sent down to Mary, and a gift of Grace from him. . . . Truly God is one God alone. It is far from his holiness that he should have a son!" (Koran 4, 172). Koran 9: 30-31 affirms this position, "They imitate the infidels of old. God confound them! How they are led astray. They worship their rabbis and their monks as gods beside God, and the Messiah the son of man. And yet they were ordered to serve one God only. There is no God but him. Exalted be he above those whom they deify beside Him." We also need to remember that the angel Gabriel was the source of information that Muhammed received for the Koran. In the *Talmud of Jmmanuel*, as we have seen, Gabriel was said to be the father of Jesus.

Written five centuries after Jesus, the Koran acknowledges a crucifixion without death is possible. Even the Jews questioned if Jesus died on the cross. Jesus did not die on the cross, according to the Koran, and the Jews were deceived. They declared, "We have put to death the Messiah Jesus, the son of Mary, the messenger of God. They did not kill, nor did they crucify him, but he was made to appear (as one crucified) to them. Those that disagreed about him are in doubt about his death: what they knew about it was sheer conjecture. . . . In reality, God lifted him to his presence: He is mighty and wise" (Koran 4:156 - 157). The Koran goes on to tell where Jesus went following the crucifixion. "We made the son of Mary and his mother a sign to mankind and gave them a shelter on a peaceful hillside watered by a fresh spring" (Koran 23, 51). This description probably is referring to a place in Kashmir.

Giving confirmation to the hypothesis that Jesus survived the crucifixion is the Koran, the most sacred book of Islam. If Jesus survived and lived in Kashmir, it would seem logical that the burial site of such a holy person would be known. As we will discover, this site *is* known.

THE TOMB OF JESUS

The historian Sheikh Al-sa'id-us-Sadig tells of two journeys made by Jesus to India and the ending of His life as Yuz Asaf in Kashmir. Sheikh Sadig wrote the text during the tenth century in today's Iran, and it was published in 1883 titled *Ikmal-ud-Din*. Another book, *The Book of Balauhar and Budasaf,* describes how Yuz Asaf died:

> "And he reached Kashmir, which was the farthest region in which he ministered, and there his life came to a close. He left the world and bequeathed his inheritance to a certain disciple called Ababid who had served him: everything he did was perfect. And he admonished him and said to him, 'I have found a worthy shrine and decorated it and brought in lamps for dying. I have gathered together the flock with the true face, which has been scattered and for whom I was sent. And now I shall draw breath in my ascent from the world, freeing

> my soul from my body. Heed the commands that were given to you, and do not stray from the path of truth, but keep firmly to it with gratitude - and may Ababid be the leader. He then bid Ababid to level off the place for him: then he stretched his legs out and lay down: and turning his head to the north and his face to the east, he passed away."

In the middle of Srinagar, Kashmir, lies the tomb of Yuz Asaf, found in the old town Anzimar, in the Khangar quarter. A rectangular building with a small porch was later built around the tomb, called Rozabal. "Rauza" denotes the tomb of a celebrated personality. An inscription above the chamber entrance states, "Yuz Asaf entered the Valley of Kashmir many centuries ago, and that he dedicated his life to manifesting the truth."

Within the building is another burial chamber, that of Islamic Saint Syed Masir-ud-Din, buried in the fifthteenth century. The larger tombstone is that of Yuz Asaf. Both tombstones are surrounded by wooden railing and several strong beams that are covered with a heavy cloth. They are aligned in the north-south direction, according to Islamic custom. Below the building floor are the actual graves located in a crypt. The remains of Yuz Asaf are contained in a sarcophagus, aligned to the east and west in accordance to Hebrew tradition, suggesting that He was not an Islamic saint. Only ascetics were buried in Hindu and Buddhist customs.

Over the centuries, worshipers placed candles around the tombstones of Yuz Asaf. After centuries of accumulation, the wax buildup was removed and a remarkable discovery was made. A pair of footprints was found carved into the stone, identifying the deceased. The relief sculpture clearly shows the scars of crucifixion wounds, demonstrating the left foot had been nailed over the right, a fact confirmed by the blood flow found on the Turin Shroud. Since, crucifixions were unknown in India as a form of capital punishment, the deceased must have been from elsewhere..

Many ancient writings in Kashmir assert that Yuz Asaf and Jesus are the same person. An ancient text describes the burial chamber as the grave of Issa Rooh Allah (Jesus, the spirit of God, the Holy Spirit). People of all denominations, including Muslims,

Buddhists, and Christians, make pilgrimages to the tomb site. Ancient Israelites called the shrine "The Tomb of Hazrat Issa Sahib," meaning "the tomb of Lord Jesus." Documents show the protective building was constructed over the crypt by 112 A.D., and the tomb has been tended by the same family since then, passed down from father to son.

In 1984, an entourage of specialists and journalists led by Holger Kersten was received by the Governor of Abdullah of the state of Jammu. He had given permission for Kersten to open the grave, and arrangements had been made for unsealing and inspecting the tomb chamber. Police protection was to be provided. On the eve of the tomb opening, an outbreak of shooting took place in the old town section of Srinagar resulting in the loss of seven lives. The chief of police urged Kersten not to open the tomb, as he could not guarantee the group's safety. Kersten agreed, and the tomb was not opened. Since 1989, tourist travel to Kashmir has been forbidden. In old town, where the tomb is located, the area has become the center for underground fighting, not a safe place to be. Also, because the tomb is located next to the Jhelum River, which often floods, Kersten remains unsure of the condition of the tomb's contents.

We now have evidence suggesting how Jesus may have survived the crucifixion, His journey to Kashmir, and His life in Kashmir. As both Kashmir tradition and the *Talmud of Jmmanuel* claim, Jesus was married and raised a family. A number of people in Srinagar believe they are descendants of Yuz Asaf. As we shall see, it does appear that Jesus left a genetic legacy.

Chapter Eleven

THE CODED GOSPELS

A Human Jesus

Scholars have been puzzled and disappointed about the lack of historical information regarding Jesus, knowing that during the first century Jewish Revolt in Jerusalem, the Romans destroyed most records concerning the Davidic legacy of Jesus, i.e. Jesus' ancestry from King David and his heirs. The Romans were unable to destroy all relevant documents, as Jesus' heirs brought important records of the Messianic heritage from the Near East to the West. Some investigators have recently discovered that the actual history of Jesus lies within the gospels themselves, written in a coded format that contains an underlying meaning. Leading the research in this field is Dr. Barbara Thiering, a theologian and former faculty member at the University of Sydney in Australia. Much of her research has been published in academic journals and in several books, including *Jesus and the Riddle of the Dead Sea Scrolls: Unlocking the Secrets of His Life Story.*

Thiering's specialty is the Dead Sea Scrolls where she found the scribes wrote using "peshers," a technique used in the time of the Old Testament. A pesher is like a solution to a puzzle providing clues that do not make sense. Those knowing the technique and possessing the necessary knowledge can solve the puzzle. Two levels of meaning were found in the Dead Sea Scroll writings. Contained in the surface material is general religious and historical matter suitable for the ordinary reader. Beneath the surface is information available to only those with special knowledge. The surface meaning, however, remained valid, not negated by other meanings. She found the words of peshers always had the same coded meaning. When Thiering analyzed the gospels, she discovered the same thing; they were written in peshers similar to the Dead Sea Scrolls.

Thiering discovered the gospels yielded a closely detailed, factual history of Jesus that is not apparent at first sight. In studying the gospels, she found a technique of interpretation similar to that used with the Dead Sea Scrolls. What she found is that the gospels serve as a parable, telling one story on the surface but with a hidden meaning beneath. By applying this technique to the actual history of Jesus found in the gospels, a whole different understanding of the life of Jesus is found, deliberately put there. Thiering claims anyone working on the gospels using these rigorous logical methods will arrive at the same conclusion.

The pesher system works like the following example. A scroll writer would take an Old Testament book such as the minor prophet Habakkuk, which deals with events in 600 B.C. when the armies of Babylonians were marching toward Judea, creating fear and panic. The scroll writer goes through the event verse by verse, explaining that it is really an event in our own time. Certain words are coded. For example, the word for Babylonian was *"kittim,"* whose hidden meaning is "Roman." So anytime Babylonia was mentioned, it actually meant Rome. In the New Testament, the pesher Jesus is defined as the "Word of God." John 1:1,14 states, "In the beginning was the Word, and Word was with God . . . And the Word was made flesh, and dwelt among us, and we beheld his glory . . ."

Peshers were also used in Acts, whose author is believed to have written the Gospel of Luke. "The apostles which were in Jerusalem heard that Samaria had received the Word of God" (Acts 8:14). One understands that Jesus was in Samaria.

Often, cryptic gospel information is introduced by the statement, "For those with ears to hear," meaning there is hidden meaning for those who know the codes. Occasionally, coded names and titles may be complex and obscure, and often straightforward, but rarely obvious. Rules of the code are fixed, and the symbolism remains constant.

Thiering believes that a group of scribes who wanted to address those with "ears to hear" wrote a scripture in the form of peshers, allowing those with special knowledge to solve the puzzle. Her hypothesis was capable of being tested. The pesher technique offers an entirely new insight into the miracles, seen as part of the surface story concealing something else. When this hypothesis is fully revealed, claims Thiering, it will be the most valuable source of the historical Jesus.

Thiering cites the pesher about Jesus turning water into wine, which can be explained to those with "ears to hear." According to the Dead Sea scrolls, there were two steps of initiation into the Essene community in Qumran where the scrolls were discovered, marked by water and wine. Members of any class could be given a form of preliminary membership through baptism by water. Only those who intended to enter the full monastic life, requiring two additional years of training, could receive the "drink of the community," meaning wine. Only celibates were allowed to participate in the wine, and those left at the water level (baptism only), were considered unclean people. These included married men, Gentiles, women, and the physically handicapped. When Jesus "turned water into wine," the pesher meant that He broke with tradition by allowing non-celibate people to receive communion. From that moment on, all adult followers of Jesus could receive communion, whether they were married, women, or handicapped. All were equal in the eyes of God.

Another pesher is found when Jesus fed the crowd of 5,000 with 12 loaves of bread, a story found in all four gospels. The pesher symbolized that ordinary men could be ministers. According to Jewish custom, only those born into the tribe of Levi could be priests. The "loaves" represent the Levites, who distributed the 12 loaves of the Presence from the holy table. Ordinary men were given Levitical powers by "eating" the loaves, and now could distribute the communion bread as did the priests. The application of the pesher technique to the gospels and Acts gives a whole different history of Jesus and of the community preceding Him and of the community from which the followers broke away.

As we will see, the hidden meaning in the gospels is quite heretical. It helps explain the virgin birth, tells of Jesus' two marriages, names His children, and confirms that He survived the crucifixion. Additionally, many circumstances involving the *Talmud of Jmmanuel* are clarified: Judas Iscariot being a scribe, the location of the burial tomb, and Jesus' son. This chapter is based mainly on the research of Barbara Thiering, and some information is based on the writings of Laurence Gardner, who wrote

Bloodline of the Holy Grail: The Hidden Lineage of Jesus Revealed. Gardner, the Prior of the Celtic Church Sacred Kindred of St. Columbia, is an internationally known sovereign and chivalric genealogist. As we will see, Jesus' lineage can be traced to our current era. To understand the biblical peshers, we first need to discover who the people of Qumran were.

THE QUMRAN COMMUNITY

In 1947, the most important discovery in modern Christian history was made at Qumran, lying just west of the Dead Sea. Several Bedouin boys in search of their wandering sheep discovered a cave overlooking the ruins of Qumran. Inside the cave were jars containing scrolls, the first of the Dead Sea Scrolls. The scrolls eventually made their way to an antiquity dealer in Bethlehem, and from there they arrived in the hands of scholars. During the following years, additional scrolls were discovered in ten nearby caves.

Many scrolls were biblical, but some were not, and were entirely new, undiscovered works. Dozens of the scrolls and fragments of hundreds more were written about the time of Christianity's origin. Titles of some scrolls were missing, but scholars titled them according to their content: "Manuel of Discipline" (Community Rule), "The War of Sons of Light and Sons of Darkness," and "Hymns of Thanksgiving." Many scholars consider the "Temple Scroll" the greatest of all, originally found in cave 11. It is the longest of the scrolls, measuring nine meters long. Written at the same time as the other scrolls, it claims to have originated from the time of Moses. The scroll contains the description of a temple as dictated by God Himself on Mt. Sinai.

A historical overview shows the buildings of the Qumran plateau were occupied between 140 B.C. and 68 A.D., except for a period following a 31 B.C. earthquake when the inhabitants moved to Jerusalem. Following their expulsion from Jerusalem in the second century B.C., Palestinian Essenes settled at Qumran. Scholars concur that the scrolls were written during this period and the era of Christian origins.

Researchers found the scroll writings to be very similar to those of the early followers of Jesus. Both the Qumran sect and early Christians lived in the immediate, small area about the same time and shared similar customs. Each group met daily for a sacred meal of bread and wine, allowing only initiates to participate. Both groups shared property, valued celibacy, and used the ritual of baptism and initiation. They each referred to themselves as "the way," "the covenant," and "sons of light." Each had a branch in Damascus, and both were governed by a bishop. They both expected a New Jerusalem and had identical architectural plans of the city. The city was a square with each of the four city walls having three gates, with each gate representing one of the 12 tribes of Israel. Many other similarities also existed between their respective writings. Scholars have concluded the Qumran sect was most likely Essene. Even before the discovery of the Dead Sea Scrolls, biblical scholars were observing that early Christianity and the Essenes were related.

Writings of the Temple Scroll told about the exclusiveness of those who could not be in the presence of God. The Qumran sect excluded men who had nocturnal emissions, men who had recent sexual intercourse, menstruating women, lepers, and the blind. In contrast, Jesus welcomed all these shunned people into His fold. Some scholars speculate the Qumran community represented the blueprint from which Christianity emerged, a split by Christians who opposed the discriminatory Qumran practice as mentioned. The Qumran sect was making preparations for two Messiahs, one from the Davidic lineage and a priestly Messiah from the lineage of Aaron.

Thiering and other researchers found similarities between life patterns of two key people in the scrolls and two key figures of the gospels. The two scroll characters were always called by several different pseudonyms, and the principal scroll figure was most often called the Teacher of Righteousness. Many of this teacher's followers had deserted him to follow another teacher. The rival had many of the same beliefs and ideas of the Teacher of Righteousness, but he was much less strict about the law. His followers were called "seekers after smooth things." In contrast to the Righteous Teacher, the rival had chosen a more relaxed way of life and less the ascetic discipline. This rival teacher became known as the "Wicked Priest." It is around these two figures, the Teacher of Righteousness and Wicked Priest, that the relationship between Qumran doctrine and Christianity revolves.

As mentioned earlier, the scroll scribes used Babylon as a code name for Rome, and the Righteous Teacher was dated from the time of a Roman oppression of the Jews. Thiering places this oppression in 6 A.D., at a time when the native kings were removed and replaced by direct rule of Roman procurators. The required census of property led to an armed uprising by the Zealots. The Teacher of Righteousness came 20 years after the oppression, the exact year being 26 A.D. About that time, in 29 A.D., Jesus began his ministry, the fifteenth year of Tiberius Caesar; The Righteous Teacher would have been a contemporary.

Thiering believes the Teacher of Righteousness was not the founder of the Essenes but was connected with a group that the Jewish historian Josephus did not regard as Essene. She believes the Teacher of Righteousness was John the Baptist, and the heretic rival, the Wicked Priest, was Jesus. In the writings, the Wicked Priest did almost everything that Jesus was accused of by His enemies.

We now need to set the political climate. Forty years before the Christian era, an ambitious and talented new king named Herod came to the Jewish people. He was not Jewish, but a mixture of Semitic races, who later converted to a version of Judaism that suited him. Herod proceeded to impose a non-fundamentalist belief upon the world. At that time Judea was a poor, small country, but in contrast, there were thousands of well-off Jews living outside the homeland in Babylon, Alexandria, and Rome. The Jewish world outside Judea was known as the Diaspora, where many wealthy Jews lived — those who had no desire to live in Judea, even though Judea was the place where God once dwelt and was the location of His temple in Jerusalem.

Herod, whose reign lasted from 37 B.C. to 4 B.C., had gained the trust of the Romans by protecting the Roman interests to the east. His passion was to make Jerusalem and Judea into a glorious land. He rebuilt the temple, restored Jerusalem, and built a summer palace on the barren cliffs of Masada, overlooking the Dead Sea.

Around Herod's time, a man of considerable stature appeared on the scene. He was called Hillel the Great and came from the Babylonian Diaspora. Hillel taught a personal and ethical renewal, expressed through baptism and water. Those baptized had become true Jews. He introduced the idea of a new covenant, the renewal of obedience to the law of Moses. Another was Menahem, a Diaspora Essene, who founded the Magians, and whose name reflected the Babylonian culture. Menahem and his order became the advisor to Herod and prophesied that Herod would become king. It was a prophecy that came true, and from that time on Herod greatly honored the Essenes.

Essene leaders assumed the names of patriarchs and angels, portraying examples of peshers. Menahem and his successors became "Isaac" of the New Israel. Hillel was known as "Abraham the Father," a term that became the Pope. "Isaac" was the patriarch of Babylon and the East. Under his direction, Jewish missionaries went out to the Diaspora, recruiting both Jews and Gentiles who needed to be circumcised.

Herod's scheme of initiation into a new form of Judaism was very successful, as Jews everywhere were joining this worldwide society. Wealthy Diaspora had no objection to paying for membership in this great society. Missionaries told them that by contributing money, God was pleased and their souls would be saved at the Last Judgement. Their contributions would free them from sin, but they had to make annual contributions. The goal was to recruit 600,000 members to form a New Israel, a project of evangelism lasting 40 years. Missionaries would take one year to recruit 100 people, and then spend three years preparing them for initiation. This money from the Jews allowed Herod to rebuild the temple and restore Jerusalem. Seventy years later, Jesus came onto the scene and objected to selling religion with the promise of salvation. He overturned the moneychanger's tables in the temple, and from that time on, there were no initiation fees but only freewill gifts.

Around 21 B.C., when Herod announced that he was going to rebuild the temple, the Essenes wrote the Temple Scroll. They gave their proposal to Herod, who did not want the conservative Essene culture to return to Jerusalem. After their rejection, the Essenes began to withdraw from Herod saying that God's plan did not include Herod as king. The Essene's plan was to restore the Davidic line to power plus the high priests of the Zadok lineage. Many Jews believed that the only true king could be from Davidic lineage. Herod agreed that a David could have power in his empire, but only in a subordinate role. He said the center of power would be in Jerusalem, but David could be a patriarch in the West, which included Rome.

The descendant of David who was willing to cooperate with Herod's plan was a man named Heli. Two generations later, he would be the grandfather of Jesus. A triarchy was modeled after the Roman triumvirate: "Abraham" would be centrally placed under Herod; "Isaac" would be in the East; the patriarch "Jacob" would head Rome and the West. Heli was given the name "Jacob," his title as patriarch. The government of the potential new kingdom was now in place. To make decisions, they met at a council table, similar to an initiate's meeting for the sacred Essene meal. The New Israel would fulfill the pattern of the old, but Judaism would be renewed by adapting to the contemporary world.

Overlooking the Dead Sea in the wilderness of Judea lies Qumran, the place of exile for the Essenes. The Essene fathers longed for the return of the great days of Israel when David ruled, and the Zadok High Priest was in the temple. Monastic members of the Qumran sect were supported by ordinary men who tithed ten percent of their income. Members of the Qumran order were required to turn over all their assets to the community after two years of training.

Important to the pesher scenario regarding Jesus, the Essenes believed they were establishing their own "temple" and "Jerusalem" at Qumran. They began to call it "Jerusalem" and the "New Jerusalem." These two forms of the name helped provide a veil of secrecy. Council meetings were held at Qumran, as this was the seat of the Essene community and its outposts.

In the peshers, outlying areas of Qumran were given names that corresponded to geographical names of Palestine. For example, when the bishop of Galilee was at Ain-Feshka on the Dead Sea, the Dead Sea was called "Galilee" by the scribes. Boat trips, according to Thiering, were taken by Jesus and the disciples on the Dead Sea, not on Lake Galilee. The gospels are vague and inconsistent about locations, yet they give exact distances where they do not seem to be needed. For example, the Gospel of John states that Bethany was 15 stadia from Jerusalem. Ain-Feshka, a place where expelled monks went for uncleanliness, as did celibates of the Diaspora, is exactly this distance from Qumran. The Essenes reproduced the original Bethany at Ain-Feshka, the same distance east of Jerusalem, when they moved to Qumran.

Khirbet Mird of Hyrcania was part of the Qumran complex, located five and one-half miles inland. The gospel pesher shows the site of Mird corresponds to the Gospel's wilderness, where John the Baptist did his baptism. "Wilderness," in Greek, means the place where individual ascetics (hermits) practiced their discipline.

The Gospel of Mark tells of Jesus going by boat to Gerasa, the place where the head of the order came for the meeting, and when He stepped out of the boat, He was there. Archaeology has located the ruins of Gerasa 36 miles inland from Lake Galilee. According to the pesher, Jesus was traveling on the Dead Sea and arrived at Ain-Feshka on the seashore.

We now have an idea how the peshers work. Thiering's research suggests geographical locations mentioned in the gospels may be metaphors for locations around Qumran. By knowing the meaning that underlies the pesher, we can get an idea what the scribes intended on a deeper level. Thiering's book does not go into detail about every pesher underlying the gospels, but she does summarize the story as interpreted from each pesher.

THE BIRTH OF JESUS

Only two of the four gospels discuss the virgin birth, leaving many questions unanswered. Paul states very clearly that Jesus was from the seed of David. Jacob Heli was now using the title David, and after him, his son Joseph used the title. When Joseph had a son, he became the successor to the Jewish throne of David. In March of 7 B.C., Jesus was born to Joseph and Mary, in a situation of ambiguity that would affect Jesus' whole life.

Celibacy was the highest way of life for the Essenes. They considered marriage and sex unholy, and even the Dead Sea Scrolls claimed that the Essenes disdained marriage. Anyone who had sexual intercourse was excluded from the temple precincts for three days. Scholars believe their young members were acquired from the ranks of abandoned and illegitimate children. For some Essenes, it was important to continue their family lines. This was true for family members of the great dynasties, such as the Zadoks and Davids, who had been the high priests of the temple and kings of Israel during the sixth century.

The Essenes practiced sex only for the purpose of having children. Mostly they lived apart from their wives, like monks in a monastery. When rules required they continue their family line, they left the monastery and prepared for marriage. For those who were to marry, a long, betrothal period of several years was required. This was followed by a marriage ceremony, which permitted them to have sex. A trial marriage lasted up to three years, unless the woman became pregnant.

When conception occurred, they waited until the pregnancy advanced to three months, and then she and her partner had a second marriage. This ceremony made the marriage permanent, as divorce was forbidden. After the second wedding, there was no sex and the husband would separate from her and return to his celibate life. For most of the marriage, the woman had to live apart from her husband.

In an Essene marriage, the woman was a virgin before her first wedding. This meant she was a member of an institution or order, much like a nun. If it happened that during the betrothal period and before her first wedding, the passion became too strong and a child was conceived, then it could be said "a virgin had conceived." This happened with Mary. She was a virgin (nun) betrothed to Joseph when she conceived before the first wedding took place. In other words, Mary the virgin conceived. The rules of the dynastic wedlock were compromised, and the birth was to be at the wrong time of year.

This created a dilemma for Joseph. If it were a boy, his son would be a descendant of King David. Joseph was advised by the angel Gabriel, the name taken by the second in command of the Qumran community. All angels in the story are men, and it was believed that priests and Levites were the incarnations of heavenly beings, gods (Elohim), and angels. Joseph was advised that he should recognize the child and proceed with the first wedding, as if it were the second marriage when the woman was traditionally pregnant. Joseph followed the instructions. The story tells that Mary conceived by the Holy Spirit. Joseph was considered a Holy Spirit by the Essenes because lower priests, kings, and princes were spirits.

This raised the question at the time whether Jesus was legitimately conceived. A conservative point of view would classify Him as an extra-nuptial child of Joseph. The Pharisees called Jesus the "man of a lie," referring to His heretical teaching as well as His illegitimacy. From a liberal viewpoint, Jesus was legitimate as He was conceived following a ceremony in June of 8 B.C., at which time Mary and Joseph were bound in betrothal.

In Essene custom, a series of ceremonies solemnified the

marriage, but sex was postponed for as long as possible. The final stage of betrothal occurred in June, and the first wedding was to be in September. In December, sex was permitted. The purpose of conceiving a son in December was to have him born in September, during the holy season. Although Jesus' conception and birth broke the Essene's tradition, supporters of Jesus said He was the true heir, but the controversy surrounding His birth pursued Him for His whole life.

According to Thiering and the peshers, Jesus' symbolic birth occured one kilometer south of the Qumran plateau, and His literal birth occurred in Bethlehem. His birth was officially classified as illegitimate. Before the earthquake of 31 B.C., while Qumran was still a monastery, there was a place where the illegitimate children were brought, destined for a future of monastic life. It was at Mird, a 16-hour walk from Jerusalem lying to the southeast. The "Temple Scroll" describes the building location lying south of Qumran, and it was called the "Queen's House." As the queen, the wife of the potential King David, she was the superior over the indigent women. In the monastic phase of Qumran, the building was known as the manger, which was a reproduction of a certain building near Jerusalem, located five stadia across the city on the Mount of Olives. Thiering says the manger symbolized Bethlehem. Following the earthquake, the manger at Qumran became the symbolic "Bethlehem of Judea."

The historian Josephus includes a passage about an account in the book of Acts. The event implies that the manger was the place where the coronation procession of the Davids began. For the coronation, the inductees rode on Solomon's mule, the process following an ancient ritual. A ceremonial donkey would be stabled on the Mount of Olives, making it the manger. When the heirs to the David and priests were expelled from Jerusalem to Qumran, a corresponding building was needed. It was placed five stadia to the south, and from this location Jesus rode the donkey in triumph into the Essene Jerusalem. When David was crowned, He was born as the adopted son of God.

Throughout Jesus' life, His legitimacy was determined according to which high priest held power. If the priest was a member of the conservative Boethus or related Caiaphus family, Jesus could not succeed, and His brother James became the true heir when he was born in September, 1 A.D. and because he was legitimate. The

Magians and Diaspora Essenes, who were more liberal and accepted Jesus' legitimacy, wanted to protect Him. They were "seekers after smooth things."

The peshers give a whole new light on the birth of Jesus. His brother James now becomes a more important figure if this is true. As we will see according to the peshers, Jesus' relationship with Mary Magdalene is much different than the gospels lead us to believe.

JESUS AND MARY MAGDALENE

Was Jesus ever married? The gospel writings contain specific passages that subtly suggest the marital status of Jesus. Thiering claims the gospel peshers definitely suggest that Jesus was married and that He had children. Dynastic regulation made it clear that the heir to the Davidic line was obliged by law to marry, and that he was required to have two sons. Marriage was mandatory to continue the hereditary House of David. Religious parameters dictated a celibate lifestyle, except for the procreation of children at regular intervals. As we will see, evidence in scripture and the Gnostic writings suggest that Mary Magdalene was the wife of Jesus.

The Gospel of Philip states, "There were three who always walked with the Lord: Mary his mother, and her sister, and Magdalene, the one who was called his companion. His sister and his mother and his companion were each a Mary." A later passage says, "And the companion of the (Savior was) Mary Magdalene. He loved her more than all the disciples (and used to) kiss her often on her (mouth). The rest of the disciples were offended and said to him, 'Why do you love her more than all of us?' The Savior answered and said to them, 'Why do I not love you like her? When a blind man and one who sees are both in the dark, they are no different from one another. When the light comes, then he who sees will see the light, and he who is blind will remain in darkness.'"

Other gospels tell of Jesus' marriage in a subtle way. Mary of Bethany anointed Jesus' head at Simon's house (Matt 26:6,7 and Mark 14:3), and she also anointed His feet, wiping them off afterwards with her hair. Thiering dates this in March of 33 A.D. Two and one-half years earlier (September of 30 A.D.) she had performed this same foot anointing ritual three months after the Cana wedding feast. On both occasions the anointing was performed when Jesus was seated at the table. These scriptural passages are an allusion to the ancient rite by which a royal bride prepared her bridegroom's table. Mary of Bethany anointed Jesus with spikenard, a very expensive and sacred ointment. To perform the rite with spikenard was the express privilege of a Messianic bride. The anointment was performed solely at the first and second marriage ceremonies. Only as the wife of Jesus could Mary have anointed both His head and feet with the sacred ointment.

Wives of the Zadok and Davidic male lines held the ranks of Elisheba (Elizabeth) and Miriam (Mary), respectively. This explains why the mother of John the Baptist was called Elizabeth, and Jesus' mother was Mary. In compliance, Jesus' own wife would have been a Mary. Mary underwent the ceremony of the second marriage only when she was three months pregnant. This would have occurred at the second anointing. At this time the bride ceased being an *almah* (virgin) and became a designated mother.

Sexual relations were permitted only in December, and husbands and wives lived apart the remainder of the year. During the period of separation, the wife was classified as a widow and was required to weep for her husband. This tradition is described in Luke 7:38 when Mary of Bethany, at the first anointment, is said to have "stood at his feet behind him weeping and began to wash his feet with tears." During the long periods of separation, the wife was given the designation of sister.

Who was Mary of Bethany? She was Sister Miriam Magdala, better known as Mary Magdalene. Gregory I, Bishop of Rome (590 - 604) and St. Bernard, the Cisterian Abbot of Clairvaus (1090 - 1153) both confirmed that Mary of Bethany was synonymous with Mary Magdalene.

Some scholars now believe the gospel wedding at Cana was in fact the wedding of Jesus. The wedding custom at that time was to have a formal host who was in full charge of the wedding feast. Authority to make decisions about the wedding rested with the bridegroom and his mother. Passages in John suggest that Jesus and His mother were in charge of Jesus' wedding. In John 2:5, Jesus' mother said to the servants, "Whatsoever he saith unto you, do it." No invited guests would have the right to give such commands, suggesting Jesus and the bridegroom were the same. This betrothal communion would have taken place in June of 30 A.D., three months before Mary first anointed Jesus' feet at Simon's house in September of 30 A.D. Only as Jesus' bride would Mary have been permitted to perform the anointment, according to Messianic custom.

No mention of Jesus' marital status is found in the New Testament, as it was deliberately removed by Church decree, writes Laurence Gardner. In 1958, an ancient manuscript was found at Mar Saba, a monastery east of Jerusalem. Within the book was found a transcription of a letter by Bishop Clement of Alexandria (150 - 215), who addressed his colleague, Theodore. Also found was an unknown section from the Gospel of Mark. Clement ordered part of the content of Mark to be suppressed because it did not conform with Church doctrine. "To them one must never give way nor when they put forward their falsifications shall one concede that the secret gospel is by Mark but shall deny it on oath. For not all true things are to be said to all men." Included in the removed portion of the gospel is an account of the raising of Lazarus. It tells of Lazarus (Simon Magus) calling to Jesus before the stone was rolled back. He was not dead in the physical sense, but was actually undergoing an initiation.

The relevance of the Lazarus incident is that it was part of the sequence of events when Mary Magdalene anointed Jesus at Bethany. John 11:20-29 describes what happened when Jesus arrived at Simon's home: "Then Margaret, as soon as she heard that Jesus was coming, went and met him: but Mary sat still in the house . . . (Martha) called Mary her sister secretly saying, 'The master is come, and calleth for thee.'. . As soon as she heard that, she arose quickly and came unto him."

The incident is described in greater detail in the portion of Mark that was suppressed by the Church. The Gospel of Mark explains that Mary did actually come out of the house on the first occasion. However, the disciples chastised her and sent her back inside to await the Master's instruction. As Jesus' wife, she was bound by a strict code of bridal practice. The custom said that she was not permitted to leave the house and greet her husband until she had received his permission. The account in John leaves Mary in her proper place without explanation, but Mark's text was held back from publication.

The suppression of the Lazarus story is why the accounts of anointing in the Gospels of Mark and Matthew are found at the house of Simon the Leper. In John this happens at Lazarus' house. As we will see, Lazarus was Simon Zelotes or Simon Magus who was unclean because he had been excommunicated. The term "leper" applied to those who were unclean, and this is why he was called Simon the Leper.

In September of 30 A.D., the date of the first wedding, Jesus was 36-1/2 years old. Jesus was observing His role as the accepted David ruler. The date of the second marriage was in March of 33 A.D., just prior to the crucifixion, at the time of the second anointing. The rules allowed a three-year trial marriage, and in December of 32 A.D., Mary conceived when sexual activity was permitted. The second marriage would be the permanent marriage, as a son would be born in September of 33 A.D., the proper season for a future king. Thiering says the pesher in the Book of Acts contradicts this by implying Mary gave birth to a daughter.

Who was Mary Magdalene? Mary's father was the chief priest, Syrus the Jairus, who officiated at the great marble synagogue at Capernaum. This was a heredity position from the time of King David restricted to the lineage of Jair (Numbers 32:41). Mary is first mentioned in the New Testament as Jairus' daughter, who was raised from death in 17 A.D., according to the pesher story. This was an initiatory raising that took place when females became the age of 14, meaning Mary was born in 3 A.D.

Prior to her marriage, Mary was under the authority of the Chief Scribe, who was Judas Iscariot. Judas was known as the Demon Priest Number Seven. The seven demon priests were established in formal opposition to the seven light priests of the Menorah. Judas Iscariot was the "demon," a name for him as a member of the Zealot party (the great real dragon with seven heads and ten horns). As Chief Scribe, Judas held the position once held by Gabriel, which included authority and supervision over celibate women before and after marriage. The New Testament calls Mary the woman "from whom seven demons had gone out." This means she was under the authority of the demon priest like the crippled women, or widows. Upon her marriage, Mary was released from the arrangement with Judas Iscariot. This is what the Bible means by "the seven demons went out of her." She was now permitted sexual activity on the regulated basis mentioned earlier.

At the age of 27, Mary was older than traditional marriagable age. Thiering raises the possibility that Mary may have been married previously, resulting in a crisis, which included the question of a valid marriage according to Essene law. Judas Iscariot, who objected at the second wedding, believed it was not valid (Mark 14:4-9, John 12:2-8). Perhaps there had been a previous marriage and a separation. Jesus' marriage was required to fulfill the rule of the dynastic order.

Mary underwent long periods of marital separation from her husband, Jesus. During these periods she was not ranked as wife, but as a sister (in a devotional sense). In her role as a sister, Mary was attached to the father, Simon Zelotes (Lazarus). In the Essene community, sisters held the same status as widows (crippled women).

Mary's and Jesus' daughter was born in September of 33 A.D. and named Tama. After her birth, Jesus remained in seclusion for three years before He emerged again in September of 36 A.D. Thiering suggests Jesus may have been involved in writing the fourth gospel, which the peshers show was written before 37 A.D. when a breach with Simon Magus (Lazarus) took place. This was the first attempt to try the two-level pesher technique, a plan to give the true history and true facts about the resurrection. Jesus may have recognized the true value of a mystery, suggests Thiering.

In September of 36 A.D., Jesus left the secluded life to join Mary, who had conceived another child. In June of 37 A.D., "the word of God increased," a phrase found in Acts 6:7, meaning according to the Pesher theory, the lineage of Jesus had continued. Her son was also called Jesus and was given the title Justus the Righteous One, a title born by James as Crown Prince. (Jesus Justus was later with Paul in Rome when Paul wrote the letters to Colossians, which included greetings from Jesus Justus.)

Jonathan Annas, also known as Stephan, became the High Priest. He changed the official status of Jesus, declaring Him the legitimate heir of David. This new status meant that He had to be associated with Agrypa, who preserved the long standing alliance between the Herod kings and Jesus' family. On Peter's advice, Jesus accepted the new Herod. Annas lost no time in announcing the status change that he and Jesus had prepared, allowing full privilege to uncircumcised Gentiles. Jesus then returned to celibate life following the birth of His son.

In June of 43 A.D., Jesus again reemerged into the world, and Mary again conceived. A second son was born in March of 44 A.D., when once again "the word of God increased" (Acts 12:24), and his name was Joseph. Following the birth of Jesus' second son, Mary Magdalene decided to leave her husband. Having fulfilled the dynastic obligation to father two sons, Jesus was released from restrictions and could again lead an unmarried life. Thiering implies a divorce took place between Jesus and Mary, followed by a second marriage for Jesus in March of 50 A.D., insinuated by a pesher statement in Acts, "the Lord opened the heart" (of Lydia, the woman who appeared in Philippi). The date was six years after the birth of His son in March of 44 A.D. The phrase "open the heart" (Acts 16:14) also suggests that Lydia was a virgin, according to the pesher.

Jesus' second marriage opened a further issue among the followers of Jesus—whether the marriage with Mary Magdalene was legal, since it appeared that Mary had been previously married. If her first divorce was not accepted, then her years with Jesus would not have been a legal marriage, and Jesus would be free to marry again.

This second marriage to Lydia was strongly criticized by the Eastern opponents of Christianity. The Book of Acts tells of Paul going to Philippi (in Macedonia) where he encountered Lydia, a "seller of purple" from Thyatira, a city in west Asia Minor and a center for Hellenistic women's order, where she was a female bishop. Thiering claims that the peshers tell of Jesus traveling with Paul around the region, and evidence suggests that Paul knew Jesus had survived the crucifixion and had become quite close to Him. Paul was of the view that Jesus was permitted to divorce and that Jesus' marriage to Mary had been legal. In fact, polygamy was usual among Jews at that time. It is under the Greek ascetic influence that Essenes introduced their strict laws of marriage. Christians were caught between normal Jewish practices and the extreme conservatism of the Essenes.

Mary was 41 years old when she gave birth to Joseph, the second son, in 44 A.D., the birth taking place in Provence (Gaul) where she had immigrated. In Revelations 12:1-17, John tells of Mary's persecution and of her flight into exile, and of the Roman harassment of the "remnant of her seed,"

> "And she being with child cried, travailing in birth, and pained to be delivered.
> And she brought forth a man child.
> And the woman fled into the wilderness, where she hath a place prepared of God.
> And when the dragon saw that he was cast unto the earth, he persecuted the woman which brought forth the man child. . .
> And the dragon was worth with the woman, and went to make war with the remnant of her seed, which keep the commandments of God, and have the testimony of Jesus Christ."

Others had joined Mary in the exile to Gaul, including Martha, and her maid, Marcella. There was also Philip, the apostle, Mary Jacob (the wife of Cleophus) and Mary Salome (Helena). They sailed across the Mediterranean and disembarked at Ratis in Provence, later to become known as Les Saintes Maries de la Mer in southern France. The Gnostics believed she fled into exile bearing the child of Jesus.

Jacobeus de Voragine in 1483 wrote in his famous text *Legenda Aurea* about St. Martha of Bethany, who was a hostess to Jesus Christ, having been born into a royal family. Her father's name was Syro, who was from Syria, and her mother's name, Eucahia. Together with her sister Mary Magdalene, they inherited from their mother three properties, including the castle Magdalene, Bethany, and a part of Jerusalem. After the "ascension" of Jesus and after the disciples departed, Martha, her brother Lazarus, her sister Mary, and St. Maxim all embarked on a ship and arrived safely in present day Marseilles. They proceeded to the region of Aix where they converted the local inhabitants to the faith.

The name Magdalene (or Magdala) is derived from the Hebrew noun Migdal meaning "tower." Mary and Martha had inherited the community's castle/tower of guardianship.

Several early books shed more light on Mary's life. *The Life of Mary Magdalene* written by Raban Maar (776 - 856), Archbishop of Mayence, relates many traditions about Mary. A copy of the manuscript was found at Oxford University in the early 1400's. The book inspired the foundation of the Magdalene College there in 1848. Another book, *Saint Mary*

Magdalene, written by the Dominican Friar Pere Lacardaire, states that Mary's mother, Eucharia, was related to the royal House of Israel. Louis XI of France, who ruled from 1461 - 1483, used this evidence to insist on Mary's dynastic position in the royal lineage of France.

As a result of Mary's presence in France, cults and shrines later evolved around Mary. The most active Magdalene cult was based at Rennes-le-Chateau in the Languedoc region. Many shrines in France have been established to honor Ste. Marie de Madeleine. Included is her burial place at St. Maximus, where her sepulcher and alabaster tomb have been guarded by Cassiante monks since the early 400's.

The church at Rennes-le-Chateau was consecrated to Mary Magdalene in 1059, and in 1096 the great Basilica of St. Mary Magdalene began at Vezelag. It was here that St. Francis of Assisi founded the Franciscan Friars Minor in 1217. The Cistecians, Dominicans, Franciscans, and other monastic orders followed a lifestyle differing from the Roman Church hierarchy, all sharing a common interest in Mary Magdalene. When St. Bernard drafted the constitution for the Order of Knights Templar, he mentioned a requirement for the obedience of Bethany, the castle of Mary and Martha.

Early Christian texts tell of Mary being the "woman who knew all," as she was the one to whom "Christ loved more than the disciples." Mary was considered an apostle endowed with knowledge, vision, and insight that far exceeded Peter's. She was the beloved bride who anointed Jesus at the sacred marriage in Bethany. The Gnostic tradition believed that Mary Magdalene was associated with wisdom, the Sophia energy. The female gnosis of Sophia was considered the Holy Spirit, represented by Mary.

The early Church disregarded all this knowledge about Mary Magdalene and discredited her; instead they exalted the mother of Jesus. Ambiguous passages in the gospels describe an unmarried Magdalene as a sinner (this actually meant that Mary was a celibate *almah* undergoing a trial betrothal, according to the peshers). The Church fathers decided that a sinful woman must be a whore, thus discrediting her.

In competition with the early Church was the universal goddess, who had many names such as Cyble, Diana, Demeter,

Juno, and Isis. It was Isis who inspired the Black Madonna, represented by 450 pieces of sacred art discovered worldwide. The Black Madonna presented a dilemma for the Church, especially those icons found in European cathedrals and shrines. It represented the strength and equality of womanhood and represented Mary Magdalene, who, according to Alexandrian doctrine "transmitted the true secret of Jesus." The long standing Magdalene cult had been associated with Black Madonna locations. She is black because wisdom (Sophia) is considered black, having existed in the darkness of chaos before creation. Sophia was considered to have been incarnated in the Queen Mary Magdalene as the Holy Spirit, as she bore the ultimate observance of the faith. The Gnostic Gospel of Philip regarded Mary Magdalene as "the symbol of divine wisdom." Gnostics believed the Holy Spirit was essentially the female element that bound the Father to the Son.

As Laurence Gardner puts it, Mary Magdalene as wife of Jesus was not only the Messianic Queen, but the mother of the true heirs. However, centuries after her death, Mary's legacy remained a great threat to a fearful Church that bypassed Messianic descent in favor of apostolic succession.

Mary died in 63 A.D. at the age of 60 in Aix-en-Provence. Today Mary Magdalene's remains are preserved at the Abbey of St. Maximus. In 1279, Charles II of Sicily, Count of Provence, disinterred Mary's skull and upper arm bone to have them set in a gold and silver display case, where they remain today. Some of Mary's other bones and ashes were kept in an urn that was vandalized during the French Revolution. Mary's cave of "solitude" is found at La Sainte Baume, an area where Mary long resided. Jesus' and Mary's lineage continues, as we will see later through the Fisher Kings.

THE CRUCIFIXION

Dr. Thiering's research of the gospel peshers comes to the same conclusion as the *Talmud of Jmmanuel* and Holger Kersten's investigation — that Jesus survived the crucifixion. Dr. Thiering provides additional insight to the location and scenario of the event. New Testament passages tell of Jesus' suffering taking place "outside the gate" and "outside the camp." They tell that the place of the crucifixion was known as the "place of a skull," suggesting a graveyard.

As mentioned earlier, Jerusalem became the pesher metaphor for Qumran. Thiering's research shows this is where the crucifixion took place, not in the real city of Jerusalem. The brief inscriptions attached to the crosses used in the crucifixion could be read easily from the vestry or city. They were written in three languages, Hebrew, Latin, and Greek, all used by scholars living there.

Thiering's pesher research found those crucified with Jesus were not thieves but two of the disciples, the Zealots Simon and Judas. The pesher also suggests that Jesus was not on the middle cross but on the western cross as King of the Jews. Simon Magus had the title of Father (Pope) in the Essene community, and he was placed on the middle cross, and Judas was the priest who hung on the east cross. Gnostic tradition tells of Simon of Cyrene (the name used for Simon Magus after his demotion) being crucified in place of Jesus, confirming that a Simon was crucified. Similarly, the Dead Sea Scrolls confirm Simon's and Judas' crucifixion, which speaks of the crucifixion of "seekers after smooth things" by the Young Lion of Wrath, meaning Pilate.

Thiering tells of vinegar being brought to Jesus, which was actually spoiled wine that had been poisoned. Shortly afterward he became unconscious and gave up the spirit.

The tetrarch Antipas knew well the rules for the Sabbath. He had gone to Pilate to change the method of execution to being buried alive. The three were to be crucified under Roman law, but if Pilate wanted to return to Jerusalem that day from Qumran, he would have to turn the victims over to the Jews operating under Jewish law. This law was found in the Old Testament that stated hanged men should not stay on the cross overnight. Pilate ordered the legs of the two men who were still alive to be broken and for them to be buried in a nearby cave to die. Jesus, who appeared to be dead, could be buried with them. Pilate let the Jews provide their own guard, not understanding the guard would be there until only the next day. Once Pilate was assured the cave was sealed and guarded, he returned to Jerusalem.

Thiering believes Jesus was buried in a cave at Qumran, belonging to His brother James (Joseph of Ariamathea). James was still the heir to the David throne because Jesus' first son had not yet been born. Simon Magus and Judas were taken down from the crosses still alive, but with broken legs. Theudas helped James carry Jesus to the cave and left a supply of 100 pounds of myrrh and aloe. The juice of the aloe plant served as a purgative that quickly neutralized and expelled the poison before it had time to kill Jesus. Myrrh was used to heal the wounds.

Thiering states the remains of the cave, or two adjoining caves, can still be seen today at Qumran, with the path still partly visible. The outer wall of the main cave can be viewed from below and beside the cliff, but the roof has collapsed. Archaeologists, looking for manuscripts in 1955, observed two linked caves, although little was left of them. (Remember the *Talmud Jmmanuel* and the two linked caves?)

The main cave was called cave seven, and to its southwest corner was cave eight. It appears that seven and eight were joined. Simon Magus and Judas were placed in cave seven dressed in white burial clothes, unable to walk. Both were Levitical celibates, called angels by the Essenes. Jesus was placed in cave eight. He had entered the cave as if dead and had come out alive.

The peshers, as interpreted by Dr. Thiering, provide additional information on the crucifixion scenario, but places it at Qumran, the pesher for Jerusalem. Physical evidence at Qumran supports the double-cave theory. Thiering added a new twist, claiming James was Joseph of Ariamathea.

THE DISCIPLES

The peshers, according to Thiering, give an entirely different insight to the role of Jesus' disciples compared with the gospel description. The least important disciples in the gospel appear to be the most important in the peshers. Although, the four gospels do not name the same twelve apostles, except for Philip, Batholomew, and Judas Iscariot, the peshers do. The apostles were an influential Council of Twelve under the leadership of Jesus the Christ, whose purpose was to defend and support the oppressed. As we will see, all the disciples held very prominent roles in Palestine, with most being trained priests, therapeutics, and teachers, according to the peshers.

James and John: Jesus refers to James and John (the sons of Zebedee) as the "sons of thunder." Their father was Jonathon

Annas, also called "Thunder," who was the son of Ananus, the Saddusee High Priest from 6 A.D. to 15 A.D. His counterpart and political rival was Simon Magus, the Samaritan Magi also referred to as Simon the Canaanite. James and John were spiritual sons (deputies) of the Ananus priests, who were under jurisdiction of Simon and held the highest patriarchal office, that of Father (Pope). Symbolic fishing was a traditional part of the baptism ritual, and priests who performed the baptism were called Fishers. Both James and John were ordained Fishers.

Simon Zelotes: Simon Magus (of Zebedee) was head of the West Manasseh Magi, a priestly caste of Samaritan philosophers who advocated the legitimacy of Jesus. Simon was a magician and master showman, who was known to levitate and perform psychokinesis. Of the twelve apostles, he was the most prominent in terms of social status, often called Simon Zelotes, the Zealot. Zealots were militant freedom fighters who opposed the Roman occupation that had usurped their heritage and territory.

Judas Iscariot: Judas was Chief of Scribes, and under his supervision and that of his predecessors, the Dead Sea Scrolls were written. One predecessor was Judas of Galilee, the founder of the Zealots. Judas Iscariot was a warlord of Qumran and head of East Manasseh. The Romans called him Judas Sicarius, the assassin with "sica" meaning "a curved daggar." Judas was second in seniority to Simon Zelotes.

Thaddaes (Theudas): Thaddaes was a son of Alphaes and was called Judas in two of the gospels. He was an influential community leader and a zealot commander. From around 9 B.C. to 44 A.D., Thaddaes was head of the Egyptian Therapeutae. His moderate national group reoccupied Qumran during the second phase, with the pesher name of Qumran at that time being "Egypt." Thaddaes was allied with Joseph, Jesus' father, but was displaced when Judas the Galilean took over Qumran from 4 A.D. to 6 A.D. He returned to a peace mission as the prodigal son and became an apostle of Jesus. In 33 A.D., Thaddaes took part in an uprising against Pilate and was later arrested with Simon Magus and Jesus. The tetrarch Anitpas offered a bribe to Pilate to have Thaddaes released, thus saving him from crucifixion. Following the crucifixion, Thaddaes looked after Simon Magus in the cave and helped resuscitate Jesus by supplying aloe and myrrh. In 44 A.D., Thaddaes was executed.

James: James was leader of the Thunder party and son of Alphaeus.

Matthew (also called Levi): Another son of Alphaeus was Matthew, who succeeded to become the High Priest but was deposed by Herod Agrippa. He was heavily involved in promoting Jesus' teachings and actively sponsored the gospels issued under his name. Being the Chief Levite Priest, he was responsible for collecting public revenues from the Jews.

Philip: Philip was the chief Gentile in the gospel period, head of the Order of Shem, and associated with the Samaritans. Jesus promoted him as the "centurion servant," and Philip was therefore given full membership at the "miracle of changing water to wine."

Bartholomew: Bartholomew was Philip's evangelical and political companion. He was Chief of the Proselytes and an official of the influential Egyptian Therapeute at Qumran.

Thomas: Being one of the most influential Christian evangelists, Thomas preached in Syria, Persia, and India. Known as the "Jesus twin," he was identified as the son of Herod the Great by Mariamme II, the daughter of the High Priest Simon Boethus. In 5 B.C., he was disinherited by Herod after his grandfather and mother plotted to poison Herod. Thomas' wife, Herodias, left him to marry his half brother, the tetrarch Antipas. Thomas supported John the Baptist's position in the dispute about Antipas' marriage. Thomas later represented the 1,000 circumcised Gentiles who lived as celibates. Near Madras at Mylapore, Thomas was lanced to death.

(Simon) Peter: Peter was a village Essene and the least influential of the disciples. Belonging to the Essene Order of Naphtali, Peter was a married man leading a sober life. Jesus associated with Simon Peter's class despite their difference in grade. Peter was a Hellenist who accepted Jesus as the David, believing that Jesus should claim only to be king (the Christ) and not the priest. Peter became loyal to Agrippa I, but later turned against Agrippa II. After becoming a widower, he joined the high order of the Nazarites, and when the Christian party transferred to Rome, Peter represented Jesus in His capacity as King. Jesus had referred to Peter as His guardian, His right-hand man. Peter was martyred by crucifixion during Emperor Nero's persecution of Christians.

Andrew: Andrew was Peter's brother, also an ordinary village Essene who held no public office. His role at the baptism ritual was strictly as a layperson.

JOSEPH OF ARIMATHEA

Jesus was conceived during the "wrong time" of year and was born before Joseph's and Mary's marriage was formalized in their second marriage. Six years later, Jesus' brother, James, was born within all the rules of dynastic wedlock. Because of the questionable birth time, Mary and Joseph took Jesus to Simon (the Essene Gabriel) for legitimization under the law (Luke 2:25-35). The Hellenists, westernized Jews, claimed that Jesus was the rightful Christ. However, on the other hand, the orthodox Hebrews claimed the rightful title lay with James,who was born six years after Jesus within all the rules of Essene wedlock. For many years the argument festered, but when Joseph, their father, died in 23 A.D., it became necessary to resolve the conflict because the "Joseph" title had to be passed down.

The "Joseph" title was given to the eldest son of each generation in the Davidic Succession. After a dynastic son of the House of Judah succeeded to become the David, his eldest son, also called the Crown Prince, became "the Joseph," which means "he shall add," denoting his royal heirship. By this hierarchial structure, James the Just became Joseph of Arimathea. Interestingly, outside the gospel, this Joseph was believed to be Jesus' mother's uncle, or Jesus' great-uncle.

Lineage from the Davidic kings was allied to the lineage of the Zadokite priest, and the prevailing Zadok was Jesus' cousin, John the Baptist. John supported James as the Christ, even though he acknowledged Jesus as legitimate and baptized Him in the Jordan River. Both John the Baptist and James were Nazarites, a sectarian term traced back to the Old Testament personalities of Samson and Samuel. Nazarites were strict ascetics, the sect of Joseph and Mary, in which Jesus was probably raised. During the gospel era, the Nazarites were associated with the Essene community of Qumran.

Because of John the Baptist's attitude, Jesus knew He had to move quickly to revive the Jewish kingdom, or He would lose out to His brother James. Jesus knew a split Jewish nation would never defeat Rome, and they therefore needed to unite with the Gentiles. Jesus wanted to integrate the two factions, but became frustrated by the stubbornness of the Jews. Tradition prophesied a Messiah to lead the Jewish people to salvation, and Jesus knew He qualified to be the long-awaited Messiah. He sought acceptance as both the King and Priest following the death of John the Baptist.

When the Hellenists were in power, James was prepared to act as successor to Jesus, and was given the title "Joseph," acknowledging that he was second in line. Under Hebrew rule, James would be the David and therefore was called "Jacob," the name for the David King. For Jewish Christians who finally accepted Jesus as the Lord (Priest and Pope), James was the David, and they called him "Jacob." Some scholars believe Arimathea refers to an alliance with Agrippa I, at which time James said "ari meth" meaning the "lion is dead," when he heard the news that Tiberius had died. Thiering, Gardner, and others claim that James is the same person as Joseph of Arimathea, traditionally referred to as "Josephes."

John of Glastonbury (the fourteenth century compiler of *Glastioniencis Chronica*) tells of Joseph of Arimathea (James) being imprisoned by the Jewish Elders following Jesus' crucifixion. This is confirmed in the apocryphal *Acts of Pilate*. Other manuscripts claim that Joseph escaped and was eventually pardoned. Years later Joseph was said to be in Gaul with his nephew Joseph, Jesus' and Mary's second son, who was baptized by Philip the apostle. Joseph is traditionally referred to as 'Josephes.'

Joseph of Arimathea (James) was quite wealthy. Early documents found in Glastonbury describe Joseph of Arimathea as a tin merchant who oversaw mining estates in England. Recorded in the 1601 *Annales Ecclesiasticae* by Cardinal Barionius are passages that Joseph of Arimathea first came to Marseilles in 35 A.D. From there he and his entourage went to Britain to preach the gospel. Gildas III (516 - 570) wrote in *De Excidio Britanniae* that the doctrine of Christianity was carried to Britain during the last days of Emperor Tiberius Caesar, who died in 37 A.D. Eusebius (260 - 340) also wrote of apostolic visits to Britain. This period corresponded to the period shortly after the crucifixion, but prior to the time of Peter and Paul. Gildas claims St. Philip was behind Joseph's British assignment.

When Joseph of Arimathea (James) and his twelve missionaries arrived in Britain, the native Brits showed much skeptism, but he was cordially greeted by King Arriragus of Siluria, brother of Caractacas the Pendragon. The King granted Joseph 12 hides of Glastonbury lands, one hide equaling 120 acres. Here they built a church on the same scale as the ancient Hebrew tabernacle. Britain boasted the first above-the-ground church, since in Rome they had to be hidden in the catacombs.

Joseph of Arimathea made a number of visits to Britain, and two were of great importance to the Church. The Reverend Lionel S. Lewis (Vicar of Glastonbury in 35 A.D.) confirmed that St. James (Joseph) was at Glastonbury in 35 A.D. The second notable visit of Joseph followed the 62 A.D. stoning and excommunication of James the Just in Jerusalem. Thiering claims it was a spiritual death and not a physical death that happened. St. Joseph is most remembered in association with Church history in Britain, while in Spain he is revered as St. James.

In 49 A.D., Joseph of Arimathea went to Britain with Mary Magdalene's elder son, the twelve-year-old Jesus Justus. Tales of the visit are still passed down there, with stories of how young Jesus walked upon the Exmoor Coast and visited the Mendip village of Priddy. Because royal blood walked upon the land of England, a stone inscription was placed in memory of his parents, Jesus and Mary Magdalene. It was eventually set into the south wall of St. Mary's Chapel, in Glastonbury. The stone on the site of the original first century chapel is inscribed with "Jesus Maria." According to the old annals, it was to Mary Magdalene that the Glastonbury Chapel was dedicated by her eldest son, Jesus Justus, in 64 A.D.

In 53 A.D., Jesus' son, Jesus Justus, was officially proclaimed the Crown Prince at the synagogue in Corinth and received his Davidic Crown Prince's title of Justus ("the righteous" or "the Just" Acts 18:17). At that time he formally succeeded his uncle, James the Just (Joseph of Arimathea), as the kingly heir. At the age of 16, Jesus Justus became the Chief Nazarite, gaining entitlement to the black robe of that office, as worn by the priests of Isis, the universal Mother Goddess.

According to the peshers, Thiering claims that Jesus went to Rome around 61 A.D. by way of Crete and Malta. About that time, Jesus Justus' younger brother had finished his education at a Druidic college and had settled in Gaul with his mother. They were later joined by James (Joseph of Arimathea), who came to live permanently in the West, having been forced out of Jerusalem in 62 A.D. The Nazarenes had been brutally harassed by the Romans, and the Sanhedrin

Council charged James with illegal teaching. They sentenced him to stoning and excommunication, and he then moved to Gaul.

Following Joseph of Arimathea's departure from Jerusalem, in 64 A.D., a major revolt by the Christians in Rome coincided with fire that engulfed Rome. Nero blamed Peter and Paul, putting them to death. Thiering states that before Paul died, he managed to relay a coded message to Timothy, assuring him that Jesus was safe, but not divulging his whereabouts.

In 65 A.D., Simon Zelotes led most of the Nazarenes out of Jerusalem, taking them east of the Jordan River and eventually into the region of old Mesopotamia. Sporadic fighting took place in 66 A.D. between the Zealots and Romans, and in 70 A.D. a massive Roman army led by Flavius Titus destroyed Jerusalem and then Qumran.

The Roman governors ordered all public records of Jerusalem to be burned, preventing later access to Jesus' family genealogy. Africanus wrote about the purposeful elimination of Messianic records: "A few careful people had private records of their own, having committed the names to memory or having recovered them from copies, and took pride in preserving the remembrance of their aristocratic origins." He called the royal heirs of Jesus the "Desposyni," heirs of the Lord. Eusebius confirmed the writings of Africanus, and said that during imperial times, the Desposyni became the heads of sects by way of a strict, dynastic progression. During the early centuries after Jesus, various Desposyni groups were harassed by the Roman Empire and later by the Roman Church. Many were hunted down as outlaws and pursued to their deaths, writes Gardner.

The truth about this selective inquisition was carefully concealed, but the mythology and tradition have survived. Gardner claims the tradition has survived by way of Grail lore, the Tarot cards, Arthurian romance, songs of the Troubadours, unicorn tapestries, esoteric art, and reverence for the heritage of Mary Magdalene. Even today, the Holy Grail remains the ultimate relic of the quest. The ultimate object of the quest is a threat to the Church that dismissed Messianic succession in lieu of their self-styled hierarchy.

Jesus' and Mary's son, Josephus, was generally disguised as Joseph of Arimathea's son or nephew, the latter being true. In either role, he was no threat to the orthodox scheme of things.

Joseph of Arimathea assumed a peripheral role in the Davidic structure and was not associated with the key Messianic heritage. When Jesus assumed the title "David," His brother became the "Joseph." Following Jesus' death, His oldest son, Jesus the Justus, assumed the role of David, and his younger brother Josephes became the "Joseph" the Crown Prince. Jesus Justus, called "Gais" or "Gesu" in Grail lore, traveled abroad to Rome and Jerusalem.

During that time, Josephes' foster father and legal guardian was James, Joseph of Arimathea. Jesus Justus' firstborn son was named Galains (called "Alain" in Grail tradition). The legacy of Davidic kingship was promised to Galains, which was formally passed to him by his Uncle Josephes. Galains became a celibate and died without children. The Grail heritage reverted to Josephes' lineage that was inherited by his son Josue, from whom the Fisher Kings (Priest-Kings) descended.

Records at Glastonbury, where Joseph of Arimethea is buried, indicate Joseph died on July 27, 82 A.D. The Cistercian monk, Estogre de Saint Graal, wrote that Joseph was buried at the Abbey of Glais, with Glais being synonymous with Glastonbury.

This all sounds confusing, especially when some of the lineage have two names. It is important, though, because the lineage of Jesus plays an important role in later world politics. These unknown facts about Jesus' lineage gave rise to some of the King Arthur legends and the Holy Grail.

Chapter Twelve

THE JESUS LINEAGE

Discovering The Holy Grail

Mystery and intrigue can best describe the lives of those who knew the secret truths about the life of Jesus. The Church had become so powerful with the backing of the Roman Empire that those with nonorthodox knowledge about Jesus feared for their lives. Following the "marriage" between the new Church and Roman Empire under Constantine in the 4th century, all the nonorthodox documents concerning the life of Jesus were destroyed. Constantine, a pagan emperor, followed the pagan cult of Sol Invictus, worshiping the sun god Sol. Syrian in origin, the cult was imposed by Roman emperors on their subjects a century before Christianity. Constantine's purpose was to create unity in both politics and religion.

Sol Invictus was essentially monotheistic, very compatible with the popular cult of Mithras and sharing some attributes with Christianity. Constantine deliberately blurred the distinction among Sol Invictus, Mithraism, and Christianity. In 321 A.D., Constantine gave an edict that the Sabbath was to be observed Sunday because this was the day people worshiped the sun god Sol. Jesus' birthday was then changed from January 6 to December 25 to correspond with the birth of Sol, and Constantine deified Jesus as the earthly manifestation of Sol Invictus. The Council of Nicea, convened in 325 A.D. by the emperor, decided by one vote that Jesus was a god, not a mortal prophet. Christianity thus became a cult of rituals, rather than ideas, and theology became secondary to politics. The following year Constantine ordered all works contrary to orthodox teachings to be destroyed. Earlier in 303 A.D., the pagan emperor had also destroyed many Christian writings. One can begin to understand why there is so little information regarding the life of Jesus. Constantine ordered new copies of the Bible, allowing orthodox scribes to revise, edit, and rewrite the material as they saw fit. Of the 5,000 manuscripts surviving today containing information on Jesus' life, not one pre-dates the fourth century.

Constantine wanted a common and unified world religion (Catholic meaning "universal") with himself as head. The Roman Church had become a hybrid to appease all influential factions. At the time of Constantine's rule, there had been many religions in the Empire, with Christians comprising only about 10 percent of the population. Christianity became a vehicle that allowed Rome to establish a political power by offering the people a better afterlife if they followed the teachings of the Church (or Roman Empire).

Mithraism was one of the most popular religions at the time of Constantine, a Syrian offshoot of the more ancient Persian cult of Zoroaster, introduced into the Roman Empire about 67 B.C. The story of Mithra has many parallels to the story of Jesus. Doctrines include a virgin birth, baptism, a sacramental meal, immortality, a savior god who died and rose, a savior who was mediator between man and God, a resurrection, a last judgment, and a Heaven and Hell. Sound familiar? Mithraism recognized the divinity of the Emperor and tolerated existing cults. The religion was finally absorbed by the less tolerant Christians. Church Fathers later asserted that Mithraism was the work of the devil intended to parody the story of Christ. They did not tell their followers that it existed long before Jesus.

To survive as a religion under the protection of the Roman Empire, the Church had to compromise its ideals by incorporating pagan beliefs into their doctrine that would win over Gentile converts. Members of the early Church considered themselves Jews and were accepted as a Jewish sect until the end of the first century. Beginning in the second century, the vast majority of converts were Gentiles, who converted from the Roman Empire pagans, and this is to whom the Church needed to appeal. Many popular religions revolved around ancient gods born of a virgin, including: Guatama Buddha (600 B.C.); Dionysus, born in a stable and turned water into wine; Quirrnus, an early Roman savior; Attis (200 B.C.); Indra (700 B.C.), born in Tibet; Adonis, a Babylonian god born to Ishtar; Krishna (1200 B.C.), a Hindu deity; Zoroaster (1500 - 1200 B.C.); and Mithra (600 B.C.). One can easily see the parallels between Jesus and the ancient gods, wondering how much of the story of Jesus is myth—based on pagan belief, fabricated to gain pagan converts.

A few people did know the truth about Jesus but were required to keep it secret or suffer the consequences. The early Gnostics knew many spiritual truths when they were competing with Christianity for orthodoxy, but they were eventually suppressed by the early Church and were considered the first heretics. The Cathars of France, considered a Gnostic offshoot, knew the truth and despised the Roman Church. They were decimated by the Albigensian Crusade, organized by the Church in the thirteenth century, because they had secrets and reportedly were in possession of the Holy Grail. As we will see, Jesus' and Mary Magdalene's bloodline evolved through the Merovingian Kings along with knowledge possessed by the Priory of Sion, a secret order that still exists, claiming to have seeded the Knights Templar, the precursors to the Freemasons.

Priory of Sion is largely responsible for releasing information about the Messianic bloodline that has stimulated a number of European authors to research this interesting hypothesis. The Knights Templar discovered a great treasure in the Temple of Solomon that changed Europe forever. Secrecy surrounded the discovery with evidence suggesting it may have included the Ark of the Covenant and knowledge that Jesus survived the crucifixion. The Templars were mainly centered in southern France, near the Cathars, in the region of Mary Magdalene's exile around Rennes-le-Chateau. They, too, were reported as guardians of the Holy Grail.

Perhaps it is wise to start at the beginning with the Nasoreans, an offshoot of the Essenes, before we try to link all these intriguing mysteries. As we will see, the true Jesus sect formed the Jerusalem Church, which lacked most of the pagan doctrines and was headed by Jesus' brother James.

JESUS THE NAZARENE

Jesus is referred to as the "the Nazarene" in nearly all the Greek manuscripts that mention Him. English versions wrongly transcribe this as Jesus of Nazareth. For example, Paul hears a voice on the road to Damascus that says, "I am Jesus of Nazareth, whom thou persecutest." The Greek manuscript has no such statement, but the Jerusalem Bible provides the correct translation: "I am Jesus the Nazarene, and you are persecuting me" (Acts 22:8). In the Acts of the Apostles, the first Christians are called Nazarenes, and Jesus Himself is called a Nazarene six times.

In the Old Testament, Numbers 6:1-13, the Nazarites were described as Jews, such as Samson and Samuel, who were bound by strict vows of obligation: "All the days of the vow of his separation there shall no razor come upon his head: until the days be fulfilled, in which he separated himself unto the Lord; he shall be holy, and shall let the locks of the hair of his head grow. . . . And this is the Law of the Nazarite" (Numbers 6:5,13).

Scholars have not found any linguistic connection between "Nazarene" and "Nazareth." However, both are used to describe Jesus, suggesting they are synonyms. No mention of Nazareth is found in the literature before Jesus' time, and if it did exist, Nazareth was but a tiny village. "Nazarene" is derived from the Aramaic root "Nazar," meaning to "discuss" or to "observe." It also means to consecrate oneself to God. Used as a noun, it symbolizes an anointed head, an observer of the sacred rites.

Other information about the Nazarenes and baptism is provided by Kersten. His research found that Nazaria constituted a branch of the Essenes, probably associated with the Ebionites, one of the original Christian communities. The Essenes used the rites of baptism that departed from the Jewish doctrine. John the Baptist was a prophet to the Nazarenes, and he was known as the "savior by Galilee." Practiced by the Hindus, ritual water immersion originated in India. The Atharva Veda states, "Whoever is not purified after birth with water of the Ganges blessed by the holy invocation will be subject to as many wanderings as years he spent in impurity." (Wanderings means the life as a spirit or after a rebirth.) Ritual immersion symbolized the release from all earthly things and the rebirth of the spirit in a pure body."

Both Pliny the Elder and Josepheus wrote that the Nazarene sect lived on the banks of the Jordan River and on the eastern shore of the Dead Sea, approximately 150 years before Jesus was born. The Nazarenes may explain the hair style worn by Jesus. Followers were permitted to wear their hair long, and both John the Baptist and Jesus wore their hair long. A Roman patrician named Lentilus wrote a letter known as the "Epistle of Lentilus" to the senate describing Jesus. The letter describes Jesus' hair as "flowing and wavy . . . it fell loose over his shoulders, and was parted in the middle of the head after the fashion of the Nazaraians."

Some scholars have speculated Jesus was an Essene. Jewish historian, Heinrich Graetz, described early Christianity as "Essenism with foreign elements." Similarities existed among Essene monks, and Buddhist monks, and some of Jesus' ways. Essene monks dedicated their lives to ascetic practices, as they were well-disciplined mystics who practiced meditation. They practiced telekinesis, clairvoyance, levitation, restoring the dead to life, and laying on of hands. Essenes also believed in a doctrine of moral causation, similar to the Indian doctrine of karma. This means the deeds of the present life affect one's position in the next life. These practices parallel those of the Indian yogis.

The Dead Sea Scrolls tell of the Essenes preparing the way for two messiahs, but neither John the Baptist nor Jesus are mentioned. The kingly messiah was to be from the Davidic lineage (Jesus' lineage) and the priestly messiah from Aaron lineage (John's lineage). The Bible does not mention the Essenes either. In fact, many of the Essene practices were contrary to Jesus teachings, and were more in alignment with John the Baptist's. The verdict is still out if Jesus was actually an Essene, but evidence strongly suggests He was a Nazarene, a subsect of the Essenes. Both John the Baptist and Jesus' brother, James, were Nazarites, the sectarian term traced back to Samson and Samuel. Nazarites were, in fact, associated with the Essene community of Qumran.

Many sects of Christianity were actually far less pagan than the politically motivated Church of Rome. The Church depended on the idols and opulent setting found in Roman ideals. Esoteric Gnostic Christians condemned the Church, as they believed spirit was good and matter was defiled. Nazarenes upheld the original mission of Jesus rather than the eccentric and embellished teachings of Paul.

From the early days of the Jewish revolt, the Nazarenes retained their religion under the leadership of the Desposyni. As confirmed by the *Ecclesiastical History* written by Eusebius, the heirs of Jesus were called the "Desposyni," a term reserved exclusively for those in the same family descent as Jesus. They were of the sacred legacy from the Royal House of Judah, a dynastic bloodline that lives on today, according to author Laurence Gardner. They flourished in Mesopotamia, eastern Syria, southern Turkey, and central Asia.

Nazarean faith was closer to the original teachings of Jesus than any of the early Christian sects. It was essentially Jewish-based rather than idolatrous entanglement with sun worship and mystery cults. They were the purest of true Christians. Nazarenes taught that God was God and Jesus was man, a hereditary human Messiah of Davidic succession. They repudiated the belief that Jesus' mother was a physical virgin; instead, she was like any other woman.

The Nazarenes became known as the Nestorians who were condemned by the Council of Ephesus in 431. They were declared heretics and banished, but had established themselves among friends in Egypt, and in Turkey, where they established the Nestorian church at Edessa in 489. Julius Africanus wrote that the Romans had purposefully destroyed the Desposynic papers that told of royal heritage at Edessa. These documents once confirmed the existence of continuing private accounts of Jesus' lineage, describing the Davidic family sects controlled by a "strict dynastic succession."

The rank of Chief Nazarite was traditionally held by the Davidic Crown Prince, who wore ceremonial black. Jesus' brother, James the Just, assumed this position of royal head of the order. Following him were the successive Crown Princes of Judah, who retained the status and the responsibilities of the office.

Many scholars, who hold that the Dead Sea Scrolls were written by Essenes at Qumran, believe these people were the Nazoreans, the original Jerusalem Church. Professor Robert Eisenman claims the leader of the Qumran community in the fourth and fifth decades of the first century was James the Just, who the Church accepts as the first Bishop of Jerusalem. If so, one can conclude that the Qumran community was the Jerusalem Church. Qumran inhabitants wore white robes, took vows of poverty, were sworn to secrecy, and claimed to have secret knowledge. They appeared to be a revolutionary group central to the Jewish revolt that eventually led to the destruction of Jerusalem and the Temple.

Hippolytus reported in *The Refutation of All Heresies* about a sect he called the Naassenes, who claimed to have beliefs passed down from James. Naassene is another form of Nasorean. "Nasrani' is an Arabic word for the followers of the major prophet Jesus. It also means "little fishes." Members of the Nasoreans traveled to holy places of the early Christian era and marked their sacred places with two arcs that formed the famous symbol of Christianity, the fish. Originally, the hallmark symbol of Christianity was the fish, not the cross.

Today, the Nasorean sect survives in southern Iraq as part of a larger Mandaean Gnostic sect. They trace their heritage back to John the Baptist and believe that Yshu Mshiha (Jesus) was a Nasorean, a rebel who betrayed the secret doctrines entrusted to Him. The Mandaean sect follows an ancient form of Gnosticism who practice initiations, ecstasy, and some rituals similar to that practiced by Freemasons. The priests of the Mandaeans today are called Nasoreans. Manda means "secret knowledge." This sect descended from the original Church of Jerusalem, and their migration out of Judah dated to A.D. 37.

Descending from the Church of Jerusalem was a sect called the Ebionites, the name the Qumran community used for themselves. Ebionism means "poor." The Ebionites, who considered themselves Jews, held the teachings of James the Just in high regard believing Jesus to have been the Messiah after the coronation by John. They also hated Paul accusing him of being the enemy of the truth. For a long period after Jesus and James, the terms "Ebionite" and "Nasorean" were interchangeable, and both were condemned by the Church of Rome. All descendants from the Jerusalem Church, except for the deviant Pauline followers, believed Jesus was a man and not a god.

The Nazoreans believed in the power of the sword to restore the rule of God. They were called "Zealots." In 70 A.D., Jerusalem fell to Titus, and the Zealots were killed or captured. Eventually, the last of the Jews who knew the secrets of the Nasoreans died when the population of Masada, located just south of Qumran overlooking the Dead Sea, committed suicide rather than surrender to the Romans. Josepheus, the historian, believed the war of 66 - 70 A.D. was caused by the tension created by the murder of James the Just. Origen, who also believed this, said "Yet as if against his will and not far from the truth, he says that this befell the Jews in revenge for Jacob the Just, who was the brother of Jesus the so-called Christ, because they killed him although he was a perfectly just man." After the Jews lost the war and the Temple was destroyed for the last time, the teachings of Jesus and the Nasoreans were replaced by Christianity.

Before the Roman destruction of Jerusalem, a great treasure was hidden in the Temple of Jerusalem, including scrolls by the Nazoreans. The "Copper Scroll" of the Dead Sea Scrolls lists huge amount of gold, silver, precious objects, and at least 24 scrolls. Within the Temple, directions were given to 61 separate caches. Over a millennium later, nine Knights Templar discovered the Nasorean scrolls and a treasure beyond their dreams. The plot now thickens!

THE KNIGHTS TEMPLAR

During the early part of the twelfth century, a discovery was made in the bowels of King Solomon's Temple that made the Knights Templar one of the most influential bodies the world has ever known. The discovery helped revolutionize Europe and commanded concessions from the Roman Catholic Church. A mystery still remains concerning the exact discovery, but speculations have flourished, ranging from a cache of gold and silver, to important documents concerning early Christianity, to the Ark of the Covenant. Whatever the discovery was, the Knights Templar became a very powerful organization and one of the most glamorous and enigmatic institutions in Western history. At their peak, they became the most influential organization in the entire Christian world, with the possible exception of the Pope.

The story begins with the First Crusade and the 1099 capture of Jerusalem by Godefroi de Bouillon, who became designated King of Jerusalem. Of the eight crusades that persisted until 1291, Godefroi's crusade was the most productive. During the Crusade Era, various orders emerged, including the Ordre de Sion (Order of Sion) established by Godefroi de Bouillon in 1099. Following his death in 1106, de Bouillon was succeeded by his younger brother, Baldwin of Boulogne, who ruled Jerusalem until 1118, and was followed by his cousin, Baldwin II du Bourg. That year the Knights Templar was founded by Hugues de Payan, a nobleman from Champagne, and eight other knights. Their publicized objective was to keep the roads and highways safe for the Holy Land pilgrims, but there was no evidence they ever policed the Bedouin (desert nomads)-infested roads. In actuality, they were the King's front-line Moslem diplomats.

The King had vacated an entire wing of the palace built upon the foundation of the ancient Temple of Solomon, which became the headquarters for the Knights. Despite their vows of poverty, they moved into luxury accommodations. For the next nine years, the Knights admitted no new candidates into their order. They had also sworn an oath of obedience to the Cistercian Abbot, St. Bernard de Clairvaux (died 1153).

The stables of Solomon were located beneath the Temple itself, large enough to hold 2,000 horses. Scholars speculate that part of the treasure was found prior to the Knight's arrival, and the Knights were there for excavation purposes. They had been deliberately sent to the Holy Land to find it. In 1112, St. Bernard joined the Cistercian Order, an order which was close to bankruptcy. However, within a few years, six new abbeys were built, and by 1153, 300 more abbeys were established. This extraordinary growth by the Cistercian Order closely paralleled the growth of the Templars. Remember the Templar's oath to the Cistercian order? Apparently, the Templars had discovered something very valuable.

In 1128, a Church council officially convened to recognize the Templars, incorporating them as a religious military order. Hugues de Payan was given the title of Grand Master. The Order consisted of warrior-monks, who were to be a "militia of Christ." They were sworn to poverty, chastity, and obedience. The Knights wore white habits of surcoats and cloaks and were instructed to cut their hair but not their beards. If captured, the Templars were not allowed to ask for mercy and were compelled to fight to their death. Only if the odds exceeded 3:1 were they allowed to retreat. Templars also agreed to owe no allegiance to either secular or ecclesiastical power, other than the Pope.

Throughout Europe, young sons of noble families flocked to join the Templar Order, as either soldiers in the crusades, travelers, ambassadors, or political consultants. All new recruits were required to donate their belongings to the Order, an example set by Hugues de Payan. Vows of poverty did not prevent the Order from accumulating wealth, as they acquired estates from all over Europe. In 1146, the Knights adopted the famous red cross as their logo. By the time of the Second Crusade, the Templars had martial zeal, were foolhardy, and had a reputation of being extremely arrogant. They were considered the most disciplined fighting force in the world, greatly feared by their enemies.

During the next century, the Templars became extremely powerful with international influence. They created the institution of modern banking and loaned large amounts of money to destitute monarchs, becoming bankers for every throne in Europe and for Moslems. Saracen (Moslem) leaders greatly respected the Templars, and the Moslem world developed a close link with the Order. Secret connections were made between the Assassins, the famous Islam sect of militants. Merchant traders became dependent on the Templars, as they had become the primary money changers. Europe's finance center was the Templar's Paris preceptory.

As time progressed, the Templars acquired more power. The Order served as a clearing house for new ideas, new science, and new knowledge. They made contribution to surveying, mapmaking, road building, and navigation. Templars had their own seaports, shipyards, and fleet of ships. The Order owned hospitals, had their own physicians, and emphasized hygiene and cleanliness. On almost every political level, the Templars acted as official arbiters in disputes, with kings even submitting to their authority.

The Templars had knowledge of great architecture realized from their discovery, largely based on sacred geometry. Skylines of European cities began to change following the construction of the great Notre Dame cathedrals with magnificent Gothic arches. This architecture was phenomenal, with some believing it was impossible as it left an impression of mystical weightlessness. Sacred geometry principles were applied to all Templar masonry construction of holy monuments. The European cathedrals were all built about the same time, though it took most of them a century to complete. Notre Dame in Paris was begun in 1163. Other Notre Dame cathedrals were built around France, with relative locations to each other replicating the

Virgo Constellation. The Notre Dame of Chartres stood on the most sacred ground, as it had been a pagan site dedicated to the traditional Mother Goddess. Pilgrims had traveled there long before Jesus. A great mystery was found in the Cistercian Gothic architecture involving the stained glass windows used in the cathedrals. Their luminosity was greater than any other and could transform harmful ultraviolet rays into beneficial light. The secret of its manufacture has never been revealed as it disappeared in the mid-thirteenth century. Tradition claims it was a product of Hermetic alchemy that science has yet to replicate. Not one piece of art in the cathedrals portrayed the crucifixion because the Templars denied the crucifixion story as described in the New Testament.

As time developed, the Templars became more arrogant, brutal, corrupt, and things began to change. In 1185, King Baudoium IV died, and the truce with the Saracens was broken. During July of 1187, the Christians were defeated at Hattin, and several months later the Moslems captured Jerusalem that nearly a century before had been captured by the Christians. In 1291, most of the Holy Land was entirely under Moslem control, and in May of that year the last stronghold, Acre, was defeated. The new Templar headquarters was established in Cyprus.

Because of the arrogant power attained by the Templars, in 1306, King Phillippe IV of France was anxious to eliminate the Templars from his territory. He was in great debt to the Order and had no control over them. They were firmly established throughout France and had become arrogant and unruly. King Phillippe IV had engineered the kidnaping and death of Pope Boniface VIII between 1303 and 1305. Then he secured the election of his own candidate, the Archbishop of Bordeau (Clement V). Together the King and new Pope conspired to bring down the Templars. They infiltrated the Order with spies, and on Friday the thirteenth, October 1307, an edict was issued to seize all Templars and their property in France. Disappointing to the King, they could not find the Order's hidden wealth, as it is believed the Templars were tipped off before the arrests. The Grand Master Jacques de Molay had burned the books and extant rules of the Order and hid the treasure. Before their capture, rumors circulated that the treasure was smuggled by night from the Paris preceptory to the naval base at LaRochelle and loaded onto 18 galleys. Tradition claims that most of it went to Scotland.

The King's spies charged that the Templars were worshiping a devil called Baphomet. Other accusations included infanticide, abortions, homosexuality, denying Christ, and repudiating, trampling, and spitting on the cross. In 1312, the Pope dissolved the Order, and in March of 1314, Jacques de Molay and Geoffroi de Charney, preceptor of Normandy, were slowly burned at the stake. Before he died, de Molay put a curse on both the Pope and King, predicting they would be dead within a year. Both died the following year.

Most Templars in England seemed to have escaped capture, and those arrested were given light sentences. The Templar land was eventually consigned to their rivals, the Knights Hospitalers. Scotland was at war with England, and the papal bull was never proclaimed in Scotland, and subsequently became a haven for Templars. Interestingly, tradition claims that most of the Templar's wealth went to Scotland, where they maintained a coherent organization for another four centuries.

Many unanswered claims and questions about the Templars remain today, one such mystery that they were sorcerers, magicians, alchemists, and secret adepts. Whether or not the claims were supported, carvings on Templar preceptories suggest they had knowledge of astrology, astronomy, alchemy, sacred geometry, and numerology. Another rumor is based on Wolfram's (between 1195 - 1220) epic romance *Parzival,*—that the Knights Templar had become the guardians of the Holy Grail, the Grail castle, and the Grail family. Yet another belief is that certain Freemasonry rites claim direct descent from the Order, and many scholars believe Freemasonry originated from the Templars as they were the authorized custodians of the Templar secrets. By 1789, the legend of the Templars had reached mystic proportion. Today in France, the Templar legacy is a thriving industry.

Many believe that the Templars had knowledge of some great secret concerning the origins of Christianity. An association existed between the Templars and Gnostics, and the Order was sympathetic to Islam, in contrast to the Church who called them all heretics. Evidence suggests the Templars tried to seek unity among race and religion with a goal of fusing Christianity, Islam, and Judaic faiths.

During interrogation, some Knights referred to the worship of Baphomet, which still remains a mystery but may have been recently solved. A code used by the Essenes in the Dead Sea Scrolls was applied to the name "Baphomet." The word transformed into the Greek word "Sophia," meaning "wisdom." Sophia is presented as the partner of God, who greatly influenced Him. She is central in Gnostic cosmology and the Jewish Kabbalah, and she is also associated with Mary Magdalene. On certain occasions, Baphomet seemed to be associated with a bearded head that the Templars worshiped. Indisputable evidence shows the Templars had secret ceremonies involving a head of some kind, but who that head symbolized remains a mystery. Today, some speculate it may have been the head found on the Turin Shroud, as the Templars were in possession of it between 1204 and 1307. Others speculate the head is symbolic of John the Baptist. In 1308, a list of charges was made regarding the power of the head, claiming the head could save them, make them rich, make trees flower, and make lands germinate.

Several writers have shown that some Templars were associated with Johannites or Mandaean Gnostics, who denounced Jesus as a false prophet and acknowledged John the Baptist as the true Messiah. Johannite Christians in the Middle East claim to have been given the "secret teachings" and true story of Jesus. Jesus is reported to have given the secret teachings to His beloved disciple John. Interestingly, both the Knights Templar and Freemasons hold John the Baptist as their patron saint, providing another link between the two. Floors of every Masonic temple have parallel lines, one representing the staff of John the Evangelical (John the Beloved) and the other symbolic of John the Baptist's staff. Both Johns are important in the brotherhood; more important than Jesus. The Scottish Rite Freemasons trace the Templars back to the Johannite sect.

Fabre'-Palaprat came into possession of an important document called the *Levitikon* that was a version of John's Gospel with strong Gnostic implications. The text consists of two parts: the first contains religious doctrines that include rituals concerning the nine grades of the Templar Order. It describes the Templars as the "Church of John," who called themselves the "Johnanites," or the original Christians. The second part of the book is like the standard Gospel of John, but it is missing the last two chapters, 20 and 21, regarding the resurrection. It eliminates the miracle of turning water into wine and the raising of Lazarus. It also eliminates any reference to Peter. The book presents Jesus as having been an initiate into the mysteries of Osiris, and tells that the secret teachings Jesus gave John greatly influenced the Knights Templar. According to Fabre'-Palaprat, *Levitikon* claims Jesus was merely a man and not the son of God, and that He was the illegitimate son of Mary.

The discovery made by the Templars at King Solomon's Temple literally changed the world. Some scholars believe they discovered the treasure hidden by the Jews before Rome destroyed Jerusalem, and the cache was not discovered by the Roman soldiers. Others believe it was documents hidden by the Essenes during the Jewish Revolt. The Old Testament tells of the Ark of the Covenant being housed in the Holy of Holies, at the Temple of Solomon. Gardner gives evidence that the treasure discovered did indeed include the Ark of the Covenant.

THE ARK OF THE COVENANT

Lying deep beneath the Jerusalem Temple was the great stable of King Solomon, which had remained sealed and untouched since biblical times. One crusader described it as having a marvelous capacity to hold more than 2,000 horses. Gardner writes, "To find and open up this capacious storeroom was the original secret mission of the Knights Templar, for it was known by Saint Bernard to contain the Ark of the Covenant—which held the greatest of all treasures—The Table of Testimony." These tablets were very important because the "Cosmic Equation" was inscribed on the Tables of Testimony. This was the divine law of number, measure, and weight. The cryptic system of the Kabbalah provided the mystical art of reading the inscription.

There is controversy surrounding the relationship between the Tables of Testimony and the Tablets of Moses. Church doctrine today states that the Tablets of Moses contained the Ten Commandments etched into stone by God himself on Mount Sinai. However, Gardner's research shows the Ten Commandments were only a part of the Tablet's content. They were the precepts God delivered to Moses and his followers. Exodus 24:12 states God said to Moses: "Come up to me into the mount, and be there: and I will give thee tablet of stone, a law, and commandments which I have written that thou mayest teach them." Three separate items are mentioned: tablet of stone, a law, and commandments. God then states in Exodus 25:16: "And thou shalt put into the Ark the testimony which I shall give thee." Later in Exodus 25:18: "He gave unto Moses . . . two tables of testimony, tablets of stone." Moses, however, broke the original tablets when he cast them unto the ground (Exodus 32:19). God then said to Moses: "Hew thee two tablets of stones like unto the first: and I will write upon these tablets the words that were in the first tablets which thou brakest" (Exodus 34:1). God then verbally restated the Ten Commandments and said to Moses: "Write thou these words" (Exodus 34: 27). And Moses wrote "the words of the covenant, the Ten Commandments" (Exodus 34:28).

A distinction was made between the Tables of Testimony written by God and the Ten Commandments written by Moses. The Church has claimed the Ten Commandments were the most important part of this interaction, and the very important Tables of Testimony have been purposefully ignored.

Exodus provides precise instructions regarding the Ark's construction. It provides information for its transportation and the specification for clothes and footwear to be worn by the bearers and overseers. Also provided is the design and materials for the tabernacle in which the Ark was to be stored. Exodus 37 to 40 gives a complete account of how these instructions were to be followed, with no allowance for mistakes or deviation from "blue prints." Construction was completed by Bezaleel, the son of Uri ben Hur of Judah.

Constructed according to Exodus' specifications, the Ark is an elaborate coffer and electrical condenser built with resinous wood, double-plated inside and out with gold. These plates of negative and positive charge can produce several hundred volts, enough to kill someone. This was experienced by Uzzah when he touched the Ark (2 Samuel 6:6-7 and 1 Chronicles 13:9- 10). The Ark also becomes an effective transmitter of sound with its two magnetic Cherubim and the Mercy Seat between them. This is how Moses communicated with God (Exodus 25:22).

The Ten Commandments and Tables of Testimony were placed in the self-protecting Ark, to be guarded by Levites, which David took to Jerusalem. It was housed in the Holy of Holies of the Jerusalem Temple built by King Solomon, assisted by Master Mason Hiram Abiff, important in Freemason rituals. Access to the Ark was forbidden, with the exception of the High Priest's visit once a year for ritual inspections.

By following the Copper Scroll's instructions, the Templar's search and excavation of Solomon's Temple were completed by 1127. They had retrieved the Ark and its contents, claims Gardner, and untold gold bullion and treasure. It had been safely stowed below ground long before the demolition and plunder by the Romans in 70 A.D. As mentioned earlier, the Copper Scrolls verified the cache of treasure and documents hidden in the Temple. At the Council of Troyes in 1128, Saint Bernard became the first official patron and Protector of the Knights Templar. International status was bestowed upon the Templars and their Jerusalem headquarters, and the Church established the Knights as a religious order. Their rise to international prominence was swift.

Rumor suggested that the Ark may have been taken to Ethiopia (Abyssinia), and today there is a sanctuary that some claim houses the Ark of the Covenant at Axum, a small Ethiopian village. However, Revelations 11:19 suggests that it remained in the "Temple of Heaven": "And the temple of God was opened in heaven, and there was seen in his temple the ark of his testament: and there were lightnings, and voices, and thunderings, and an earthquake, and great hail." A television documentary on the Discovery Channel in March 2000 suggested there may have been more than one Ark of the Covenant, with one or more Arks being located beneath the Rosslyn Chapel in Scotland, a chapel having both Masonic and Templar connections.

Approximately 30 percent of the Templar holdings were in Languedoc, the region of the Cathars. Cathars were known adepts of occult Kabbalah symbolism, knowledge necessary for the Templars to decipher the Ark's message. Gardner claims the Knights Templar transported the Ark and treasure to the Languedoc region, the final destination of the Jerusalem find. The Church came to this conclusion as well, and Gardner believes this is part of the reason for the Cathar persecution by the Church.

THE CATHARS

Languedoc is located in the mountainous foothills of the Pyrenees in southern France. This was the home of the Cathars, a Christian sect having Gnostic overtones. A deep mystery surrounded this religious group that originated almost directly from the heresies established and entrenched in France at the beginning of the Christian era, according to the authors of *Holy Blood, Holy Grail.* The Cathars were extremely wealthy, and rumors persisted that they were in possession of a mystical treasure kept at Montesegur, a stronghold situated on top of steep cliffs. The Cathars were also linked to the Holy Grail and the cult surrounding it. Wolfram von Eschenbach, in one of his Grail romances, declared that the Grail Castle was situated in the Pyrenees. The treasure was never found, but speculation varied that the treasure was the Holy Grail, or the Ark of the Covenant, or sacred documents regarding early Christianity, or proof that Jesus survived the crucifixion, or proof that Jesus and Mary Magdalene had children. Whatever the secret was, it made the Roman Church very uneasy, resulting in the Albigensian Crusade, the first European holocaust, Christians against Christians.

In the early thirteenth century, Languedoc was not officially part of France, but was an independent principality ruled by a small number of noble families. Within this small principality flourished the Cathar culture that was the most advanced in the Christian world, with the possible exception of Byzantium. Education was greatly esteemed, with philosophy and intellectual activities earnestly pursued. Greek, Arabic, and Hebrew were all studied, and schools were devoted to the Kabbalah. They practiced a civilized religious tolerance.

However, the Roman Church was not held in the highest esteem in Languedoc because the Church considered the Cathar population to consist of heretics. Both the nobility of northern Europe and the Church were aware of their vulnerability resulting from Cathar beliefs. The Cathars became a threat to Roman authority, as it began to displace Roman Catholicism in that region.

Some Cathars believed Jesus was pure in spirit and could not have been crucified. However, most Cathars regarded Jesus as a prophet, no different from other prophets, who was a mortal man who suffered on the cross. All Cathars repudiated the significance of both the cross and crucifixion. The cross symbolized the god of evil, whom they called "Rex Mundi." They refused to worship the cross and denied the sacraments such as baptism and communion. Writings about the Cathars suggest that the Cathars knew that Mary Magdalene was the consort of Jesus, and most medieval French townspeople knew about their relationship, long before the discovery of the Gnostic gospels. Additionally, the Cathars disliked John the Baptist, calling him a demon and a rival of Jesus.

Cathars were ordinary men and women who found freedom in their religion, compared with heavy restraints imposed by the Roman Church. They condemned procreation but tolerated sexuality, as they practiced both abortion and birth control. They lived a life of extreme devotion and simplicity. Most practiced meditation and strict vegetarianism. When traveling, they always went in pairs. Many nobles of Languedoc were attracted to the Cathar philosophy. In 1145, Saint Bernard journeyed to Languedoc with the intention to preach against the heretics. Instead, he was so impressed by them in contrast to the Church corruption, he reported to the Pope of their exemplary lifestyle.

Cathars comprised a multitude of diverse sects, with an underlying doctrine of reincarnation and recognition of the feminine principle in religion. They rejected the orthodox Church and denied the validity of all clerical hierarchies. As the earlier Gnostics, Cathars insisted on individual responsibility for spiritual growth, acquired by direct and personal knowledge, which preceded all creeds and dogma. Cathars were dualists, believing in the conflict between good and evil. They believed in two gods. The good god, who was disincarnate, was the god of love. Love was incompatible with power and the material creation associated with power. Like early Gnostics, the Cathars believed the physical universe was the result of the god of evil. They believed the purpose of man's life was to transcend matter and attain union with the principle of love.

The Church pronounced anathema on the Cathars in 1179, but needed an excuse to direct public opinion against the Cathars. During January of 1208, a papal legate was murdered in Languedoc, and the Church wrongly blamed the Cathars. Pope Innocent III ordered a crusade against the Cathars. In 1209, 70,000 knights and foot soldiers descended on Languedoc, destroying crops, razing towns, and slaughtering the population. Many Catholics living in Beziers had been warned of the invasion but chose to remain in support of their friends the Cathars. They too were killed with one crusader saying: "Kill them all. God will know his own." They proceeded to destroy other towns in the region, leaving a trail of blood and death in Europe's first genocide.

The Church Crusaders were promised remission of all sins, a place in Heaven, and all the booty they could plunder. A crusader was required to fight no more than 40 days. However, Cathars were mainly pacifists, so they had to employ a large number of mercenaries at considerable expense during the 40-year war. Countless thousands of Cathars were burned at the stake, and by the end of the holocaust, more than 100,000 Cathars lost their lives. This debacle by the Roman Church provided the impetus for the Inquisition that later followed.

In January of 1244, nearly three months before their final defeat, two *parfaits* escaped from the fortress carrying the Cathar's material wealth of gold, silver, and coin. It was first brought to a fortified cave in a mountain and finally to a castle stronghold. This treasure vanished, never to be heard of again. On March 16, 1244, just before their final defeat, four *parfaits* made a daring escape by ropes down the sheer face of the mountainside at Montesegur. Tradition has them carrying a sacred treasure that some believe may have been manuscripts, secret teachings, or religious objects. Whatever it was, they did not want the treasure to fall into the Church's hands. Was it the Holy Grail? The mystery picks up six centuries later at Rennes-le-Chateau.

THE MYSTERY AT RENNES-LE-CHATEAU

We now have two legends regarding a mystical treasure in the region of Languedoc, that of the Cathars and that of the Templars. Interestingly, Languedoc is the region where Mary Magdalene lived following Jesus' crucifixion. Several miles to the southwest of Rennes-le-Chateau was Mount Bezu, where the ruins of a Knight Templar preceptory lay. East of the village were the ruins of the Chateau of Blanchefort, where the twelfth century Grand Master of the Knights Templar had lived. Much of the story regarding Rennes-le-Chateau is based on the research of Baigent, Leigh, and Lincoln found in the book, *Holy Blood, Holy Grail.*

On June 1, 1885, the tiny village of Rennes-le-Chateau located in the Pyrenees foothills of southern France in Languedoc was blessed with a new parish priest, Berenger Sauniere. The village would never be the same. Well versed in Latin, Greek, and Hebrew, Sauniere hired a peasant girl, Marie Denaraud, as a housekeeper who worked 18 years for him. Following his arrival at Rennes-le-Chateau, Sauniere wanted to restore the village church, which had been consecrated to Mary Magdalene in 1059. The church stood upon a foundation of an older Visigoth structure that dated to the sixth century. During the restoration, Sauniere removed the alter stone that rested on two archaic Visigoth columns, one of which was hollow. Inside he found four parchments preserved in sealed wooden tubes. Two of them comprised genealogies dating from 1244 and 1644. The other documents had been composed in the 1780s by Abbe Antoine Bigou, who was the personal chaplain to the noble Blanchfort family. The parchment from Bigou's time appeared to be a code written in Latin texts from the New Testament, in which the words ran incorrectly together with no spaces between them. However, some text could be easily deciphered without a key. One deciphered text said: "To Dagobert II King and to Sion belongs this treasure and he is there dead." Realizing he discovered something of major importance, Sauniere brought the parchments to the Bishop of Carcassonne and was then sent immediately to Paris, where he met with several ecclesiastical authorities, including Abbe Bieril, director of the Seminary of Saint Sulpice. During his three-week Paris stay, rumors spread that Sauniere had an affair with a well-known French performer, Emma Calve. Upon his return to Rennes-le-Chateau, Sauniere excavated an intriguing carved flagstone, beneath which lay a burial chamber with skeletons. He also discovered in the church graveyard a headstone for Marie, Marguise d' Hautpoul de Blanchefort, with a coded inscription consisting of deliberate errors in spacing and spelling. It was an anagram for a message concealed in the parchments referring to Nicolas Poussin and David Teniers, both artists whose works hung in the Paris Louvre. Sauniere tried to eradicate the tombstone inscription after realizing the burial chamber and grave were for the same person.

It appears that Sauniere found something of value. Following these mysterious discoveries, Sauniere made a hobby of taking long hikes into the countryside collecting rocks of no value.

Another passion was collecting worthless postage stamps. He then opened a number of shadowy accounts in various banks, and then began sending all kinds of mail throughout Europe, the postage alone exceeding his previous annual income. By the end of his life in 1917, Sauniere was spending several million pounds a year. Much of it went back to the community for roads, water works, and so forth.

Inside the church entrance, Sauniere erected a hideous statue which represented the demon Asmodeus, representing the custodian of secrets and guardian of hidden treasures. Jewish legends claim the demon was the builder of Solomon's Temple. Sauniere installed garishly painted plaques on the church walls, depicting the stations of the cross deviating from the scriptural account. For example, on Station VII was a child with Scottish plaid. Sauniere also collected rare china, precious fabric, and antique marble. Routinely, he provided his parishioners with great banquets. The church became suspicious of the large amount of money Sauniere was spending, but when they questioned him, they were met with defiance. Finally, the church accused Sauniere of illicitly selling masses and tried to remove him. Refusing to leave, the Vatican exonerated him and Sauniere was reinstated.

On January 12, 1917, Marie, Sauniere's housekeeper of 18 years, ordered a coffin for Sauniere, though his parishioners later declared him in good health. On January 17, he suffered a stroke at the age of 61, the date that was coincidently on the Blanchefort tombstone. While on his death bed, a priest visited Sauniere for the last rites, and emerged shaken, said to never smile again after Sauniere confided to him a secret. Sauniere died on January 20, and the next morning his body was placed upright in an armchair for mourners to pass by for last respects.

His will declared him penniless, as all his wealth had been transferred to his housekeeper, Marie Denarnaud. She continued to live comfortably until 1946 when she burned her money in defiance of the government. She had promised the purchaser of her villa that she would confide to him before her death a secret that would make him not only rich but powerful. In January of 1953, Marie suffered a stroke, and she carried her secret to the grave.

Since the Cathar holocaust of the thirteenth century, legends of great hidden treasures spread throughout the region. Tradition indicates the Cathars possessed something of great and sacred value. Also were legends of the vanished Templar treasure and stories about how the Grand Master Blanchefort commissioned mysterious excavations in abandoned gold mines. Hitler knew about these legends, and in 1940 - 41, the Germans undertook a number of fruitless excavations.

Between the 5th and 8th centuries, much of modern France was ruled by the Merovingian dynasty, which, as we will see shortly, carried Jesus' bloodline. One ruler was King Dagobert II, who married a Visigoth princess. Documents claim that Dagobert amassed great wealth from his military conquests, supposedly concealed in the surrounding Rennes-le-Chateau. If Sauniere discovered this treasure, it would explain the coded reference concerning Dagobert.

Another treasure possibility may have been the legendary treasure of King Solomon's Temple. In 70 A.D., contents of the Holy of Holies were sacked by the Roman soldiers and taken to Rome. In 410, Rome was invaded by the Visigoths, with the historian Procopius writing that Alaric the Great made off with "the treasure of Solomon . . . in the olden times they had been taken from Jerusalem by the Romans." The treasure may have changed hands several times from Jerusalem, to Rome, to the Visigoths, to the Cathars, and to the Knights Templar. The coded inscription said it belonged to Dagobert II and Sion.

Sauniere's discovery was a monumental secret of historical importance. It seemed to involve more than riches, a secret that was very controversial—perhaps knowledge, suggesting Sauniere's wealth could have come from blackmail, a payoff for silence. Even the Vatican was afraid of him, so it appeared more religious than political. Could the blackmail money have been coming from the Church?

The authors of *Holy Blood, Holy Grail* produced a British television documentary on Rennes-le-Chateau on BBC. After it aired, they received a letter from a retired Anglican priest, who claimed the treasure did not involve gold but "incontrovertible proof" that the crucifixion was a fraud and that Jesus was alive in 41 A.D. The authors visited the priest who told them, "This proof had been divulged to [me] by another Anglican cleric, Canon Alfred Leslie Lilley." He died in 1940, but once associated with Emile Hoffet, Abbe Bieril's nephew of the Paris circle who had met with Sauniere.

While in Paris, Sauniere purchased a print of Nicolas Poussin's, the great seventeenth century painter mentioned in the coded inscription. The painting was titled "Les Bergers d' Arcadie" and consisted of three shepherds in the foreground gathered around a large tomb inscribed with "Et in Arcadia Ego." In the background was a mountainous landscape matching that around Rennes-le-Chateau. Surprisingly, during the 1970s an actual tomb was discovered, identical to that in the painting, in the village of Arques, six miles from Rennes-le-Chateau, and three miles from the Chateau of Blanchefort. The *Holy Blood, Holy Grail* authors wondered if the tomb inscription in the painting was an anagram. In English it read "And in Arcadia I." After the BBC television documentary, one viewer rearranged the letters to "I Tego Arcana De," which meant "Begone! I conceal the secrets of God."

Speculation still varied over Sauniere's discovery and whether it was the Cathar treasure, the Jerusalem Temple treasure, the Holy Grail, or even the tomb of Jesus. The Priory of Sion claimed that Sauniere's discovered parchments also provided genealogical information of Jesus' lineage to the Merovingian dynasty. Whatever Sauniere found made him very wealthy. Sauniere's activities also suggested he was looking for something else. Some speculate that the legendary treasure was brought to Rennes-le-Chateau from Montesegur, but some suggest he was looking for the remains of Mary Magdalene.

Much of the symbolism at Rennes-le-Chateau was associated with Masonic tradition. Evidence suggests that Sauniere was affiliated with the Rectified Scottish Rite Order, a branch of Freemasonry that specifically claimed descent from the Knights Templar. Sauniere placed a great emphasis on Mary Magdalene, even naming his library tower after her. Also, the tomb in Nicholas Poussin's painting was thought to be the local "Arques tomb," of which local legend claims was the resting place of Mary Magdalene or a marker pointing to it. Researchers speculate that Sauniere was in search of Mary Magdalene's burial site. Mary Magdalene, according to legend, lived her life not in Provence but in Languedoc, around Rennes-le-Chateau. Whatever Sauniere was looking for still remains a secret, but the Priory of Sion seems to have more answers than anyone.

PRIORY OF SION

The Priory of Sion first became known to the public in the early 1960s, and to the English-speaking people through the book *Holy Blood, Holy Grail*. The Priory has been described as a quasi-Masonic or chivalric order with certain political ambitions. Founded in 1099 during the First Crusade, the Priory claims to be behind the creation of the Knights Templar. Their basic purpose was to restore the Merovingian bloodline to power, the bloodline of Jesus.

Their notoriety came in a mysterious way. Since 1956, a quantity of relevant material to the Jesus' mystery was leaked to the public in a piecemeal fashion, according to the authors of *Holy Blood, Holy Grail*. A series of books, pamphlets, and other documents related to Sauniere and Rennes-le-Chateau began to appear in France. By drawing attention to the intrigue of this area, the Priory hoped to stimulate further research. Underlying all the information, there consistently appeared to be a hidden secret. Topics included works about the Cathars, Templars, Merovingian dynasty, Rose-croix, Berenger Sauniere, and the Rennes-le-Chateau, all suggesting they possessed some secret knowledge. Much of the information came through Pierre Plantard, whom we will discuss later. This mystery put authors' Baigent, Leigh, and Lincoln on the path to solve it.

The research of Baigent, Leigh, and Lincoln found a secret order was behind the Knights Templar, who used a variety of names, and are known today as the Priory of Sion. The Order was directed by a sequence of grand masters, all using the title John. The Priory remained unscathed after the dismantling of the Knights Templar in the early fourteenth century. Since 1956, they have been responsible for disseminating literature, as earlier mentioned. Their primary objective remains to restore the Merovingian dynasty and bloodline to France and other European nations.

The bloodline had perpetuated itself from King Dagobert II and his son Sigisbert IV. Godfroi de Bouillon was of this heritage, and he captured Jerusalem in 1099 during the First Crusade. Following de Bouillon's death, Baudouin accepted the crown offered him and became the first official King of Jerusalem. He and his descendants were elected kings, not kings by blood. One document leaked to the public was *Dossier Secrets*, which stated the Ordre de Sion was founded by Godfroi de Bouillon in 1090, nine years before the conquest of Jerusalem. The text states that King Baudouin owed his throne to the Order.

Until 1188, the Ordre de Sion and the Knights Templar Order are said to have shared the same grand master. Then the Ordre de Sion selected its own grand master with no connection to the Templars. The name Prieure de Sion was adopted with the subtitle Ormus. Ormus was part of Zorastrian thought and also found in Gnostic texts. Masonic teachings say Ormus was an Egyptian sage, a Gnostic adept of Alexandria. In 46 A.D., Ormus and six followers were converted to a form of Christianity by Mark, Jesus' disciple. The teachings of early Christianity had been fused with the older mystery schools. In that same year, Ormus conferred his new symbol, a red (rose) cross. Both the Knights Templar and Rosicrucians (an organization of Christian mystics) adopted this new symbol.

Dossier Secrets included three lists of names, including a list of Templar grand masters from 1118 to 1190 and a list of grand masters of Prieure de Sion, which included some surprising names. On the list was Nicholas Flamel (the great alchemist: 1398 - 1418), Leonardo da Vinci (1510 - 1517), Robert Fludd (1595 - 1637), J. Valentin Andrea (an early Rosicrucian: 1637 - 1654), Robert Boyle (1654 - 1691), Isaac Newton (1691 - 1727), and Victor Hugo (1844 - 1885). The list of grand masters appeared to be accurate according to the *Holy Blood, Holy Grail,* but seemed to be derived from inside information.

The *Dossier Secrets* also mentioned the former rulers of England, the Stuarts, who were deeply involved in promoting Freemasonry during their stay in France. They were considered the source of the Scottish Rite form of Freemasonry. The Scottish Rite promised initiation into greater and more profound mysteries handed down by Scotland. Charles Radclyffe succeeded Isaac Newton, and *Dossier Secrets* suggests Scottish Rite Freemasonry was originally promulgated by him. In 1775, he founded the first Masonic lodges on the continent in Paris.

According to the Priory documents, every grand master adopted the name Jean (John), including the four women on the list, who assumed the name Jeanne (Joan). Grand masters, by assuming the name John or Joan, implied an esoteric and Hermetic papacy based on John, in contrast to the exoteric one based on Peter. The authors of *Holy Blood, Holy Grail* did not know which John the assumed name was based upon. Was it John the Baptist? John the Evangelist of the Fourth Gospel? Or John the Divine of Revelations?

For years there was a bitter chasm between the Catholic Church and the Freemasons. In 1958, Pope Pius XII died, and the new Pontiff was Cardinal Angelo Roncalli of Venice, who chose the name John XXIII. A book written in 1976 titled *The Prophecies of Pope John XXIII* was about prophetic poems. The book states that Pope John XXIII was secretly a member of the Rose Croix, with whom he affiliated in Turkey as papal nuncio in 1935. During his term as Pope, he directed the Roman Catholic Church to the twentieth century, and the book claimed that he revised the Church position toward that of Freemasonry.

Most grand masters of the Priory of Sion were connected by blood or personal association with families in the Prior documents and especially with the House of Lorraine. All names on the list were nominally Catholic but held unorthodox religious views, such as beliefs in the occult. Over the years, the Priory of Sion had been involved in European and world politics. Members of the Priory, which have included French leaders Charles de Gaulle and Francois Mitterand, did not believe Jesus died on the cross, and that Jesus and Mary Magdalene were married.

The later Priory publications explained their role in the Berenger Sauniere scenario at Rennes-le-Chateau. They claimed Sauniere was only a pawn. The real force behind the events was Sauniere's friend, Abbe'Henri Boudet, who was an official in the village of Rennes-le-Bains. The Priory of Sion publications suggest that Boudet was the person who gave Sauniere all his money, a total of 13 million francs between 1887 and 1915. Rennes-le-Bains guided Sauniere in the construction and restoration of the church, including the strange stations of the cross. Sauniere's housekeeper, Marie Denarnaud, was actually Boudet's agent, and through her, Boudet gave Sauniere instructions and money. Only in 1915 did Sauniere realize the real secret for which he acted as a custodian. It was now implicit that Boudet was working for the Priory of Sion.

As the authors pursued their research, new documents continued to be deposited in the Bibliotheque Nationale in Paris that gave new clues to the researchers. The documents appeared to pave the way for another astonishing disclosure that involved the Merovingian dynasty. One article said that "without the Merovingians, the Prieure de Sion would not exist, and without the Prieure de Sion, the Merovingian dynasty would be extinct." One bulletin written by M. Burrus charged, "The Merovingians' descendants have always been behind all heresies from Arianism, through the Cathars and the Templars to Freemasonry. . ." The Priory publication titled *The Treasure of the Golden Triangle* (*Le Tresor du Triangle*) stated the upper degrees of Freemasonry were actually the lower degrees of Prieure de Sion.

M. Plantard de Saint Clair was listed as Secretary General of the Priory. When asked the purpose of the Order, he answered: "The society to which I am attached is extremely ancient. I merely succeed others, a point in a sequence. We are guardians of certain things. And without publicity." Off the record, Plantard declared to BBC that the Priory of Sion did hold the lost treasure of the Temple of Jerusalem, the booty plundered by the Roman legions in 70 A.D. He said when the time was right, the items would be returned to Israel. Plantard, who is of Merovingian lineage, said the treasure was spiritual, part of a secret.

M. Paoli wrote a book, titled *The Undercurrents of a Political Ambition,* regarding his research into the Priory. He wrote: "We have, on the one hand, a concealed descent from the Merovingians, and on the other, a secret movement, the Prieure de Sion, whose goal is to facilitate the restoration of a popular monarchy of the Merovingian line." Paoli believed the Merovingian claim was legitimate.

In 1977, another Priory document appeared, *The Circle of Ulysses,* under the name of Jean Delaude. A question was asked about the plans of Prior of Sion, to which he responded, "I do not know, but it represents a power capable of taking on the Vatican in the days to come."

In summary, the Priory of Sion appeared to be a secret society in possession of wealth acquired by the Romans from the Temple of Solomon. Some of the most influential people of France once belonged to this mysterious society. They also held knowledge and secrets that they were gradually revealing to the world. One such secret included that of the Merovingian lineage.

THE MEROVINGIAN HERITAGE

As the Western Roman Empire fell into decline, the greatest threat to the Roman Church came from a Desposynic royal strain in Gaul. They were the Merovingian dynasties, the male descendants of the Fisher Kings from the Jesus lineage. Much of the history regarding the era comes from the *Fredegar Chronicles*, an exhaustive seventh century historical work. Coincidently, it can be found in the Bibliotheque Nationale in Paris, where literature from the Priory of Sion is deposited. Fredegar, who died in 660, was a Bergundian scribe who chronicled the period from the earliest days of the Hebrew patriarchs until the establishment of the Merovingian kings. To accomplish this monumental task, Fredegar used a variety of Church records and state annals.

During the middle of the second century A.D., King Lucius, the great grandson of Arviagus, who had given Joseph of Ariamathea 12 hides of Glastonbury land, revived the spirit of the early British disciples, writes Laurence Gardner, who based much of his research on Fredegar's works. King Lucius was said to have "increased the light" of Joseph's first missionaries and was known as Lleifer Mawr (the Great Luminary). His daughter, Eurgen, was the first link between the two key Davidic successors, that from Jesus and that from James (Joseph of Arimathea). This happened when Eurgen married Aminadab, the great grandson of Jesus and Mary Magdalene (from the line of Bishop Josephes).

King Lucius was credited for many accomplishments. Many Gaulish Christians had fled to Britain, especially to Glastonbury, to escape Roman persecution, where they sought aid of King Lucius. Lucius was credited with building the first Glastonbury Tower on St. Michaels Tor in 167 A.D. King Lucius was also responsible for establishing the first Christian Archbishop in London and the first church in London, the Church of St. Peter.

The Fisher King's lineage evolved to establishing the Merovingian dynasty. The Fisher King Faramund (reigned 419 - 430) married the Chief Genobaud's daughter, Argotta. Faramund is often regarded as the true patriarch of the French monarchy. He was the grandson of Boaz, in the direct Messianic succession from Josue's (Jesus's grandson, son of Josephus) son, Aminadab, of Jesus lineage, who had married King Lucius' daughter, Eurgen of the Armimathaes line. Argotta descended from King Lucius' sister, Athildis, who had married the Sicambrian chief, Marcomer, around A.D. 130. From Faramund and Argotta, the Merovingian succession was seeded. It was dually Desposynic! Faramund and Argotta's son, Clodion, became the next Guardian (Lord) of the Franks in Gaul.

Clodion's son, Meroveus, was proclaimed Guardian at Tournai in 448. After him, the line became known as the mystical dynasty of Merovingians, as they became King of the Franks. The kings did not reign by coronation nor appointment, but by the accepted tradition that corresponded to Messianic right through the succession of Fisher King (Priest King) Faramund.

Meroveus was a semi-supernatural person of mythical proportion. Tradition has Meroveus being born of two fathers. When already pregnant by her husband, King Clodion, Meroveus' mother went swimming in the ocean. Here she was seduced/raped by an unidentified creature from beyond the sea. Following Meroveus' birth, two different bloodlines flowed in Meroveus' veins. Because of this dual bloodline, Meroveus was said to have superhuman power. The resulting dynasty was cloaked in an aura of magic, sorcery, and the supernatural. Their monarch became known as the Sorcerer Kings, who practiced esoteric acts. They healed with their hands, were clairvoyant, and communicated with animals, and they had knowledge of magical spells that protected and enlightened them. The dynasty heirs were born with a distinctive birthmark, a red cross situated over the heart or between the shoulder blades. They were called the long-haired kings, like Samson, and they believed their hair contained the essence and secret of power.

Merovingians claim descent from Noah and from ancient Troy. Their ancestors traced back to ancient Greece, specifically to the region known as Arcadia, and ancient Troy had been settled from Arcadia. Later, Merovingian ancestors established themselves on the Danube and Rhine Rivers toward the advent of the Christian era. Under Merovingian rule, the kingdom of the Franks flourished. They were not barbarians, but they encouraged secular literacy.

They could be brutal, but they were not warlike. Over time, the Merovingians accumulated great wealth.

On their twelfth birthdays, the heirs were automatically regarded as Merovingian kings. There was no public ceremony or coronation, as power was simply assumed. The king was essentially a ritualized figure, a priest king. Merovingian rulers were polygamous, and occasionally enjoyed harems of great proportion. The Merovingian kings were known as the Priest Kings, an embodiment of the divine and incarnation of God's grace. They engaged in ritual practices. For example, skulls of the Merovingian monarchs were ritually incised, similar to that of the high priests of early Tibetan Buddhism, allowing the soul to escape at death.

The most famous Merovingian ruler was Meroveus' grandson, Clovis I, who reigned between 481 and 511. Under Clovis, the Franks were converted to Roman Christianity. Following the conversion, Clovis presided over a unified empire, a "Holy Roman Empire," a pact he made with the Church, allowing the Church to expand with great power. Clovis had many adversaries, including the Visigoths, who adhered to Arian Christianity, that denied Jesus' divinity and insisted on His humanity. In 507, Clovis defeated the Visigoths, whose empire straddled the Pyrenees as far north as Toulouse. The Visigoths fell back and established their capital at Rhedae, now the village of Rennes-le-Chateau. In 511, Clovis died, and the empire was divided among his four sons.

We now come to the era of Dagobert II, involved in the discovery by Saurniere. Dagobert II was born in 651, son of a Merovingian King, and heir to Austrasia. After Dagobert's first wife died, he married Giselle de Razes, the niece of the King of the Visigoths. The marriage was celebrated at Rhedae, and the Merovingian bloodline was now allied to the royal bloodline of the Visigoths. Around Rennes-le-Chateau, Dagobert acquired considerable territory in what is now Languedoc, and he was proclaimed King of Austrasia, but was later murdered by his servant. His body was exhumed in 872, and moved to the Church of Saint Dagobert. With the murder of Dagobert, the power and influence of Merovingian dynasty effectively ended. At one time historians under Church pressure tried to eliminate Dagobert from the history books. Was it because he was Desponsynic?

However, after the end of the Merovingian dynasty, the bloodline continued. Dagobert and Giselle de Razes had a son named Sigisbert IV, who carried on the Merovingian bloodline. According to Prior documents, Sigisbert IV was rescued by his sister and taken to the domain of his mother, the Visigoth princess. He adopted the nickname of Plantard, and under the name of Plantard, the lineage was perpetuated. By denying the existence of Dagobert, any line of descent would have been invalidated, as the Church had destroyed many records that related to this lineage.

Centuries later, Godfroi de Bouillon, of Merovingian blood, inaugurated the Crusades and captured Jerusalem. He was a descendant of the Plantard family, who founded the Ordre de Sion. According to the *Dossier Secrets*, de Bouillon was a descendant of the tribe of Benjamin that had left Israel two millennia earlier. In the *Dossier Secrets* footnotes were many references to one of the 12 tribes of Israel, the tribe of Benjamin at the time of Moses. When the land of Israel was divided among the 12 tribes, the territory of the Tribe of Benjamin included the sacred city of Jerusalem. The Bejamites did go into exile, to Greece and then Arcadia. The Prior of Sion documents claim the Merovingians descended from the tribe of Benjamin by way of Arcadia. Thus, Godfroi de Bouillon would have been reclaiming his ancient and rightful heritage when he captured Jerusalem.

In Arcadia, the cult of the Mother Goddess survived and prospered. The goddess worshiped was Demeter, followed by Diana. During classical times, Arcadia was ruled by the powerful militaristic state of Sparta, which had absorbed much of the older Arcadian culture. Similar to Merovingians, the Spartans gave magical significance to hair, which became a sacred symbol denoting physical vigor. Both apocrypha books of the Maccabees emphasized the link between the Spartans and Jews, explicitly stating they were brethren from the family of Abraham. The Semitic Phoenicians were the great sailors of the Mediterranean, and in the ninth century B.C., the Kings of Tyre intermarried with royalty from Israel and Judah. Phoenician trade routes included southern France, and today there are many Semitic names in various locales around France. Prior documents suggest that the Merovingians and various noble families of southern France descended from Semitic lineage.

The female lineage of the Merovingians emerged from the Sicambrian Franks, who were associated with Arcadia before migrating to the Rhineland. They called themselves the "New Image" (People of the New Covenant), just as the Essenes of Qumran had been known. It was the Arcadian legacy that was responsible for the sea beast legend, the Bristea Neptunis that symbolically represented the Merovingian ancestry. The sea-lord was King Pallus, a god of old Arcadia whose predecessor was Oceanus. Legend tells of the immortal sea-lord to be ever incarnate in a dynasty of ancient kings whose symbol was a fish, the traditional symbol of Jesus. The fish became the emblem of the Merovingian kings along with the lion of Judah, and the Merovingian king lineage became known as "the vine."

By the time of the Norman conquest of Britain in 1066, the French Merovingians had been ignored for three centuries. However, it was the Royal House of Stuart that emerged as the most significant reigning dynasty in the Desposynic succession. In 1371, the early Stewarts became the Kings of Scots, and the royal branch later adopted the French corruption of the name, Stuart. Laurence Gardner writes that in sovereign terms, the Stewarts' conjoined legacies were of great significance. Their Scots lineage was of the Arimathea lineage and their Briton heritage was from Jesus Himself, through the Fisher Kings. In 1306, the Scots crowned Robert I Bruce, who defeated Edward II of England in the 1314 English invasion of Scotland. They were helped by the Knights Templar who had escaped to Scotland from the continent. After defeating Edward at Bannockburn, Bruce declared his nation independent and a home was secured for the exiled Templars.

The Grail Knights and Templars were appointed guardians of the Stewart Sangrael in Scotland and proctor of the Stone of Destiny. Just south of Edinburgh, at Roslin, the Templar legacy is still found today. Here stands the fifteenth century Rosslyn Chapel associated with the St. Clair family, who built a castle nearby. Tradition says that deep beneath this castle fortress are sealed vaults that still contain some Templar treasure brought from France during the Templar flight from the King of France. Legend also has important documents concealed in a vault beneath the Rosslyn Chapel that shed light upon the Templars and Freemasons. During the 1307 flight from France, part of the

Templar fleet had gone to Portugal and reincorporated as the Knights of Christ. As mentioned earlier, some believe the Ark of the Covenant may also be hidden at the Rosslyn Chapel.

The Stewarts emerged as a unique Grail dynasty, long known as the "House of Unicorn." The Desposnynic unicorn was incorporated into the Royal Arms of Scotland. Tradition indicates the unicorn was symbolic of the virile Jesus. The mystical beast was also the foremost symbol of the Albigensian Cathars, and medieval legend equates the unicorn with fertility and healing. The Cathars believed the horn of the unicorn would purify false doctrines perpetuated by the Roman Church.

Early development of Masonic lodges in Britain was directly allied to the House of Stuart. During their later exile, the Stuart kings were at the forefront of Scottish Rite Freemasonry, founded on the most arcane knowledge and universal law.

The Jesus lineage had been secretly tracked over the centuries and now is being released to humanity. The Fisher Kings and Merovingian heritage were seeded by Jesus, and the seed continues through the Stuarts of Britain and other royalty of Europe that has married into this heritage. Not forgotten, however, is Mary Magdalene, whose legacy was remembered through the Black Madonna and Priory of Sion.

THE BLACK MADONNA

The Black Madonna found throughout Europe has remained a mystery and somewhat of an embarrassment to the Church. Traditional thought believes the Black Madonna represents the Virgin Mary, but those in the know claim she represents Mary Magdalene, and a cult with pagan undertones developed around her. The authors of *Holy Blood, Holy Grail* uncovered documents in the Bibliotheque Nationale, supposedly planted by the Priory of Sion, that concerned the Black Madonna. A poem in the documents claims the Mother Goddess of Christianity is Mary Magdalene to whom the church at Rennes-le-Chateau was dedicated.

The Black Madonna cult is central to the Priory. To them, she represents both Isis, the Egyptian goddess, and Mary Magdalene, and her name is "Notre-Dame-de-Lumiere." In other words, the title Notre Dame conferred to the great cathedrals in

France (built by the Templars) refers to Mary Magdalene. Mary Magdalene is extolled as a saint in France, and medieval legends say she even brought the Holy Grail to France. Worship of the Black Madonna was encouraged by the Merovingians. But why? About 65 percent of the Black Madonnas are found in France, mainly southern France. Another interesting finding in the Provence region of southern France is the large number of John the Baptist churches. Mary Magdalene sites also contain a larger than average number of John the Baptist churches. But why?

Isis is Mary Magdalene's counterpart in pagan lore, while the god Osiris is Jesus' counterpart. Another interesting finding is that the archetype that fits most closely with Jesus' life story is that of the Egyptian god, Osiris, consort of Isis. Picknett and Prince, authors of *The Templar Revelation: Secret Guardians of the True Identity of Christ* believe Jesus and Mary Magdalene were living out the story of Osiris' death and resurrection. They believe that Jesus was trying to introduce goddess worship to the people of Israel.

A mysterious document surfaced among the family archives of the Montgomery family, now termed "The Montgomery Document," that supports the findings of *Holy Blood, Holy Grail*. It tells of Yeshua ben Joseph (Jesus, son of Joseph) being married to Miriam (Mary) of Bethany. Because of a revolt against the Romans, Miriam was arrested. Because she was pregnant, Miriam was released and then fled Palestine for Gaul where she gave birth to a daughter. Miriam of Bethany was described as a priestess of a female cult, similar to the Merovingian worship of the goddess Diana. Was it a coincidence that the Notre Dame of Paris was erected upon the foundation of a Diana temple? Other famous churches in France were built on sites sacred to ancient goddesses.

Jesus' words "In my Father's house are many mansions" (John 14:2), have puzzeled many Christians. This phrase is explicitly Osirian and comes directly from the *Egyptian Book of the Dead*. Osiris was killed on a Friday, and his dismembered body was scattered. After three days he rose again, thanks to the magical intervention of Isis and the god Thoth. The cosomolgy of the Gnostic Pistis Sophia text matches that of the *Egyptian Book of the Dead*. For example, the greatest Egyptian celebration came on December 25, the birth of Isis' son Horus. Her other son Aion was born on January 6, the date when the Orthodox

Church celebrates Christmas. Also, the Lord's Prayer originated as the prayer of Osiris to Amon. Mary Magdalene was revered by a European underground movement because she founded her own church, based on the Isis/Osiris religion.

Saint Bernard was devoted to both the Virgin Mary and especially Mary Magdalene. He wrote over 90 sermons linking the "'Bride" with Mary of Bethany (Mary Magdalene), and he was known to have a love for the Black Madonna. When Saint Bernard created the Templars, he required his knights to "the obedience of Bethany, the caste of Mary and Martha."

Additional evidence has shown that the relationship of Jesus and Mary was a marriage involving a child. It appears Mary was a very evolved soul, whose followers worshiped her through the guise of the Black Madonna. So important was this relationship that it was equated to the one in Egyptian mythology of Isis and Osiris. Perhaps the patriarchal view of the Church was one of the main reasons why it took nearly two millennia for women to attain equal status in much of the world. If the Church had recognized Mary Magadalene for who she was, perhaps the suffering of women for all these centuries could have been prevented.

THE HOLY GRAIL

An enigma has arisen over the past millennia regarding the Holy Grail, popularized in Grail romances. No one knows exactly what the Holy Grail is, or even if it actually existed. One thread common to the story of Jesus' lineage is the Holy Grail, and in some way the Grail legends always relate to Jesus. Some legends claim the Grail was the cup from which Jesus and His disciples drank at the Last Supper. Another tradition says it was the cup in which Joseph of Arimathea caught Jesus' blood as He hung from the cross. It has been characterized as a plate, a stone, a casket, a jewel, an aura, and a vine. In stories, the Grail is often accompanied by a blood-tipped spear. As mentioned earlier, the Holy Grail has been equated with the Turin Shroud. Tradition claims the Cathars were in possession of the Grail, and later the Templars became custodians.

No reference to the Grail occurred for 1,000 years, until the peak of the Crusades. The Grail status peaked when the Frankish

Kingdom was in full glory, when the Templars were at their zenith, and when the Cathar heresy was gaining momentum that threatened to displace the Church's creed.

The Grail legacy is associated with early Judaic Christianity, but has never been recognized by the Church, which considers it an unproclaimed heresy. Pagan tradition, blasphemy, and unholy mysteries have also been associated with the Grail. Because of its strong female theme, the Roman Catholic Church has openly condemned the Grail legends. Gardner claims the Church despised the notion of chivalry and the songs of the Troubadors because they placed womanhood on a pedestal of veneration, contrary to Catholic tradition. Perhaps the main reason the Church objected to the Grail was the connection the Grail Family had to Messianic lineage. In Sir Thomas Malory's fifteenth century account of the Grail, he states that the Grail champions are Bors, Perceval, Lancelot, and his son, Galahad, who are said to be from Messianic background. Malory described Galahad as "a very young knight of King's lineage and the kindred of Joseph of Arimathea, being the grandson of King Peller."

Scholars agree that the Grail romances were founded upon pagan doctrines, derived from the cults of Tammuz, Attis, Adonis, and Osiris in the Middle East. In Irish and Welsh mythology, the Grail legends refer to death, rebirth, and renewal. During the twelfth century, when the Grail romances underwent significant transformations, they became associated with Christianity and Jesus. For nearly a century, volumes of romance stories and poems appeared involving a relic linked mystically to Jesus. A cult developed, closely paralleling the rise of the Templars. Legends of the Grail abound.

Most scholars claim the Grail romances date from around 1188, around the time of Jerusalem's fall and the separation of the Priory Sion from the Knights Templar. The Grail was supposedly brought to Glastonbury, England by Joseph of Arimathea, and legend also has Mary Magdalene bringing it to France. By the fifteenth century it was a cup she brought, but earlier legends do not mention a cup, but imply something much more. One of the earliest Grail authors, Chretien, did not specify what it was, but said it was made of gold and encrusted with gems. Wolfram von Eschenbach wrote *Parzival* between 1195 and 1216, and he emphasized the guardians of the Grail and Grail family were the Knights Templar. He maintained his

Grail story was the correct version. Through his poems, von Eschenbach emphasized that the Grail is a means of concealing something of great consequence. He reiterated the need for secrecy and linked it specifically to the crucifixion. In the book of *Perlesvaus*, the Grail involves a secret entrusted to a select few that related to Jesus. King Arthur seems to have lived in Gaul during the late fifth century at the peak of the Merovingian dynasty. Von Eschenbach also insisted Arthur's court was at Nantes in France, not Britain. Arthur means "bear," and the term "bear" also refers to the Merovingian line. Some scholars today believe the Grail romances refer to the Merovingian era.

The authors of *Holy Blood, Holy Grail* suggest the Grail itself may actually refer to the royal bloodline of the Merovingian dynasty. If the Grail family and the Merovingian bloodline were one and the same, the Templars would indeed be the guardians of the Grail. The Grail romances stress the importance of Jesus' blood. Sangrael became the Holy Grail, the Blood Royal. As Gardner puts it, the Sang Real was carried by the uterine chalice of Mary Magdalene.

In King Arthur legends, the Davidic lineage was represented by the Fisher Kings of the Grail family. Anfortas denoted the patriarchal line, according to Gardner's research, and it was identified with the Hebrew name Boaz, great grandfather of King David. Boaz was the name given to the left-hand pillar of King Solomon's temple, a symbol used today in Freemasonry. Within the traditional Grail stories, there is a consistency of Jewish names such as Josepheus, Lot, Galahad, Urien, Jonas, and so forth. All the legends digress to tell of the Fisher Kings that we now know to be of Jesus' lineage.

The Chapel of St. Michael in Glastonbury was established by King Lucius on an ancient pagan site, on a ley line that connected to other churches. The Michael in the title refers to the Archangel Michael. As mentioned in a previous chapter, the angelic title of Michael was the Zadokite priest in Essene tradition. John the Baptist held this priestly office during the time of Jesus. Following the death of John, Jesus, on many occasions, tried to gain recognition as a priest. According to Gardner's research, only at the ascension was His priesthood formalized, when Jesus was carried to the "Kingdom of Heaven" (the high monastery) to become High Priest (Hebrews 5:6). At that time His dynastic role became dually Messianic, that being a priest king, a "Fisher King" in Grail lore. For the first time since the time of King David and the High Priest Zadok, the kingly and angelic titles were combined. Jesus became both the David and Michael. Hebrews 6:20 states, "Whither the forerunner is for us entered, even Jesus, made an high priest for ever after the order of Melchizedek." Remants of the "Prince Melchizedek Document" discovered with the Dead Sea Scrolls indicate Melchizedek and Michael were the same. Following that time, the dynastic Melchizedek (Melchi-Zadok) successors lay with Jesus' own male line, those descending through the Fisher Kings. This lineage of the Davidic bloodline, the Royal Blood of Judah, became known as the "Grail Family." During the early years, they were not actual monarchs but priest kings by right. In the fifth century, when the descendant Fisher King married Princess Argotta, heiress of the Sicambrian Franks, the Christine line began its great rise to prominence. The senior descendant in the Grail line became the dynastic "Michael," an office held by John the Baptist.

Similar to the Philosopher's Stone in alchemy, the Holy Grail has been identified as the key to knowledge and the sum of all things. It represents a repository of spiritual wisdom and cosmological knowledge. Its power included rejuvenation and provision, as the Grail was a teacher, healer, and provider.

The Knights Templar were thought to be the guardians of the Grail. The Order had given a public face to the inner circle, just as the Holy Land was opened up to European travelers. Essentially, the Templars were a mystery school, operating on a hierarchy and through secret initiation. Scholars believe the vast majority of Templars were none other than Christian soldiers, as they appeared to the public. They were a front to the inner circle, who furthered research into esoteric and religious matters, whether it be Jewish, Islamic, or Christian. They sought the secrets of the universe.

The Grail Keepers knew of the great secret, the sacred lineage of Jesus and Mary Magdalene. Both the Templars and Priory of Sion kept the secret well. The Grail legends were basically Gnostic ideals that emphasized that each individual, and not the Church, is responsible for the state of his or her soul. After two millennia of keeping this sacred secret, the Priory of Sion feels the world is now ready to know the truth of Jesus' lineage, the Holy Grail.

EPILOGUE

Over the last two millennia, the Church has been the most powerful institution that has withstood the test of time. Overall, Christianity has influenced the civilized world more than any other religion. Countless wars have been fought in the name of Christianity, and along with the Crusades and Inquisition, have killed millions of people to accomplish their goal of maintaining orthodoxy. One has to ask the question if all these atrocities would have occurred if the teachings of Jesus had not been corrupted?

The myth of Jesus began during the early centuries following the crucifixion. If the Proto-orthodox Church wanted to survive, it needed to compromise and appeal to the pagan masses and incorporate their beliefs. Doctrines from competing religions such as Mithracism and Constantine's religion of Sol Invictus were also incorporated into this new religion of Christianity. Politics played an important role in determining orthodoxy, especially during the Council of Nicaea where one vote decided that Jesus was God and not man.

To reinforce the correctness of Church doctrine, scribes edited out many of the New Testament truths that contradicted the created Church myth of Jesus. Once orthodoxy became established, it was impossible to change. No matter what the truth, the orthodox doctrine ruled. Those who did not subscribe to the Church myth were called heretics, often punished with the penalty of death. Staying alive became more important than spiritual truth. This is one of the reasons secret societies later developed, such as the Knights Templar, Rosicrucians, and Freemasons, providing a place where they could pursue spiritual truths.

During the past one and one-half centuries, science began to unravel some of the Church myths. Discoveries in Tibet found documentation of Jesus' lost years. Other documents surfaced suggesting that Jesus survived the crucifixion. Biblical analysis, especially in the Gospel of John, suggests how this might have occurred. Science underlying the Turin Shroud suggests the body wrapped in the linen was alive. Evidence explained how the Church manipulated Shroud evidence to preserve the myth of

Jesus' resurrection. Evidence from France indicates that Jesus and Mary Magdalene were married with children, and their legacy has been documented by the Priory of Sion. Other evidence surfaced that Jesus lived His remaining years in Kashmir, He had a family, and His grave is in Srinagar.

One of the biggest Church myths is that of the resurrection, a belief that when resurrection occurs, all the physical atoms and molecules of the deceased body will recombine to reform the physical body. Scientifically, it may be difficult to do if the body has decayed or been burned. The early Christian Gnostics claimed resurrection was a spiritual resurrection, not a physical resurrection.

The most important truth ignored by the Church was the concept of reincarnation. Biblical evidence has been presented that the early scribes had not completely edited out all references to rebirth. The pure teachings of Jesus were similar to those of the Buddha, and the evidence suggests that Jesus studied the philosophy of Buddhism while in India. We have seen that ancient, unedited, Aramaic manuscripts reinforce the teachings of reincarnation by Jesus, plus demand a respect for all animal life. The concept of reincarnation explains all the inequalities of life because the soul's purpose is to perfect itself through life situations in various incarnations.

I am not here to condemn the Church because Christianity as we have known it was meant to be exactly as it has been in the Universal Plan for our soul's evolution. However, the time has come to correct the myth of Jesus created by the Church and live by the teachings of Jesus. This means an end to war and a respect for all humanity and animal life. Jesus promised to return, and hopefully upon His return, we will have established the foundation of the new Golden Age, the millennium of peace.

REFERENCES

Listed below the reference material are the subheadings of the chapter with the reference numbers indicated.

CHAPTER ONE: THE EARLY CHURCH

(1) Ehrman, Bart D., *The New Testament, A Historical Introduction to the Early Christian Writings,* Oxford University Press; New York, 1997.

(2) Ehrman, Bart D., *The Orthodox Corruption of Scripture,* Oxford University Press; New York, 1993.

(3) Halliday, W.R., *The Conflict Between Paganism and Christianity in the Fourth Century,* Clarendon Press; Oxford, 1963.

(4) Koester, Helmut, *Introduction to the New Testament History and Literature of Early Christianity,* Fortress Press; Philadelphia, 1982.

(5) Losiy, Alfred F., *The Birth of the Christian Religion and the Origins of the New Testament,* University Books; New Hyde Park, New York, 1982.

(6) Pagels, Elaine, *The Gnostic Gospels,* Vintage Books; New York, 1989.

(7) Treadgold, Donald W., *A History of Christianity,* Nordland Publishing Company; Belmont, MA, 1979.

(8) *Merriam Webster's Collegiate Dictionary,* Tenth Edition; Springfield, Massachusetts, 1993.

Topic Headings and References:

Introduction (6)

Roman and Pagan Influence (1) (3) (7)

The Church's Beginning (1) (5) (4) (7)

The Struggle for Orthodoxy (2) (7) (8)

CHAPTER TWO: THE NEW TESTAMENT

(1) Ehrman, Bart D., *The New Testament, A Historical Introduction to the Early Christian Writings,* Oxford University Press; New York, 1997.

(2) Ehrman, Bart., *The Orthodox Corruption of Scripture,* Oxford University Press; New York, 1993.

(3) Gruer, Elmar R., and Kersten, Holger, *The Original Jesus: The Buddhist Sources of Christianity,* Element; Rockport, MA, 1995.

(4) Koester, Helmut, *Introduction to the New Testament History and Literature of Early Christianity,* Fortress Press; Philadelphia, 1982.

(5) Merriam Webster's Collegiate Dictionary, Tenth Edition; Springfield, Massachusettes, 1993.

(6) Pagels, Elaine, *The Gnostic Gospels*, Vintage Books; New York, 1989.

Topic Heading and References

Establishing the New Testament (1) (4) (5)
The Corruption of Scripture (1) (2)
The Quelle (3) (6)

CHAPTER THREE: THE EASTERN INFLUENCE

(1) Gruer, Elmar R., and Kersten, Holger, *The Original Jesus: The Buddhist Sources of Christianity*, Element; Rockport, MA, 1995.
(2) Head, Joseph, and Cranston, Sylvia, *Reincarnation: The Phoenix Fire Mystery*, Theosophical University Press; Pasadena, 1994.
(3) Pagels, Elaine, *The Gnostic Gospels*, Vintage Books; New York, 1989.

Topic Headings and References

Introduction (1)
New Testament Similarities with Buddism (1)
Rebirth (1) (2)
Similarities Between the Teachings of Jesus and Buddha (1) (3)

CHAPTER FOUR: THE GOSPEL OF THE NAZIRENES

(1) Baigent, Michael, Leigh, Richard, and Lincoln, Henry, *Holy Blood, Holy Grail*, Dell Publishing, New York, 1982.
(2) Ewing, U.C., *The Prophet of the Dead Sea Scrolls*, 1963.
(3) Findlay, Adam, *The History of Christianity - In the Light of Modern Knowledge*.
(4) Forsstom, John, *The King of Jews*.
(5) Goodspeed, Edgar, *History of Early Christian Literature*.
(6) Schonfield, Hugh, *The Passover Plot*, 1965.
(7) Sconfield, High, *Jesus Party*, 1974.
(8) Thiering, Barbara, *Jesus and the Riddle of the Dead Sea Scrolls: Unlocking the Secrets of His Life Story*, Harper; San Francisco, 1992.
(9) Wauters, Alan and Van Wyhe, Rick (Editors), *The Gospel of the Nazirenes*, Essene Vision Books, Patagonia, AZ, 1997.
(10) Wilson, Ian, *Jesus, the Evidence*.

Topic Headings and References

Intoduction (9)
The Nazirenes (8) (9)
Historical Accounts of the Nazirenes (1) (2) (3) (4) (5) (6) (7) (9) (10)
The Nazirean Gospel (9)

CHAPTER FIVE: THE TALMUD JMMANUEL

(1) Deardorff, James, *Celestial Teachings: The Emergence of the True Testament of Jmmanuel (Jesus),* Wild Flower Press; Tigard, OR, 1990.

(2) Meier, Edward A., *The Talmud of Jmmanuel: The Original Book of Matthew,* Wild Flower Press; Newberg, OR, 1992.

Topic Headings and References

Introduction (1) (2)
The Deardorff Research (1)
Was there an Aramaic Gospel? (1)
Jesus in the East (1) (2)
A Different Portrayal of Jesus (1) (2)
Rebirth, Destiny, and Perfection (2)
The Scientific Analysis (1) (2)
Epilogue (1)

CHAPTER SIX: THE EARLY LIFE OF JESUS

(1) Kimball, Glenn, *Hidden Stories of the Childhood of Jesus,* BF Publishing;, Houston, TX, 1997.

Kimball's Sources

(1) *The Gospel of the Birth of Mary* (Written by Matthew in the Fourth Century.)

(2) *Protovangelion* (Jesus' brother James was credited with writing this.)

(3) *The First Gospel of the Infancy of Jesus Christ* (Thought to have been written by Thomas.)

(4) *The Thomas Gospel of the Infancy of Jesus Christ.*

(5) *History of Joseph, the Carpenter, or Death of Joseph.*

CHAPTER SEVEN: JESUS IN INDIA

(1) Gruber, Elmar R. and Kersten, Holger, *The Original Jesus: The Buddhist Sources of Chrisitianity,* Element; Rockport, MA, 1995.

(2) Kimball, Glenn, *Hidden Stories of the Childhood of Jesus,* BF Publishing; Houston, TX, 1997.

(3) Notovitch, Nicholas, *The Unknown Life of Jesus Christ,* 1894.

(4) Notovitch, Nicholas, *The Life of Saint Issa: Best of the Sons of Men,* 1894.

(5) Pagels, Elaine, *The Gnostic Gospels,* Vintage Books; New York, 1989.

(6) Prophet, Elizabeth C., *The Lost Years of Jesus,* Summit University Press; Livingston, MT, 1984.

(7) *Apocryphal Acts of Thomas*

Topic Headings and References

Introduction (6)
The Saga of Nicholas Notovitch (3) (6)
The Life of Saint Issa (3) (4) (6)
The Aftermath (6)
Early Christianity (3) (5) (6) (7)
The Wise Men (1) (2) (6)

CHAPTER EIGHT: THE TURIN SHROUD

(1) Heller, John H., *Report on the Shroud of Turin,* Houghton Mifflin Company; Boston, 1983.
(2) Kersten, Holger, and Grubar, Elmar R., *The Jesus Conspiracy: The Turin Shroud and the Truth about the Resurrection,* Element; Rockport, MA, 1992.
(3) McCrone, Walter, *Judgement Day for the Turin Shroud,* Microscope Productions; Chicago, 1996.
(4) *Merriam Webster's Collegiate Dictionary,* Tenth Edition; Springfield, MA, 1993.
(5) Nickell, Joe, *Inquest on the Shroud of Turin,* Prometheus Books; Buffalo, NY, 1983.
(6) Wilson, Ian, *The Shroud of Turin: The Burial Cloth of Jesus Christ?,* Image Books; New York, 1966.
(7) Wilson, Ian, *The Mysterious Shroud,* Doubleday & Company; Garden City, NY, 1986.

Topic Headings and References

Introduction (2)
The Shroud (2)
History (2) (4) (6)
The Science of the Shroud (1) (2) (3) (5) (6) (7)
The Church Conspiracy (2)

CHAPTER NINE: THE CRUCIFIXION

(1) *Apocryphal Acta Pilata*
(2) *Apocryphal Gospel of Peter*
(3) Kersten, Holger, and Gruber Elmar, The Jesus Conspiracy, *The Turin Shroud and the Truth about the Resurrection, Element*; Rockport, MA, 1992.

(4) Meier, Eduard A., (Editor) *The Talmud of Jmmanuel: The Original Book of Matthew*, Wild Flower Press; Newberg, OR, 1992.

Topic Headings and References

All Topic Headings (3)
Introduction (3) (4)
Death on the Cross (2) (3)
The Centurion (3) (1)
The Talmud Jmmanuel (4)

CHAPTER TEN: THE POST-CRUCIFIXION

(1) *Apocryphal Acts of Thomas*
(2) Kersten, Holger, *Jesus Lived in India*, Element; Rockport, MA 1994.
(3) *The Koran*
(4) Meier, Eduard A., (Editor) *The Talmud of Jmmanuel: The Original Book of Matthew*, Wild Flower Press, Newberg, Oregon, 1992.

Topic Headings and References

Introduction (2)
The Journey (1) (2)
The Kashmir and Jewish Connection (2)
Jesus and the Koran (2) (3)
The Tomb of Jesus (2) (4)

CHAPTER ELEVEN: THE CODED GOSPELS

(1) *Apocryphal Gospel of Phillip*
(2) *Apocryphal Acts of Pilate*
(3) Barionius, Cardinal, *Annales Ecclesiasticae*
(4) Gardner, Laurence, *Bloodline of the Holy Grail, The Hidden Lineage of Jesus Revealed,* Element; Rockport, MA, 1996.
(5) Gildas III, *De Excidio Britanniae*
(6) Lacardiaire, Pere, *Saint Mary Magdalene*
(7) Maar, Raban, *The Life of Mary Magdalene*
(8) Meier, Eduard A., (Editor) *The Talmud of Jmmanuel: The Original Book of Matthew*, Wild Flower Press; Newberg, OR, 1992.
(9) Thiering, Barbara, *Jesus and the Riddle of the Dead Sea Scrolls: Unlocking the Secrets of His Life Story,* Harper; San Francisco, 1992.
(10) Voragine, Jacobeus de, *Legenda Aurea*

Topic Headings and References

Introduction (4) (8) (9)
The Qumran Community (9)
The Birth of Jesus (9)
Jesus and Mary Magdalene (1) (4) (6) (7)(9) (10)
The Crucifixion (8) (9)
The Disciples (4)
Joseph of Arimathea (2) (3) (4) (5)

CHAPTER TWELVE: THE JESUS LINEAGE

(1) Baigent, Michael, Leigh, Richard, and Lincoln, Henry, *Holy Blood, Holy Grail*, Dell Publishing; New York, 1982.
(2) *Dossier Secrets*
(3) Eschenbach, Wolfram von, *Parzival*
(4) Eusebius, *Ecclesiastical History*
(5) *Chronicles*
(6) Garner, Laurence, *Bloodline of the Holy Grail: The Hidden Lineage of Jesus Revealed*, Element, Rockport, MA, 1996.
(7) Hippolyus, *The Refutation of All Heresies*
(8) Kersten, Holger, *Jesus Lived in India*, Element, Rockport, MA, 1994.
(9) Knight, Christopher and Lomas, Robert, *The Hiram Key*, Element, Rockport, MA, 1996.
(10) Picknett, Lynn, and Prince, Clive, *The Templar Revelation: Secret Guardians of the True Identity of Christ*; Simon and Shuster, 1997.
(11) Paoli, M., *The Undercurrents of Political Ambition*
(12) *Pistis Sophia*
(13) Ronacalli, Cardinal Angelo, *The Prophecies of Pope John*
(14) Thoth, *Egyptian Book of the Dead*

Topic Headings and References

Introduction (6) (9)
Jesus the Nazarene (1) (4) (6) (7) (8) (9)
The Knights Templar (1) (3) (6) (9)
The Ark of the Covenant (1) (3) (10)
The Cathars (1) (3) (10)
The Mystery at Rennes-Le-Chateau (1) (10)
Priory of Sion (1) (2) (10) (11) (13)
The Merovingian Heritage (1) (2) (5) (6)
The Black Madonna (1) (10) (12) (14)
The Holy Grail (1) (3) (6) (11)

INDEX